AF580665

Music Librarianship in America

Edited by
Michael Ochs

Cambridge, Massachusetts

Eda Kuhn Loeb Music Library

Harvard University

Papers of a symposium held 5–7 October 1989 to honor the establishment of the Richard F. French Librarianship at Harvard University.

Originally published in the *Harvard Library Bulletin*, N.s., vol. 2, no. 1, Spring 1991

0-8108-3521-5

Copyright 1991 by the President and Fellows of Harvard College.

The paper used in this publication meets the minimum requirements of the American National Standard for Information Sciences—Permanence of Paper for Printed Library Materials, ANSI Z39.38-1984. ∞

Contents

Part 3: Music Librarians and American Music

Part 4: Music Librarians and Performance

Introduction

The following papers were commissioned for a symposium, *Music Librarianship in America*, that was held at Harvard University on 5–7 October 1989. The purpose of the symposium—to explore the larger aspects of music librarianship—was accomplished by examining important issues from the viewpoint of senior practitioners and by looking at the profession through the eyes of leading figures in neighboring disciplines. In the papers and discussions presented here, a score of distinguished representatives from the fields of musicology, ethnomusicology, history, publishing, arts administration, performance, composition, criticism, librarianship, and library education consider the role of music librarians and their contributions to musical life.

The symposium honored the establishment at Harvard of the Richard F. French Librarianship, the first music library chair to be established in the United States. Sessions were attended by over 275 music librarians, musicologists, librarians from other disciplines, and students, representing thirty states and three foreign countries. Participants viewed exhibitions of musical treasures from the Eda Kuhn Loeb Music Library, the Isham Memorial Library, and the Houghton Library. They also heard three concerts: "A Black Gospel Music Celebration," featuring Shirley Caesar, Larry Watson, and the Reverence Gospel Ensemble of the Berklee College of Music; "Musicque de joye," instrumental and vocal music of the Renaissance performed by the Boston Camerata, directed by Joel Cohen; and a recital by the Dutch organist Ewald Kooiman.

The symposium was sponsored by the Harvard College Library and the Department of Music. Primary funding was generously provided by the Council on Library Resources. The symposium and the concurrent music festival also received financial support or contributions in kind from the American Musicological Society, the Boston Area Music Librarians, the Massachusetts Institute of Technology Libraries, the Music Library Association, the Amelia Peabody Foundation, and the following Harvard University organizations: the William E. B. DuBois Institute for Afro-American Research, the Divinity School, The Memorial Church, and the Office for Government, Community, and Public Affairs.

Richard F. French and Harold Samuel helped shape the symposium and define its goals. The distinguished organizing committee, which the editor of these proceedings was privileged to chair, consisted of Rodney G. Dennis, Lewis Lockwood, Christoph Wolff, and Yen-Tsai Feng. The exceptionally skillful editorial work of Ruth Tucker unobtrusively permeates these pages.

Michael Ochs

Prologue: Meeting the Challenge

Susan T. Sommer

Susan T. Sommer is coordinator of the General Library of the Performing Arts, The New York Public Library at Lincoln Center, and adjunct associate professor at the School of Library Service, Columbia University. She is past president of the Music Library Association and a former editor of the Association's journal, *Notes*.

Richard F. French has had great meaning in my life, as he has in the lives of many other individuals in the field of music, including numerous contributors to this volume. In the 1950s when I was a beginning graduate student and very much in awe of almost everyone, certain people were particularly important to me. I had a part-time job as a general dog's body for Noah Greenberg and the New York Pro Musica Antiqua, on whose board of directors Dick French served. The generosity of spirit that pervaded the entire organization began with Dick and the other board members. One cannot imagine a greater group of heroes to someone starting out in the field of musicology: they made me feel like a full partner in their endeavors at a crucial time in my life. Since then, Dick has remained a good friend and a generous one, as he has to so many in the library and musicological world.

Summarizing the papers that follow—indeed even to attempt summarizing Milton Babbitt's contribution alone—is clearly an impossible task. Instead I will draw a few conclusions about issues that are raised and attempt to address the question that poses itself, "So what?" More specifically, what are the present challenges to music librarians, and what should we be doing to meet them?

In his keynote paper, Harold Samuel places musicological and academic concerns about libraries in a historical context; many of the other contributors address their subjects similarly. Expanding the canon is a recurrent theme that is raised first in Part I, "Music Librarians as Custodians of Cultural History." We are repeatedly urged to broaden our horizons, to look at areas that other parts of the discipline of musicology are exploring—non-Western musics, non-print materials, interdisciplinary ideas—and to respond accordingly in our libraries. We are also exhorted to emphasize our role as gatherers: to collect everything and, in effect, keep it forever, using the latest techniques of preservation. In this way we can discharge our responsibilities toward the historians of today and those of the future.

Though there is some mention of technology in the first group of papers, there is almost none after that—no great discussion of on-line access points, electronic collecting, or of the organization and preservation of materials in libraries. I take this to mean that our scholarly colleagues trust us to know and apply technology, and that we can concentrate on matters a great deal more fundamental.

In the sections "Music Librarians and Music Scholarship" and "Music Librarians and American Music," many of the themes introduced in Part I are continued and expanded—into art history, ethnomusicology, popular music, and Native American music. Here the traditional canon is significantly redefined to transcend our usual collecting modes ("crossing the great divide"), giving us new problems to face. We are reminded of the power that music librarians have, not merely to respond to music publications but to influence them. Similarly, what we collect for the future

Richard F. French, photographed in 1985 by Rodney Smith.

will influence the future's view of the present. We are asked to be scholarly music librarians "with the mantle of learning lightly worn." And we are instructed in the ways, both subtle and unsubtle, in which we can encourage performances of American music. Finally, we are confronted with the increasingly important role played by non-print materials. It is no longer enough to collect and disseminate mainly books and published scores, and only peripherally archival, sound, and video materials; the latter must be accorded full importance, notwithstanding the considerable problems we may encounter in dealing with them.

The section "Music Librarians and Performance" is in many ways a spectacular performance in itself, by three individuals very much concerned with performance and live music. The participants testify that music librarians can serve as a source of inspiration by helping patrons find materials that are unavailable or even unknown outside our libraries. But music is not really music when it remains on the page. For a few of us—as for Milton Babbitt sitting in the New York Public Library at Fifty-eighth Street or at Forty-second Street—it becomes music when it goes through our eyes to our brain and we "hear" it. For most others, however, hearing requires the intervention of another human being. It is up to us to see that the music gets to the intermediary—in this case, the performer.

The participants in the final section also point out that besides introducing users to the published and unpublished repertoire, libraries sometimes serve as venues for live music, and thus librarians can encourage composers to create more music. Although the papers in this section tend to express rather personal views of music librarianship, they are no less thoughtful or valid than the more formal papers.

As a coda, Richard French entreats us to ask new questions about music—a role common to composers, performers, musicologists, and music librarians—and to suggest new ways in which to interrogate the world—the purpose of this symposium. Finally, Michael Ochs reflects on the past, present, and future of our profession.

The Music Library Association (MLA) fosters the work that music librarians are doing—the committees, the roundtables, the programs themselves come into being because they represent tasks that we are undertaking or ideas that we have conceived. In contemplating what is said in the papers that follow and, at the same time, looking at MLA's administrative structure and programs, I concluded that we music librarians are indeed addressing the challenges. There are, of course, standing committees that address and redefine longstanding concerns of the profession. But there are also roundtables and working groups that materialize out of the imaginations of our colleagues; they come into being because a number of people who are deeply concerned about a subject are also willing to do something about it. We have roundtables on American music, on band material, on film music, on jazz and pop, for example. We have special groups working on questions of bibliographic control, interlibrary cooperation, and reference methods.

In another sense our libraries themselves have been—and are—meeting the challenge by anticipating it. Many of the non-librarians taking part in this symposium call for libraries to expand their vision by reaching out to encompass historical documents of popular and world music, but from these papers and discussions we learn that many libraries have already done so.

Several participants comment on the role of serendipity in finding unexpected treasure in libraries. It is indeed exciting to find something valuable, something whose existence you never knew of, lying unnoticed in a box at the back of the library stacks. But someone was responsible for taking in and keeping that box, buying that journal you didn't know you would want, acquiring that collection of popular music or ethnic records. That someone was—and will be—the music librarian.

Music librarians do not have all the answers. We know we never will, but we are trying to ask all the right questions. A major value of the symposium papers published here is the contribution they make toward defining those questions. And as every scholar and reference librarian knows, the first and most important problem is not "What is the answer?" but "What is the question?"

Whence Music Librarians?

Harold E. Samuel

It is fitting that this symposium brings together the users of music libraries with music librarians, for it was the users—musicologists, mostly—who played such a large role in establishing the Music Library Association (MLA) in 1931 and developing it in the early years. So the musicologists can be proud of this landmark in the life of their stepchild.

At an April 1934 meeting of the MLA at Vassar College, seven of the nineteen persons attending were musicologists: Otto Kinkeldey of Cornell University, Harold Spivacke and Oliver Strunk of the Library of Congress, Paul Henry Lang of Columbia University, George Sherman Dickinson of Vassar College, and Hugo Leichtentritt and G. Wallace Woodworth of Harvard University. Among the non-musicologists present were Eva Judd O'Meara, who had been instrumental in organizing the founding meeting at Yale in 1931, Margaret Mott of the Grosvenor Library in Buffalo, John Windle of the Newberry Library in Chicago, Gladys Chamberlain of the New York Public Library, and Barbara Duncan of the Eastman School of Music. Other musicologists active in the founding years were Carleton Sprague Smith of New York Public, Glen Haydon of the University of North Carolina, and Charles Warren Fox of Eastman. In fact, the first six presidents of MLA were musicologists; of course Spivacke, Strunk, Kinkeldey, and Smith were also librarians.

Harold E. Samuel is librarian of the Music Library and professor of music, Yale University. He is a former editor of *Notes: Quarterly Journal of the Music Library Association.*

To a large extent the musicologists were looking out for their own interests. They were aiding and abetting the establishment and the enrichment of collections that contained the tools of their research. But they also participated centrally in such "library matters" as indexing *Denkmäler*, devising a music classification scheme at Vassar, inducing the Library of Congress to print cards for music, and inaugurating a mimeographed bulletin for members. The bulletin, edited by O'Meara, became the first series of *Notes*, a publication that to this day has remained the leading international bibliographic journal in the field of music and a cohesive element for music librianship in the United States. Over the years, *Notes* has indeed held MLA together.

In 1941 Glen Haydon reported to the Association at a meeting held at Harvard that he had visited sixteen music libraries recently and found inadequate holdings at most of them. Presumably these included the seven to ten universities that were offering a Ph.D. in musicology at that time. During MLA's first decade, its membership grew considerably: forty-two persons attended the meeting at Cincinnati in 1940. That year MLA had 175 members in twenty-eight states and one in Canada. Almost a third of the membership (52) were from New York State. Massachusetts had twenty members. Clearly more and more libraries across the country were engaging specialists for their music holdings. After World War II, when states upgraded their teachers' colleges and normal schools to branches of enlarged state university systems, new positions were created both for music librarians and music faculty, and new music collections were established. Today MLA has almost 1,200 individual members, and perhaps as many as 600 of them have primary responsibility for a music collection. This rapid infusion of young members as well as the pace of technological change made it necessary at annual meetings to concentrate on technical matters. Although complexities of automation now often dominate MLA conference topics, the basic aims of librarianship—to have the right book in the right place at the right time and to create tools to direct the user to that material—remain as they were in the past. The technical aspects of music librarianship do not generally appeal to musicologists, who no longer attend our meetings. (The last full-time musicologist to serve as president of MLA was Wiley Hitchcock, in 1965 and 1966.) We still need their assistance in other ways, however.

One way musicologists can help is in recruiting persons to the field of music librarianship. Since they are acquainted with large numbers of students, musicologists can identify those who might contribute to our profession. What are we looking for? First of all, the prospective music librarian must have the proper personality and temperament for librarianship. Libraries are service organizations, and not everyone enjoys or is even capable of giving service. In a paper presented at a meeting of the American Library Association in 1937, Otto Kinkeldey listed four goals for the training of a music librarian: (1) acquaintance with the organization and operation of a library, either by means of a degree program in library science or on-the-job training; (2) ability with foreign languages—at least an elementary knowledge of French, German, and Italian; (3) a working knowledge of music bibliography; and (4) a love of music and a basic knowledge of music history and theory.[1] These accomplishments would get a person a job today, too, though on-the-job training is no longer acceptable as an alternative to a master's degree in library science, which now takes precedence over the other requirements. But the vast majority of today's music librarians do have the other qualifications, and the extent to which they possess them will probably determine the size of the collections they will come to manage. As positions in musicology become more difficult to obtain, more holders of doctorates in musicology are turning to music librarianship. Obviously one need not abandon research to become a librarian. Why, however, aren't more people attracted to the field? We in the profession know the variety and challenges of our occupation and enjoy them; musicologists could relay this message to students.

Teaching faculty have always been, and must continue to be, helpful in building and maintaining library collections. This is not so important at the several institutions with "elite" collections, whose librarians usually anticipate the needs of degree programs and of faculty research. Faculty assistance with acquisitions can be very important in college libraries, whose goals differ from those of research libraries. At any rate, it is probably no longer financially feasible to develop exhaustive collections such as already exist in our major music centers. Not only would the costs be unreasonable, but too much of the material is no longer available. Particularly

[1] Otto Kinkeldey, "Training for Music Librarianship: Aims and Opportunities," *ALA Bulletin*, 31 (August 1937), 459–463.

with limited budgets, materials must be carefully selected to support degree programs in history, theory, and performance. Unfortunately some college and university libraries do not have music collections adequate for their degree programs. Here the faculty can play a major role, providing the impetus and advocacy for improving library holdings.

When a student somehow gets an urge to pursue a topic—an urge often inspired by a teacher—the library should have what the student needs or what makes further investigation possible. Therein, of course, lies a goal of education: enticing students to pursue topics independently, without a teacher's supervision. Among general library holdings, music scores can complicate the pursuit of a topic. Books can be read in a reading room; records can be listened to in a record library; but scores must often be taken from the library to a place for performance. Ideally students in performance should read through bushels of scores to become acquainted with the literature; singers should study orchestral music and orchestral musicians should study the song literature. Motivating such students is difficult; they need continuous encouragement from the faculty.

These matters were discussed by Otto Kinkeldey at a meeting of the Music Library Association here at Harvard in 1948. Kinkeldey's talk, "The Music Teacher and the Library," was followed by a talk titled "The Graduate Student and the Library" given by a young Harvard instructor, Richard F. French.[2]

Regarding another matter, Kinkeldey reminded the Cornell community in a librarian's annual report that a university has three essential components: faculty, students, and library. Accrediting agencies, such as the Middle States Association and, for music, the National Association of Schools of Music (NASM), attempt to assure adequate library holdings. Librarians, however, are seldom included on accrediting teams, whose faculty members would perhaps be the first to admit that they are not fully qualified to judge a library's holdings and procedures. NASM pays lip service in its *Handbook* to the importance of libraries but in fact does little about them. Although it would be difficult for the Music Library Association to play the role of national watchdog in assuring strong library programs, the Association should participate in the accrediting activity of NASM.

A final point. Donald Grout, at the 1941 MLA meeting, gave a paper titled "The Music Library and Musicology." He began by quoting Archibald MacLeish, then Librarian of Congress, who defined civilization as "a spider that hangs itself from its past on a continuously lengthening thread." Grout then asked permission to describe musicologists as a nest of spiders—"a group of industrious and possibly annoying insects, whose ever-lengthening thread of communication with the past is maintained by the music library. It is obvious that for the development of musical scholarship no single factor can possibly be of greater importance than the music library. We depend on you [music librarians] for our very existence."[3]

Grout continued by emphasizing the importance of source materials for the musicologist, and he advocated three long-term programs: (1) selecting a limited special field of source materials and collecting heavily in it (as the Library of Congress has done with opera librettos); (2) collecting photographic copies of primary sources (as the Isham Memorial Library at Harvard has done); and (3) "collecting

[2] Both papers were subsequently published in the *Proceedings of the Music Teachers National Association*, 42 (1948), 81–92.

[3] Donald J. Grout, "The Music Library and Musicology," *Notes*, 1st ser., no. 11 (Aug. 1941), 3–12.

and preserving material relative to American music, both past and present." He realized that little or no interest in American music existed then, but that "when such research is undertaken—as it eventually must be—it will be based on the material available in local archives: records of the musical life of a community or a region, its concerts, its musical organizations, its teachers and its performers, the manuscripts and papers of its local composers—in short, material which will enable us to learn what music was composed and performed, when, by whom, under what circumstances, and with what relationship to the whole social life of the people."[4] Grout anticipated by twenty to thirty years the rise of interest in the sociology of music, which we attribute to the influence of ethnomusicology. Paul Fromm made a plea similar to Grout's at an MLA meeting in 1966. Now, of course, it has become permissible to study American music. Scholars must scramble for materials, just as scholars had to scramble thirty or so years ago when it became permissible to study the nineteenth century, whose materials our libraries had not been collecting because there was no demand for them. We now have demand for musical Americana, much of which is in manuscript form and belongs in archives. Our major regional research libraries should be seeking out music sources, past and present—at least those from their own geographical areas. The Library of Congress and the New York Public Library have been collecting American music for decades, as have, on a smaller scale, other libraries and archives around the country (they are identified in Donald Krummel's *Resources of American Music History*).[5] This collecting must include all styles of music. Last fall, the Yale School of Music hosted a meeting of the Canadian and United States chapters of the International Association for the Study of Popular Music. For many the meeting was a revelation, as seventy-five persons from around the country gathered to present and discuss over fifty papers on topics concerning popular music.

Those are some of the ways in which teachers and librarians in the past have influenced each other and in which faculty members today can be helpful. The influences will surely continue to our mutual benefit.

4 Ibid., 10–11.

5 D. W. Krummel, et al., *Resources of American Music History* (Urbana: University of Illinois Press, 1981).

Expanding Our Musical Heritage

Charles Hamm

When I arrived at Princeton many years ago to begin work on a Ph.D. in musicology, all books, monographs, editions, periodicals, and other materials considered necessary for successfully completing the degree had been collected in a large study-seminar room. I went around the entire room taking each volume off the shelf in turn and transferring onto index cards what I took to be the most relevant information about each. This preparation for general examinations was considered eccentric by my fellow students, but it proved effective. The word "canon" was never used then, but the ideology, though never articulated, could not have been clearer. The corpus of music and literature on music necessary for the pursuit of musicology was finite: it was all here in this room; and once our apprenticeship was completed and we moved out into the hard world of academia, our success would be measured by whether or not our own work would one day be brought into this room.

The Firestone Library stacks were situated just outside the door of our sanctuary, and occasionally, when none of my professors or fellow students was about, I would sneak a look at a score by John Cage or Charles Ives, or at a book about southern folk hymnody, or a bound collection of nineteenth-century sheet music. I felt like a teenager browsing through a collection of pornography.

Charles Hamm, the Arthur R. Virgin Professor of Music at Dartmouth College, is the author of *Music in the New World*.

I have no recollection of Princeton's music librarian in those days. If there was one, that individual's duties must have been almost completely routine: learning which bodies of music and which individual composers were part of the musicological canon, then trying to obtain all available editions of the appropriate music and the relevant literature about it.

We graduate students would sometimes speculate about where we might find jobs once we left Princeton. Would we be lucky enough to go to Berkeley or Yale or Illinois or Smith, where we would find a library comparable to the one upon which we had become dependent? Or would we have to take a job at some lesser institution, where the library would be inadequate for our continuing research and teaching? What would become of us in such a place? How could we possibly do what we then knew musicologists were supposed to do?

But all of us, musicologists and librarians alike, inhabit a different planet today. The boundaries of the subject matter of musical research have constantly expanded as a result of at least four separate but related factors:

1. Since I was a graduate student, the discipline of musicology has proliferated astronomically, producing a veritable army of scholars and graduate students and spilling over from the handful of major research universities, where it was once concentrated, into state schools, smaller private colleges, schools of music, and even conservatories. One consequence of this growth has been a demand for more and

more topics for dissertations and faculty research. The graveyard of music formerly ranked unworthy of inclusion in the musicological canon has been desecrated, and once-scorned composers and even entire repertories have been resurrected as grist for dissertations, papers, articles, lectures, courses, even books.

2. The development of four allied disciplines has expanded the horizons of historical musicology. Though some early German scholars had suggested that the music of other cultures should be studied within the context of musicology, this attitude did not prevail in the New World, where the field of ethnomusicology had to be reinvented as a separate discipline, allied as much with the social sciences as with the humanities, and having its own organizational structure and journal. In many schools, however, ethnomusicology has been included under the general umbrella of musicology, and it has consequently redefined and enriched the subject matter, methodology, and research materials of the discipline as a whole. Likwise with the study of American music: in recent decades it has developed its own organizational structure (the Sonneck Society), its own journal (*American Music*), and to some extent its own scholarly profile. In most schools it is now part of the general program in musicology, whose horizons it has helped to expand. Music theory has a similar history; even though it too has developed its own scholarly society and publications, and a distinctive analytical and speculative methodology, it has been integrated into many programs of musicology. Most recently, popular music studies have followed a similar pattern; inventing an organizational structure (the International Association for the Study of Popular Music) a journal (*Popular Music*), and an intellectual profile quite different from that of historical musicology. Yet courses in popular music, and the people who teach them, are commonly situated in the musicology divisions of schools that have ventured into this area.

3. The contextual perspective of recent European thought has modified traditional approaches to musicology. The dominant character of American historical musicology, described variously as positivist, empirical, and humanistic, was shaped primarily by the work of certain German scholars of the nineteenth and early twentieth centuries. But much European musicology has taken quite different directions in the postwar decades. The writings of the Frankfurt School, chiefly those of Theodor Adorno and Walter Benjamin, have proved to be seminal for many younger Europeans, particularly in France, Great Britain, Scandinavia, and Germany itself. Socialist countries, at times isolated intellectually from the West and subjected to quite different ideological climates, have produced individual scholars of brilliance and originality, such as Bence Szabolcsi, János Maróthy, and László Somfai. Jacques Attali, John Blacking, and other contemporary Europeans, approaching music from perspectives that could be loosely labeled neo-Marxist, have had considerable impact on the latest generation of students on the Continent. These various trends all stress contextual study rather than analysis of music as an autonomous object. As Clifford Geertz wrote recently, "It is perhaps only in the modern age and in the West that some people have managed to convince themselves that technical talk about art, however developed, is sufficient to a complete understanding of it; that the whole secret of aesthetic power is located in the formal relations among sounds, images, volumes, themes, or gestures."[1] These

[1] Clifford Geertz, *Local Knowledge: Further Essays in Interface Anthropology* (New York: Basic Books, 1983), p. 96.

approaches, which tend to resonate with gender studies, semiology, deconstruction, and other recent trends in interdisciplinary scholarship and literary criticism, have thus far had more impact on younger American scholars than on their elders.

4. Much recent musical scholarship has drawn on methodologies and types of discourse from other academic disciplines. At the same time, scholars from other disciplines are increasingly involved in research and writing on music. Recent contributors to the journal *American Music* come from American studies, musical performance, sociology, composition, English, folklore, and music librarianship; the latest issues of Cambridge University Press's journal *Popular Music* have included articles by authors identifying their primary fields as American cultural history, information technology, ethnomusicology, film studies, linguistics, communications research, criticism and interpretive theory, experimental psychology, English, philosophy, architecture, sociology, music criticism, journalism, Spanish, and, of course, musicology.

Each of these four trends has brought with it a demand for different materials needed for scholarship, and taken together they have expanded almost beyond belief the range and quantity of the reference and research materials that the music librarian might be asked to acquire or provide access to in support of such scholarship.

A bit reluctantly at times, but inexorably, we are being dragged into the electronic global village of the late twentieth century. With microfilming, international computer cataloging of musicological literature, computerized databases, computer scanning of documents, faxing, and similar marvels, musicologists in every part of the country have the possibility of equal access to a growing repository of materials. And it is not difficult to guess where all this is leading. Fifteen years ago I could not have conceived of a library such as the one we now have at Dartmouth, one with a computerized on-line catalog that provides the sole access to information about the collection with far greater detail and flexibility than was possible with the old card catalog. Today it may be difficult to imagine a library where computers provide instant access to a single copy of a book or a piece of music held in a central location such as the Library of Congress—the entire document, not just the title or abbreviated information—but the technology already exists to bring this about. It seems clear that eventually the chief concern of librarians will no longer be with acquisition, but with access.

The study-seminar room at Princeton is still there, but I cannot imagine students preparing for general examinations or selecting dissertation topics today by using only the material contained in that room. It would take a hundred such rooms to house the material that students might need, depending on the directions of their research.

A recent study commissioned and published by The Research Libraries Group in an effort to "obtain a broad view of the shape of each [of eight] disciplines—how its dominant concerns have evolved over the last 15–20 years, and what its new frontiers are—and to determine the relationship between these trends and the data requirements of the discipline"[2] concludes:

> Undoubtedly the most striking trend in the humanities is the spread of interdisciplinary work into the corners of virtually every discipline . . . [appearing] to signal

[2] Constance C. Gould, principal author, *Information Needs in the Humanities* (Stanford, Cal.: Research Libraries Group, 1988), p. 1.

> a re-evaluation of the 19th-century German model on which the present departmental structure is based. A related phenomenon is the increased interest in all aspects of culture, from popular to elite.[3]

> [Although the] focus of musicology has been on "early" music, particularly that of the Renaissance and Baroque periods, later composers and music [are] now receiving more attention . . . [and] the study of . . . American music and the music of other non-European cultures is "beginning to penetrate the musicological establishment."[4]

> The interest in "low" culture as well as "high" is evident in virtually all of the disciplines, and has a decided effect on the types of information researchers seek. In history, scholars seek information about popular culture through materials ranging from comic almanacs to radio shows. In the history of art, the culture producing the art has come under scrutiny. In literature, the "canon" is no longer confined to standard literary works.[5]

> Because most ethnic music does not have written scores, ethnomusicologists are wholly dependent on sound recordings. The contemporary genres of film music, jazz, and rock music are increasingly the subject of study; here, too, sound recordings are essential. Videotechnology, applicable to research on both contemporary music and traditional genres such as opera, will be relied upon more in the future.[6]

This institutional reaffirmation of my own observations makes it possible for me to offer the following comments with more conviction.

Relationships among scholarship, librarianship, and technology are far more complex today than they were when I began my schooling, and will become even more complex and interdependent in the future. No longer do scholars define the character and scope of musical research, and librarians then acquire what is necessary to satisfy these needs, with technology helping in this acquisition. Today, instead, music librarians and technology itself are playing an increasingly active role in determining the directions and character of musical research. For one thing, more and more music librarians are themselves trained and practicing scholars, with degrees in musicology or related fields and membership in scholarly societies in addition to the MLA. Furthermore, music librarians have tended to be more concerned with evolving technology than have musicologists, and they have taken important initiatives in adapting this technology to the acquisition of materials in order to provide access to an ever-broadening range of information.

Music librarians also help shape the direction of musical research in the mere assembly and organization of collections, particularly when this is done in the teeth of musicological opinion. Charles Ives lay outside the canon when I was a student, and John Kirkpatrick must have been a lonely figure for many years as he worked his way through the Ives Collection at Yale; but the judgment on Ives has been reversed, and these days one can sometimes find as many musicologists gathered at the Ives Collection as in the reading room of the New York Public Library. It was librarians who first gathered collections of American sheet music, tunebooks, and hymnals of the eighteenth, nineteenth, and twentieth centuries, and it was music librarians who brought up from basements and other storage areas these materials that were earlier unwanted and unused by musicologists and theorists.

Furthermore, I would argue that certain new modes of musicological research, and even specific projects, have resulted from the available technology itself, rather than from the abstract theorizing of musicologists concerning the discipline's

[3] Ibid., p. 52.

[4] Ibid., p. 40.

[5] Ibid., p. 52.

[6] Ibid., p. 44.

development. For example, the vast cataloging project of Renaissance manuscripts at the University of Illinois would have been unthinkable without the technology of microfilming. The recent comprehensive computer cataloging and indexing of American theatre materials held in Baker Library at Dartmouth College—a project initiated by the library staff and supported by the National Endowment for the Humanities—has generated types of research that before would have been inconceivable. Joel Whitburn's various computer-produced compilation-indexes of *Billboard* charts over the years have substantially altered some popular music research agendas in the 1980s. In my own case, I wouldn't have dared to embark on one of my present research projects without having available the databases of several large sheet music collections (including the one at Dartmouth College). Using a small number of keywords, I can search through tens of thousands of American popular songs to identify a large collection of songs belonging to the particular genre that is the focus of my research.

Though the idea did not originate with John Cage, he said it as well as anyone else: "Only the present is fixed; the past is always changing." By the middle of the twentieth century, historical musicology, in league with other academic disciplines, had constructed an impressively reasoned image of the past that *was* in fact relatively fixed, at least in broad outline, with only details to be filled in. Now, at century's end, we are somewhere quite different, much more aware of how little we still know about the past, much more aware of how many additional dimensions and how much more material must be brought to our study of music and musical life.

To sum up, the past ain't what it used to be, and it never was. In order to understand and preserve our musical heritage, scholars and librarians, working together, need to identify every possible source of information pertaining to our musical life, and then use all available technology to acquire or gain access to it—all of it. It's far more complicated and difficult this way, but it's also more fun. And I think if I were beginning my career these days I might choose to be a music librarian.

Preserving Our Heritage for the Future

Dena J. Epstein

Dena J. Epstein is assistant music librarian (ret.), University of Chicago, and a former president of the Music Library Association. She is the author of *Sinful Tunes and Spirituals: Black Folk Music to the Civil War*, and the editor of *I Came a Stranger: The Story of a Hull-House Girl*, by her mother, Hilda Satt Polacheck.

Historians are supposed to be concerned with the past, not the future. But the rapid technological changes that have altered printing, publishing, and library processes—such as microcomputers, optical disks, telefacsimile, and cassettes, both audio and video—will inevitably influence the methodology of historians.[1] How much influence they will have is another matter altogether. The fantasy that was popular in the literature not too long ago of the "paperless" library where all literature was entered into a central computer lies at one extreme.[2] In this scholarly Shangri-la, the historian sits in the comfort of home or office developing an idea. Punching a few buttons on a personal computer will instantly bring forth all relevant literature. It has even been conjectured that the computer could "automatically launch an empirical investigation and make suitable generalizations."[3] A few more buttons could edit and document the paper, another button could order a printout, and a new contribution to scholarship would emerge, ready to be entered into the central computer for the edification of other scholars.

This fantasy seems now to have fewer enthusiastic advocates than it once had. Humanistic scholars use a varied vocabulary that can make on-line retrieval difficult if not impossible. Moreover, on-line databases frequently lack retrospective files whereas historians depend on older material in a variety of subject fields that may be needed by only a few widely-scattered readers.[4] These problems may be solved as more retrospective files become available, but it seems unlikely that complete automation of research library collections will occur. The historian enthusiastically welcomes the very real help that technology can provide in expediting such tedious tasks as collating, indexing, compiling concordances, editing, and the like. Conversely, the disadvantages of electronic media—their inherent instability and the problems presented by equipment obsolescence—should not be ignored. Historians will continue for the foreseeable future to rely on print as their basic resource and means of communication.

1 "Contemporary Technology in Libraries," Beth M. Paskoff, issue ed., *Library Trends*, 37 (1989).

2 F. W. Lancaster, *Toward Paperless Information Systems* (New York: Academic Press, 1978), and his *Libraries and Librarians in an Age of Electronics* (Arlington, Va: Information Resources Press, 1982). See also George R. Jaramillo, "Computer Technology and Its Impact on Collection Development," *Collection Management*, 10 (1988), 1–13.

3 C. W. Churchman, *The Design of Inquiring Systems: Basic Concepts of Systems and Organization* (New York: Basic Books, 1971), p. 117, quoted in Lancaster, *Libraries and Librarians in an Age of Electronics*, p. 135.

4 Peter Stern, "Online in the Humanities: Problems and Possibilities," *Journal of Academic Librarianship*, 14 (1988), 161–164.

The task of the cultural historian was well described in Richard Altick's *The Scholar Adventurers* as the solving of

> a vast and tangled puzzle—the contradictions, the obscurities, the very silence which the passage of time leaves behind in the form of history. To repair the damage done by those who in past ages have falsified, distorted, or destroyed the written record . . . requires detective talents—and staying power—of the highest order. . . .
>
> Research is frequently dull and laborious beyond description. . . . Much of it ends in despair. . . . But the same research has nevertheless provided us with an understanding . . . which was impossible fifty or a hundred years ago.[5]

Historical interpretations can vary widely over time as social patterns change. Cultural history, however historians try to protect it, is affected by prejudice and political myopia. When I began my research in the history of African-American folk music in the early 1950s, most scholars regarded such a search as an exercise in futility. "There is no trustworthy evidence before the Civil War," wrote one expert;[6] "The Negro is not distinguished by culture from the dominant group. Having completely lost his ancestral culture, . . ." wrote another.[7] Given the voluminous literature on slavery, it seemed incredible that nowhere was there a contemporary description of music, dancing, and instruments. At that time, much of the contemporary literature was disregarded as being unreliable. This was particularly true of the slave narratives, published recollections of fugitive slaves written before the Civil War. Ulrich Phillips, the most influential historian of the South in his generation, damned these writings as a group: "Ex-slave narratives in general . . . were issued with so much abolitionist editing that as a class their authenticity is doubtful."[8] A healthy skepticism about his judgments has, however, been justified by time. At least two of the most maligned narratives have been subsequently authenticated from contemporary records, such as census lists and legal documents.

Solomon Northup's *Twelve Years a Slave* includes a vivid, first-hand account of the life of a slave fiddler (figure 1), while Harriet Jacobs's *Incidents in the Life of a Slave Girl, Written by Herself* describes the John Canoe festival at Christmas in antebellum coastal North Carolina, a celebration better known in the West Indies.[9] Thus, slave narratives, originally judged wholly unreliable, are now considered a highly valued primary source.

Music historians now accept the view that music is influenced by the life around it. Almost everyone is aware that Charles Ives was an insurance executive as well as a composer and that Benny Goodman received his early training in a settlement house music school at Hull House. A recent history of music in late medieval Bruges drew upon "its social, cultural, intellectual, economic, urban, liturgical, and ecclesiastical histories"—not an easy task.[10] Music librarians cannot be expected to

5 Richard D. Altick, *The Scholar Adventurers* (New York: Macmillan, 1960), pp. 2–3.

6 D. K. Wilgus, *Anglo-American Folksong Scholarship Since 1898* (New Brunswick, N.J.: Rutgers University Press, 1959), "Appendix 1: The Negro-White Spiritual," pp. 345–364.

7 E. Franklin Frazier, *The Negro in the United States*, rev. ed., (New York: MacMillan, 1957), pp. 680–681, quoted in Lawrence W. Levine, *Black Culture and Black Consciousness: Afro-American Folk Thought from Slavery to Freedom* (New York: Oxford University Press, 1977), p. 443.

8 Ulrich Bonnell Phillips, *Life and Labor in the Old South* (Boston: Little, Brown, 1941), p. 219.

9 Solomon Northup, *Twelve Years a Slave*, ed. Sue Eakin and Joseph Logsdon (Baton Rouge: Louisiana State University Press, 1968), and Harriet A. Jacobs, *Incidents in the Life of a Slave Girl, Written by Herself*, ed. Jean Fagin Yellin (Cambridge, Mass.: Harvard University Press, 1987).

10 Paula Higgins, review of *Music in Late Medieval Bruges*, by Reinhard Strohm, *Journal of the American Musicological Society*, 42 (1989), 152.

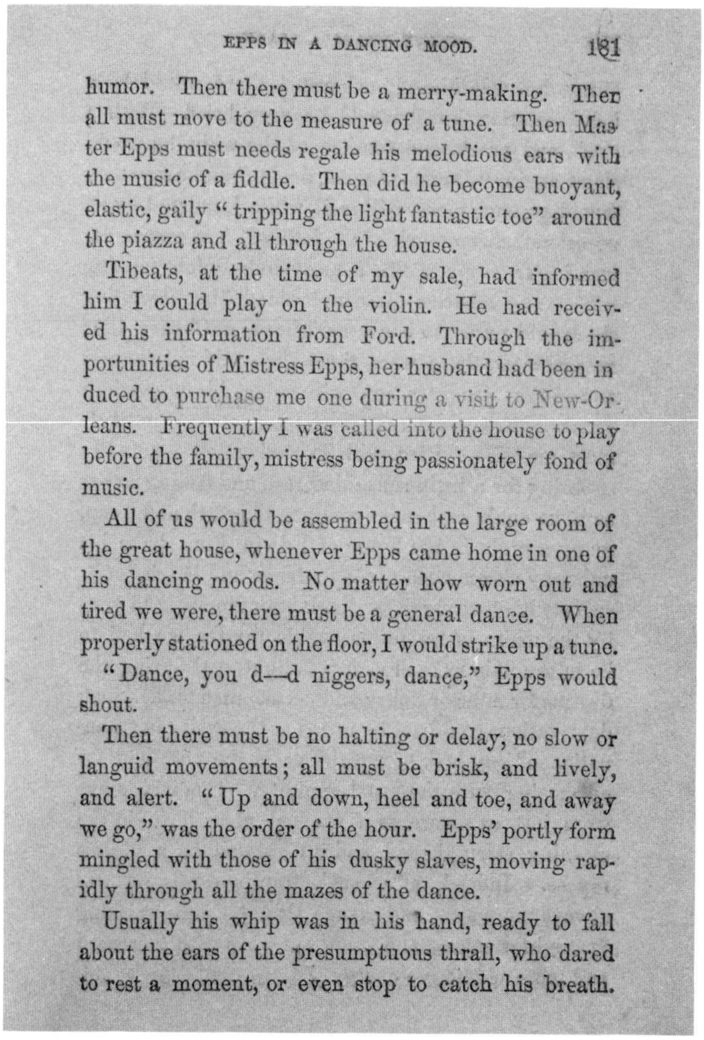

EPPS IN A DANCING MOOD. 181

humor. Then there must be a merry-making. Then all must move to the measure of a tune. Then Master Epps must needs regale his melodious ears with the music of a fiddle. Then did he become buoyant, elastic, gaily " tripping the light fantastic toe" around the piazza and all through the house.

Tibeats, at the time of my sale, had informed him I could play on the violin. He had received his information from Ford. Through the importunities of Mistress Epps, her husband had been induced to purchase me one during a visit to New-Orleans. Frequently I was called into the house to play before the family, mistress being passionately fond of music.

All of us would be assembled in the large room of the great house, whenever Epps came home in one of his dancing moods. No matter how worn out and tired we were, there must be a general dance. When properly stationed on the floor, I would strike up a tune.

"Dance, you d—d niggers, dance," Epps would shout.

Then there must be no halting or delay, no slow or languid movements; all must be brisk, and lively, and alert. " Up and down, heel and toe, and away we go," was the order of the hour. Epps' portly form mingled with those of his dusky slaves, moving rapidly through all the mazes of the dance.

Usually his whip was in his hand, ready to fall about the ears of the presumptuous thrall, who dared to rest a moment, or even stop to catch his breath.

Figure 1. From Solomon Northup's Twelve Years a Slave *(1855; originally published 1853).*

have all these resources at their fingertips, let alone in their libraries, but they should be aware of the widening boundaries of music scholarship and should help direct scholars to appropriate materials.

The effort that has gone into reconstructing the musical life of Renaissance Florence or medieval Bruges may also be necessary to recapture the musical life of the United States in the recent past. Examples of the thoughtless destruction of potentially valuable research materials may provide object lessons for music librarians of today and tomorrow. Consider the treatment given to the records of the Federal Music Project of the New Deal's Works Projects Administration. Although widely recognized as the most extensive program of government support for music that the United States has ever seen, its historical record is widely scattered and incomplete. We do not know how much was simply discarded. When the project was terminated, many records were sent to the National Archives and the Library of Congress, but many more, including concert programs, orchestral scores and parts, oral history transcripts, and collections of folk music and texts, were left elsewhere. The Illinois State Historical Library, for example, holds the archives, in thirty-six boxes, of the Federal Music Project in Illinois from the years 1935–43.[11]

[11] D. W. Krummel et al., *Resources of American Music History* (Urbana: University of Illinois Press, 1981), p. 111.

One portion of the project that is well worth serious study is the Composers' Forum-Laboratory, "a workshop to encourage new musical compositions by American artists. . . . A composer whose work was chosen . . . could rehearse the performers and conduct the orchestra. . . . Following the performance, the audience would discuss the work."[12]

The roster of composers represented on the programs of the Forum in New York City alone reads like a "Who's Who in Twentieth-Century American Music": Marc Blitzstein, Ernest Bloch, Henry Brant, Carlos Chávez, Aaron Copland, Ruth Crawford Seeger, Paul Creston, Hanns Eisler, Howard Hanson, Roy Harris, Mary Howe, Otto Luening, Walter Piston, Quincy Porter, Wallingford Riegger, William Schuman, Roger Sessions, and Virgil Thomson. William Schuman, who received the first performance of his serious music there, in October 1936, said that he had "gained ten years by the experience."[13] The success of the Forum-Laboratory idea in New York led to its establishment in other cities, including Boston, Philadelphia, Cleveland, Detroit, Chicago, Milwaukee, Minneapolis, Oklahoma City, and Los Angeles.

There is, surprisingly, no history of this significant effort, hardly even an awareness that it existed. *Amerigrove* mentions it in passing in a brief paragraph on the Works Progress Administration.[14] The only hint about the location of some of its records that appears in the index to *Resources of American Music History* is an ambiguous entry, "Composers' Forum," referring to the New York Public Library.[15] We do not know what works were performed or how the audiences reacted.

Besides the Composers' Forum-Laboratory, the Music Project established performing companies—orchestras, bands, dance and theatre orchestras, chamber ensembles, vocal groups, Negro choruses, and opera companies—that were separate from those sponsored by the Theatre Project and its dance companies. Most of the Theatre Project materials are now housed at George Mason University in Virginia, where an effort is being made to encourage their reserach use. The Writers' Project and the Theatre Project have received some attention, but so little has been written about the Music Project that the Library of Congress bibliography on the WPA published in 1982 includes only a meager list of titles. The section "Where Is It Now?" omits the Music Project altogether.[16] What a heartbreaking example of the neglect and destruction visited upon our heritage! Fortunately research has begun on the history of the Music Project in one city, Los Angeles.[17]

In addition to distortion and destruction, historians must cope with the enormous gaps in the historic record caused by the neglect of large sectors of the population. Ignored or forgotten were women, African-Americans, immigrants, and the poor, along with their creations—non-European and popular cultures. The histories of

[12] Marguerite D Bloxom, comp., *Pickaxe and Pencil: References for the Study of the WPA* (Washington: Library of Congress, 1982), p. 45.

[13] Ashley Pettis, "The WPA and the American Composer," *Musical Quarterly*, 26 (1940), 101–112. A list of the composers whose works were performed and of media of performance is given on pp. 103–104.

[14] *The New Grove Dictionary of American Music*, s.v. "Works Progress Administration (WPA), Federal Music Project of the."

[15] *Resources of American Music History*, p. 257.

[16] Bloxom, *Pickaxe and Pencil*, pp. 51–71. Milton Meltzer in his *Violins and Shovels: The WPA Arts Projects* (New York: Delacorte Press, 1976) claims that "transcripts of the discussions in New York and Boston were made and copies filed with the Library of Congress" (p. 96), but no transcripts were reported to *Resources of American Music History*.

[17] Catherine P. Smith, "Operas, Grand and Light: Produced by the Federal Music Project in Southern California, 1936–1939" (paper presented at the Annual Conference of the Sonneck Society for American Music, Nashville, April, 1989); and Stephen M. Fry, "Sources for the Study of the WPA Music Project in Los Angeles," in *California's Musical Wealth: Sources for the Study of Music in California* (Santa Barbara: Music Library Association, Southern California Chapter, 1989).

the past that dealt only with the great masters or the upper classes left a sadly distorted picture.

With regard to women, progress has been made, but no impartial evaluation of their accomplishments has yet been made. For instance, the biographical sketch of Fanny Mendelssohn in *The New Grove* of 1980 reads in part:

> Fanny is said to have been as musically gifted as her brother. . . . However, her historical importance consists in her having provided . . . much essential source material for the biography of Felix. . . . Six of her songs were published under her brother's name. . . . Most of her compositions, however, . . . were never printed.[18]

Why her songs were published "under her brother's name" and why most of her works were never published at all is not explained. This article is not a reprint from earlier editions but was written expressly for *The New Grove* by Karl-Heinz Köhler, of Weimar, Germany. Perhaps it represents some progress, since there is no entry at all for Fanny in the German music encyclopedia *Die Musik in Geschichte und Gegenwart*. A proper evaluation of Fanny Mendelssohn as a composer will require examination of those manuscripts that have remained unpublished for almost one hundred and fifty years.

On occasion even the resources of the greatest research libraries will not be sufficient to resolve a problem. Take the need to verify the performance of Florence Price's Symphony in E minor by the Chicago Symphony Orchestra in 1933, the first performance of a symphony by an African-American woman. All accounts agreed on these facts, but the program book of the orchestra makes no mention of the work. It was necessary to consult the orchestra's scrapbooks to learn that a special series of concerts was given in honor of the Century of Progress Exposition, sponsored by a Friends of Music organization. These concerts, played at the Auditorium Theater rather than at Orchestra Hall, did in fact include the performance of the symphony.

Manuscript materials still in private hands frequently are needed to resolve research questions, and the historian must both locate them and persuade owners to grant access. Many such queries go unanswered, but others are welcomed. I still remember being told by Lucy McKim Garrison's surviving daughter-in-law that I was the first person ever to inquire about a woman in the Garrison family, although they were inundated by queries about the men. Lucy was a practicing musician in a small way, but the key to her history lay in that of her family and her husband's family. Tracing a married woman if one does not know her husband's name can be next to hopeless. Serendipity and luck may be as important as diligence and skill.

Serendipity, the gift of finding something valuable that we are not looking for, can be among the happiest moments in the life of an historian, especially if it solves a puzzle that had baffled us for years. I had inherited some books that had belonged to Thorvald Otterström, a name that probably is not familiar to many of you. Otterström was a Danish theorist who settled in Chicago in 1892, composed many chamber works and songs, wrote several textbooks, and created a number of new scales as an alternative to atonality.[19] The *National Union Catalog* lists forty-seven entries under his name, including a canon, chorale and fugue for large orchestra published in Berlin in 1930. Among the books I inherited was an 1867 edition of *Slave Songs of the United States* and an annotated copy of Samuel Coleridge-Taylor's *Twenty-Four Negro Melodies* (figure 2). What had these books to do with a founder

[18] *The New Grove Dictionary of Music and Musicians*, s.v. "Mendelssohn (-Bartholdy) [Hensel], Fanny."

[19] These are described in his *A Theory of Modulation* (Chicago: University of Chicago Press, 1935).

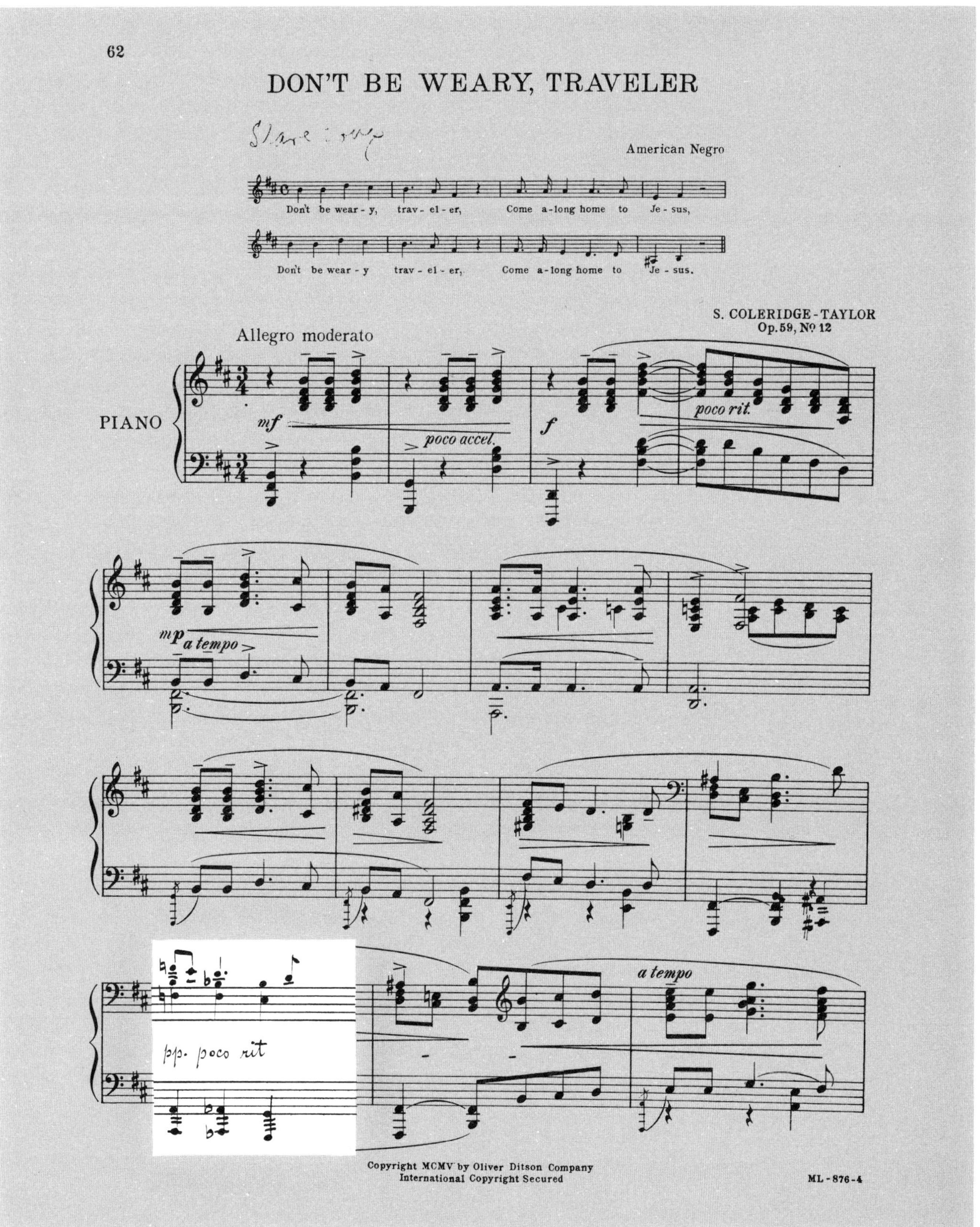

Figure 2. Samuel Coleridge-Taylor's Twenty-four Negro Melodies *(1905) showing emendations by Thorvald Otterström.*

of the Bruckner Society in America, a scholarly and austere theorist? Why had he made those careful annotations? No explanation presented itself, and I abandoned the problem. Recently, however, in examining the repertory of the Chicago Symphony Orchestra, I found a work by Otterström, *Suite—American Negro*, performed by the orchestra in 1916 and repeated in 1918, 1927, and 1936. The program notes made it clear that the thematic material was drawn from those two books. I hope the Orchestra still has the score and will let me examine it.

Music librarians can be of great assistance to historians by alerting them to new technology that may be of use to them, such as the "American Memory" program of the Library of Congress, which will "disseminate historical documentation and images of artifacts in its collections to libraries throughout the country." Stored on laser videodiscs and compact discs will be "Visions of America: Seeing the Nation through the Lens of Popular Art and Culture," including "20 hours of ethnic folk music and 3,000 Currier and Ives prints."[20]

Wilmarth Sheldon Lewis wrote in his *Collector's Progress*: "Every great library has tens of thousands of books that may not be called for once in a decade. Paradoxically, it is these books that make it great."[21] The problems inherent in providing access to little-used material must be solved in constructive ways such as relying upon storage facilities, collection sharing, networks, and consortia rather than resorting to simple deaccessioning. Cultural history is full of horror stories, like the Bodleian Library's discarding its first folio of Shakespeare's plays when a new folio appeared. Old city directories can date publications and instruments through addresses. Railroad timetables can plot the itinerary of a touring musician. Newspaper advertisements and old programs document repertories, while family Bibles and tombstones can establish dates of birth and death. Our cultural heritage will be preserved for the future in many forms: manuscripts, prints, microtexts, recordings, electronic formats, optical discs, and others. Locating the necessary material, in whatever form it may have, remains the mutual task of the librarian and the scholar.

[20] " 'American Memory' Translates Culture to the Electronic Age," *Library Journal*, 114 (1989), 20.

[21] Wilmarth Sheldon Lewis, *Collector's Progress* (New York: Knopf, 1951), p. 252, quoted in David H. Stam, " 'Prove All Things: Hold Fast That Which is Good!': Deaccessioning and Research Libraries," *College and Research Libraries*, 43 (1982), 11.

Choosing What Not to Preserve

James B. Coover

The trouble with our time is that the future is not what it used to be.
—Paul Valéry

If the title of this essay raises expectations of forthcoming advice about weeding and deaccessioning—or more specifically about what to do with quaint Edwardian books on "modern music" and embrittled nineteenth-century scores—disappointment is sure to follow. The peculiar notion behind this paper is that difficult question all librarians face: since we cannot save everything, what can we safely—even guiltlessly—discard?

For the better part of a sabbatical I stalked an answer to that question and wrestled with the idea of "de-perpetuation." No revelations were granted me, no fresh, immutable guidelines suddenly evolved, nor any ways to perform triage without regret. It probably should have been obvious at the outset that, just as one order of selection policies will not work for every library, neither will any generalized *un*-preservation guidelines, and it was pointless to struggle towards them. Semantics is too much the hobgoblin. The many articles about selection that divide a literature into classes and urge selectors to choose for each one materials that are important, good, basic, needed, and permanent, founder on these spongy words.

Their antonyms—unimportant, bad, peripheral, inessential, and impermanent—are just as useless when it comes to deciding what *not* to preserve. Were we to agree about what materials fit those negative descriptions and act accordingly, items so branded might someday no longer exist anywhere—an outcome that surely none of us wants. Our research experiences and those of our libraries' users lead us, instead, to hope that together we can somehow save at least one copy of everything ever printed. In an essay on conservation Donald Krummel wonderingly asks, "How can we ever wish to save anything less than the totality of the record of civilization?"[1]

Historically, of course, our preservation statistics are not very good. Probably half the printed records since Gutenberg have been lost, mostly through neglect.[2] The

James B. Coover is director of the music library and Albert, Jr., and Henrietta Ziegele Professor of Music, State University of New York at Buffalo. He is a former president of the Music Library Association. His latest books are *Music at Auction: Puttick and Simpson (of London), 1794–1971* and *Antiquarian Catalogs of Musical Interest.*

1 D. W. Krummel, "Kepler and his Custody: Scholarship and Conservation Policy," in *Conserving and Preserving Library Materials*, ed. K. L. Henderson and W. T. Henderson, Allerton Park Institute, 1981 (Urbana-Champaign: University of Illinois, 1983), pp. 165–179. Just preceding the quotation, Krummel writes, "Rather than proposing that there is any such thing as 'permanent research value,' we might better remember that not anything—and therefore everything—has potential value."

2 Maurice Rickards, "History's Other Half," *Private Library*, 3d ser. (1980), 8. David Stam lists some of the obvious causes: (1) most lost paper records vanished because they seemed useless, outdated, disheveled; (2) others were victims of war and natural events; (3) vast numbers were lost inadvertently; (4) still others were destroyed through the acts of censors who served nations, religions, and other groups trying to support their omniscience and positions of power, or school boards, the American Legion, and others attempting to squelch ideas they did not like. " 'Prove All Things: Hold Fast That Which is Good': Deaccessioning and Research Libraries," *College and Research Libraries*, 43 (1982), 7–8.

works of Daniel Heartz, Howard Brown, Claudio Sartori, and others, and the *Einzeldrucke* volumes of the *Répertoire International des Sources Musicales* emphasize this negligence by citing sources that no longer exist and some that survive only as *unica*. To preserve what we now own is a daunting enough challenge, especially in view of estimates that at least seventy-five million books are at present brittle and endangered. But simultaneously saving the many publications produced in our own time presents an even more intimidating dare as well as a grand opportunity.

So let us talk first of cooperative collection management and preservation, and the impact of technology on them in the future—the distant future, the most stimulating context in which to pose this nettlesome question of what not to preserve.

Forecasting, of course, is chancy. Alvin Toffler warned us in *Future Shock* that science rides a train rushing through unexpected switches while sitting in the caboose facing backwards.[3] Even so, we must try to look beyond present-day technologies, guess at the nature of music libraries in the future, and speculate about what the musicians and scholars of the next millenium would like us to save for them today.

We can suppose that performers will not be obsolete: the traditional repertory will still need them. Electronic performance may so predominate, though, that historians and critics will outnumber live artists.[4] Artificial intelligence systems (simulated cognition systems, if you prefer) running on hypercube multiprocessors will be pervasive. Composers may create by making faces and talking to interactive computer monitors (which may talk and grimace back!),[5] while theorists analyze those creations by the same means. Kindergarten through twelfth-grade classrooms, largely electronic, will require fewer animate music educators. Optical memory cards the size of a credit card will hold scores, videos, sound recordings, analyses, and commentaries for large-scale works, even whole genres of music.[6] And—lest we forget—almost everyone alive will have grown up enjoying "the Library of Congress on a laptop."[7]

These are, admittedly, humdrum speculations, but they ought to foster conjecture about music libraries beyond the next decade.[8] Imagining in that frame is, of course, not easy, because how to future-think is not a skill taught by most library

3 Alvin Toffler, *Future Shock* (New York: Random House, 1970).

4 MIDI software is already used lavishly in commercial recording studios and has eliminated jobs for many live performers. See Travis Charboneau's "Music's Electronic Future," *The Futurist*, 21 (1987), 35–37.

5 "Automated intuition and brain-type metalanguages will reduce composition to asking properly phrased questions," predicts Randolph N. Jackson in "The Future of Electronic Music," *Computer Music Journal*, 13, no. 1 (1989), 10–11.

6 Something similar is already available. In 1989 Warner New Media of Burbank, California released a performance of Mozart's *Magic Flute* on CD-ROM that includes the audio, "textual information downloaded into RAM and accessed during the appropriate music segments," English and German versions of the libretto, variants of some passages, definitions, and comments, including "A Tour Through the Opera" by Roger Englander, all for sixty-six dollars! See also Lois F. Lunin's "Optical Memory Cards—Rounding the Corner?" *Bulletin of the American Society for Information Service*, 14 (1988), 35.

7 Steve Cisler, "Taking the Ship Out of the Bottle," *Electronic Library*, 6 (1988), 329–330.

8 Compared, for example, to the notion behind Hans Moravec's recent *Mind Children: The Future of Robot and Human Intelligence* (Cambridge, Mass.: Harvard University Press, 1989) in which the author foresees, among other "advances," an attainable semblance of immortality for those humans willing to have their corporeal existence transferred—and extinguished—as their brains are downloaded, one microscopically thin slice at a time, into robots, which then take on human identities. Toffler (*Future Shock*, pp. 434–436) talks of a sophisticated computer system dubbed OLIVER (for On-Line Interactive Vicarious Expediter and Responder) that "will be nothing less than your mechanical alter ego. . . . Pushed to the extreme of science fiction, one can even imagine pin-sized OLIVERs implanted in baby brains, and used, in combination with cloning, to create living—not just mechanical—alter egos."

schools. (And the future is an ever-faster moving target;[9] just thirty years ago, IBM was extolling punched card sorters!) The thousands of citations served up in volumes of *Library Literature* during the 1980s are little help; few future-oriented librarians touch on matters much beyond the next decade.

Nor do there seem to be many library-oriented futurists. Those supposedly in the vanguard, the science-fiction writers, mention libraries infrequently, and when they do, extrapolate mainly from familiar twentieth-century developments.[10] The indexes to science-fiction literature disclose painfully few references to libraries.[11] The physical book that we know is obsolete. Ephemeral image and sound replace old-fashioned reading.[12] In post-nuclear-holocaust stories, elderly survivors sometimes try to interest the young in books from the old days, and most fail. In George Stewart's *Earth Abides*—a barbarous earth where reading is passé—an old man who is about to die takes his grandson for a poignant last look at the crumbling walls and contents of the Berkeley library.[13]

Some high-tech science fiction depicts gigantic, paperless datastores that contain all facts, all knowledge, and machinery that provides instantaneous, three-dimensional retrieval. Jorge Luis Borges, in his "Library of Babel," writes: "It was proclaimed that the library composed all books . . . everything which can be expressed, in all languages. Everything is there."[14] The scholar hero in Robert Silverberg's *The World Inside*, one of the few citizens allowed to read about the old days, taps into a similar galactic databank—he knows not where or by whom maintained.[15] Piper's *Cosmic Computer* encompasses all human knowledge and instantaneously scans, combines data, forms associations, reasons accurately, produces new facts, and predicts future happenings.[16] When he wishes, the hero of Mack Reynolds's *Commune 2000 A.D.* activates a "library-booster" that furnishes immediate on-screen access to all the important governmental and commercial collections in the world. "There was infinite room . . . . So why not store it all, all accumulated information . . . everything, no matter how trivial."[17]

9 I. F. Clarke, "The First Law of Futures," *Futures*, 19 (1987), 197–208. The quote is on page 200. Duane Webster concurs in "Closing the Gap Between Desirability and Achievability," *Journal of Academic Librarianship*, 15 (1989), 201: "Thinking imaginatively about the future of research libraries is hard work. Projecting the present into the future is easier than conceiving a radically transformed future . . . . Reacting to the problems of the moment has limited our ability to shape a more desirable future."

10 Colin Steele, "From Punched Cards to Robots," *Wilson Library Bulletin*, 62, no. 2 (October 1987), 30.

11 I am indebted, therefore, to Colin Steele's article (note 10) and Peter Suedfed and Lawrence M. Ward's "Dark Futures: Psychology, Sci-Fi, and the Ominous Consensus," *Futures*, 8 (1976), 22–39, for aiming me towards much of the science fiction mentioned here. Both articles are entertaining; the latter also paints some very gloomy scenarios. The authors note, for example, that interfacing humans and machines will increase in complexity because the reaction times are different by a ratio of about one to one hundred; but the worst future problem is predicted as a monumentally dense population in which increasingly fewer persons can cope with the "information glut," therefore with life itself (p. 27). Fredrik Pohl in his "Information: Science-Fiction or Fact?" *American Documentation*, 16 (1985), 101, attributes the accuracy rate of science fiction predictions to the principle underlying an old French saying that holds that even a broken clock is right twice a day. Make enough predictions and some are bound to be correct.

12 James Thorpe, "The Future of the Book," in *Books and Prints, Past and Future* (New York: Grolier Club, 1984), pp. 61–69. Elsewhere the author wonders if monks in scriptoria five hundred years ago ever fretted about the future of the manuscript. Furthermore, Charles Krauthammer, in a brilliant essay titled "Disorders of Memory," *Time*, 3 July 1989, 74, posits that "having just now transcended paper and entered the radically ephemeral world of video, [our culture] finds itself living in an ever moving pastless present . . . . Pastlessness is inherent in video."

13 New York: Houghton Mifflin Co., 1949.

14 Jorge Luis Borges, "The Library of Babel," in *Labyrinths*, ed. Donald A. Yates and James E. Irby (New York: New Directions, 1962, 1964), pp. 51–58.

15 Robert Silverberg, *The World Inside* (Garden City, N.Y.: Doubleday, 1971).

16 H. Beam Piper, *The Cosmic Computer* [original title *Junkyard Planet*] (New York: Ace Books, 1963).

17 Mack Reynolds, *Commune 2000 A.D.* (New York: Bantam Books, 1974).

As early as 1963, however, Hal Draper cleverly lampooned immoderate faith in such interstellar databases in his "MS FND IN A LBRY."[18] The manuscript, discovered by an expedition from another galaxy, chronicles the demise, eons earlier, of a multi-galactic, biped civilization. Its cumulated knowledge had been preserved on storage devices smaller than atoms, called "nudged quanta," housed at first in a building twenty-five miles square and two miles high (planted in an ocean to save parking space). When the structure expanded to a height of one hundred miles, cosmic radiation "defarraginated the scanning diffusers," forcing the transfer of the storage devices to artificial planets. To manage so much information, indexes were collected in files, and files in catalogs, so that a citation such as C3-F5-I4 referred to an index to indexes to indexes to indexes in a certain file of files of files of files of files, in turn found in a catalog of catalogs of catalogs. Like them, bibliographies of bibliographies of bibliographies and histories of histories of histories inexorably multiplied beyond the second and third powers. The civilization prided itself that "although hardly anybody knew anything any longer, everybody now knew how to find out everything." Controlling the immense hierarchy was a single drawer containing all knowledge about knowledge. It was the point of access to all the others. But when some junior librarian misshelves it, whammo! civilization, no longer able to communicate, comes apart. Similarly, in Murray Leinster's *Forgotten Planet*, a single mislaid card file in the galaxy's central records results in a lost planet.[19]

Scientists are turning these and like fantasies into reality. "Inventing the Future," some call it.[20] Envisioned are modems, for example, that work at five hundred *million* baud; flat-wall, tactile, holographic monitors that will let us feel Gutenberg's vellum, a Cobden-Sanderson binding, or Stradivari's varnish. Others foresee microscopic robots prowling about inside us zapping suspicious bacteria with atom-sized laser guns. Eventually, as Daniel Hillis suggests, machines will design their successors, and "after a while, we won't understand how they work."[21] Easier to imagine are trucks that load, drive, and unload themselves; anti-aging drugs, happiness pills, and intelligence boosters; scanners that translate; and home robots with personalities that converse, cook, clean, and uncomplainingly do windows. Doctors already practice surgical procedures on three-dimensional digital images and writers create floppy-disc novels with hypercards, while one of our oldest technological wonders continues its long and lonely journey beyond our solar system.[22]

A more radical flight of fancy is needed to imagine that among all the libraries, archives, national music centers, antiquarian dealers, publishers, private collectors,

[18] Hal Draper, "MS FND IN A LBRY," in *17 X Infinity*, ed. G. Conklin (New York: Dell Books, 1963), pp. 52–58.

[19] Murray Leinster, *Forgotten Planet* (New York: Crown, 1984).

[20] This is the subtitle of Stewart Brand's *The Media Lab: Inventing the Future at MIT* (New York: Viking, 1987)—a book that any librarian concerned about the future will find interesting. The description of the work being done at this emporium of "imaginetics" and its scientists' visionary ideas about future information communications in a tightly-wired world are fascinating and sobering. I find it unsettling to discover no entry for "Libraries" in the index.

[21] Brand, *The Media Lab*, p. 189.

[22] Ruth M. Davis, president of the Pymatuning Group working with the National Library of Medicine on digital scanning and storage is another, along with those working at MIT's Media Lab, who looks to science fiction for ideas about our future in "Where will Technology Put the Library of the 21st Century?" *Bulletin of the Medical Library Association*, 75 (1987), 6. She predicts that satellites will someday be "superb preservation sites[s] for library holdings in both digital and analog format" and reminds us of Teilhard de Chardin's early twentieth-century description of a "noosphere," a band of organized information orbiting the earth.

and ordinary musicians in the world, everything worth preserving is, in fact, being preserved. Attaining such a state of grace requires some drastic changes—changes that would include the microfilming or digital storage by all printers and publishers of the items they produce, and codification and commitment by libraries to the goals, terms, and procedures of large coordinated collection development schemes.[23]

We spend too many of our resources buying too much of what everyone else buys. Allocations lag behind needs, so we tend to concentrate on the works of the "masters" while acquiring fewer works by and about the *Kleinmeister*, despite their rapidly multiplying numbers. With befitting expressions of pain, old serials get canceled and new ones passed over. The latest *Urtext* score, a new book about its creator, a piece by one of the three John Adamses, or a Renaissance series from Garland Publishing are all practically automatic purchases. If a reviewer tells us that something "belongs in every self-respecting music library," every you-know-what buys it.

The overlap among comparable institutions can reach nonsensical dimensions, though according to several—albeit not unchallengeable—studies, some heavily-replicated titles are seldom or never used.[24] The redundancy intimates that we slight other genres. Nineteenth-century vocalises and instrumental tutors, for instance, along with other now-decaying "common readers" of various times, and thousands of seldom-performed twentieth-century works, may be among those endangered species. It is probably fair to say that we are not collectively acquiring enough works of secondary or tertiary importance to guarantee their availability in at least one library in the future.

What we discard raises real fears, too. Several years ago it was reported that Harvard "removes about forty-five thousand volumes each year" from its shelves.[25] Are we justified to wonder if these titles are all replicated, and will be preserved, in other collections? Should we be concerned about their disposition: are they preserved on microfilm, sold to dealers or to other libraries, transferred to storage, or given to another institution like the Center for Research Libraries? Another disquieting article, in the *New York Times* for 9 July 1989, reports that the Library of Congress keeps only seven thousand of the thirty thousand-plus items it receives every day.[26] Do the other twenty-four thousand—about nine million a year—end up in a trashbin or as recycled paper, lost to us forever? We hear repeatedly that there are over forty thousand serial titles current today in the sciences alone and that, inevitably, some of them will not be acquired and preserved by any library.

We wonder, then, how such events can occur while library leaders march us into the future behind banners that proclaim "Access, not Collections." If they depend on LC and Harvard to supply the "collections," they need to waken and contemplate some very sizable shortfalls. To focus on access almost to the exclusion

23 "There is increased recognition that each academic library is acquiring a shrinking fraction of available recorded knowledge relevant to the academic programs," says Rita Kane in "Public Service Issues in the 1990s," in *Target '95, Phase I: Perspectives* (Berkeley: University of California Library, 1989), p. 1.

24 The most famous of these studies is probably that conducted by Allen Kent and others, *Use of Library Materials: the University of Pittsburgh Study* (New York: M. Dekker, 1979).

25 Oscar Handlin in "Research Libraries in a Changing Universe: Four Points of View," by Pauline Atherton Cochrane, Oscar Handlin, Hendrik Edelman, and William Herbster," comp. and ed. Dan C. Hazen and J. Gormley Miller, *College and Research Libraries*, 45 (1984), 214–225.

26 That represents decision-making at record—and reckless—speeds.

of ownership seems a dogged disregard of common sense.[27] There is no way around it: access presupposes a collection that exists somewhere and is electronically reachable.

But even such circumstances will probably not be adequate for scholars from the historical disciplines and the humanities. They want the actual books and journals in their hands. They need to flop about randomly in footnotes, indexes, tables of contents, and multiple texts—not struggle to access electronically bits and pieces of information from some remote storage facility. Humanistic scholarship works that way. It is engagingly inefficient. It sputters along by fits and starts, chases blind leads, wanders far afield, and is shot through with speculation and serendipity, workings totally at odds with the idea of electronic remote access. Daniel Bell extols the notion of "ambient context"—what one finds on the shelf on both sides of the primary target—and emphasizes how essential it is to the work of humanists and social scientists.[28]

Delightful surprises lurk in that ambient context, but they are hard to discover on-line—at best a clumsy mode of exploration. Even hypertext "adventuring," though hailed as better than browsing by some advocates, seems woefully jejune when applied to most historical tasks. No process thus far has managed with great efficiency to ferret out and make accessible the *ideas* in our literature, either aural or printed.[29] And those are what humanists seek—ideas not data, processes not facts, nuances not conclusions, the "meaning" that rolls on after the sentences have ended, and the insights wedged perhaps between those sentences. You would think that in this nanosecond computational world they would have been better served by now. We may agree with Patricia Battin when she says that the "Electronic Scholar" deserves "the opportunity to rummage round . . . in the bibliographic wealth of all recorded knowledge," but we would caution her that the humanist finds rummaging at a terminal neither efficient nor intellectually very stimulating.[30]

In the context of present circumstances and in view of future predictions, it seems to me what we ought *not* to preserve is only that which we are assured someone else will. This conclusion will accord small comfort to those who crave bold yardsticks for making instant decisions without pain; and it also decrees work. As a simple

27 For some library leaders, "access, not collections" does not stand as such a Manichaean imperative. Richard De Gennaro, for example, takes a much more rational view of it in his "Technology and Access in an Enterprise Society," *Library Journal*, 114, no. 16 (1 October 1989), 40–43. He, of course, sits atop one of the great collections in the world at the New York Public Library [and subsequently at the Harvard College Library]. For others who control smaller, less consequential collections the shibboleth may be more wish than conviction. As Peter Briscoe and others point out in "Ashurbanipal's Enduring Archetype: Thoughts on the Library's Role in the Future," *College and Research Libraries*, 47 (1986), 121–126: "Lately it has become fashionable to say that access to information, not ownership, is what is important. This is a dangerous oversimplication. Access always presumes or depends on ownership by some party. . . . Research libraries in particular have a fundamental responsibility to collect virtually all recorded knowledge and make it available for use."

28 Daniel Bell, "Gutenberg and the Computer: *Disparate de Miedo* (The Folly of Fear)," in *Books and Prints, Past and Future* (New York: Grolier Club, 1984), pp. 125–146. His views are echoed by many authors including Richard Halsey in his "Recall—Research—Renewal: A Message of Necessity for the University Library," in *Future of Libraries: Panel Discussion . . . Papers from the Millionth Volume Celebration* (Albany, N.Y.: SUNY, 1982), p. 23, and Sue Stone in her "Humanistic Scholars: Information Needs and Uses," *Journal of Documentation*, 38 (1982), 292–313.

29 For example, does any Library of Congress subject heading come near capturing the idea of Barbara Tuchman's book, *The Donkeys*? Is there a keyword search strategy that will find material on "indeterminancy in music"? Or the "diabolical"? What will we retrieve if we ask for data on the "Diet of Worms" (an example offered years ago by Jesse Shera to exhibit the shortcomings of much keyword searching)? A marked advance is the provision of space on the *RILM Abstracts* form for abstractors to add "additional index terms" for names, places, and concepts "that do not appear in the title or abstract."

30 Patricia Battin, "The Electronic Library," *Collection Management*, 9 (1987), 140.

first step, for example, we should check the *National Union Catalog* and the records in the RLIN and OCLC databases before discarding any title. We need to increase our use of field 583 in MARC records where preservation decisions and intentions can be recorded.[31] We need to conclude cooperative agreements about who will preserve certain materials, whether they be large, special collections en masse, or individual books, scores, and recordings. Music librarians need to rejuvenate and extend the cooperative brittle-book preservation project directed several years ago by Victor Cardell.[32]

Cooperative collection development arrangements have been around for a long time. One enacted for New York State in 1981 now involves 140 libraries.[33] Two-thirds of the libraries belonging to the Association of Research Libraries were, by 1983, participating in some kind of resource sharing and collection development activities. These are American traditions going back as far as the post–World War II Farmington Plan.[34] Music librarians, however, have only recently turned to cooperative plans on any significant scale. Some music libraries have competed with each other—quietly, in a refined way (but competed nonetheless)—for a kind of chimerical self-sufficiency, each fearful that they might be found lacking a title listed in a major reference source, such as Heyer, Duckles, Baker, or the *Harvard Dictionary*.[35] That situation will change. A conspectus developed by Michael Keller and others for the Music Program Committee of the Research Libraries Group may indeed be the first formal step towards meaningful cooperation. It aims for "collaborative interdependence."[36] The raw results have already helped some libraries tune their collection building to others' strengths and weaknesses.

More recently, that committee surveyed libraries' collecting levels for twentieth-century scores and recordings. On a list of over twenty-five hundred composers' names compiled by David Day, John Roberts, and others, each library marked the names of composers whose works they were committed to buy—or willing to buy—at a comprehensive level. (The word "comprehensive" did pose semantic problems.) The results revealed overlapping emphasis on the works of dozens of the most distinguished composers. And though RLG libraries do, of course, purchase the works of many composers selectively, the survey was not designed to account for that. It would be scant comfort to have such data, in any case; even a superficial comparison of composers' work-lists with the records in the RLIN database reveals that some pieces are bought by many libraries while others—lesser works—by few or none. If that encourages some library to acquire those neglected

31 Margaret M. Byrnes, "Preservation and Collection Management: Some Common Concerns," *Collection Building*, 9, nos. 3–4 (1989), 43. Byrnes also offers one of the best discussions to date of preservation needs and the related potentials of optical disc technology.

32 It sought to identify libraries willing to guarantee the eternal preservation of certain titles, so that other libraries were free to discard their brittle copies.

33 Joseph F. Schubert, "Coordinated Collection Development for the Purposes of Resource Sharing," *Collection Management*, 7 (1985), 75–83.

34 Paul Mosher, "Cooperative Collection Development Equals Collaborative Interdependence," *Collection Building*, 9, no. 3–4 (1989), 29. See also Richard Dougherty's powerful essay on the topic, "Resource Sharing Among Research Libraries: How It Ought to Work," *Collection Management*, 9 (1987), 79–88.

35 Anna Harriet Heyer, *Historical Sets, Collected Editions, and Monuments of Music: A Guide to Their Contents*, 3d ed. (Chicago: American Library Association, 1980); Vincent H. Duckles and Michael A. Keller, *Music Reference and Research Materials: An Annotated Bibliography*, 4th ed. (New York: Schirmer Books, 1988); Theodore Baker, *Baker's Biographical Dictionary of Musicians*, rev. Nicolas Slonimsky, 7th ed. (New York: Schirmer Books, 1984); *The New Harvard Dictionary of Music*, ed. Don Michael Randel (Cambridge, Mass.: The Belknap Press of Harvard University, 1986).

36 Paul Mosher, "Cooperative Collection Development."

titles, the RLIN database will have improved our collective efforts. But if not, musicians ten years from now may not be able to find those scores.[37]

Any progress in cooperaton should release some time and money that might be used to extend the boundaries of what each library collects. Altered collecting priorities, however, can be difficult to conceptualize, sell to faculty, or implement.[38] The prospect of increased attention on musical ephemera is beguiling. To many persons, though, ephemera, with their troublesome nature, look like prime candidates for unpreservation.[39] They muddle even the most well-designed triage.

The adage "today's trash, tomorrow's treasure" is no longer just the plaintive rallying cry of ephemerists feeling put-upon. Most of us are now aware that the trash consists of primary sources for social history. They are documents created for specific occasions by the actual participants, in obvious contrast to most of the material in our libraries' "ML" and "MT" classifications, which are secondary sources—observations set down after events, most by non-participants. The first European and American documents printed from movable type were ephemera.[40] Of the thirty-five to forty thousand works printed between 1475 and 1640 listed in the revised *Short Title Catalogue*, about ten percent are ephemera.[41] They were, and are, rarely intended for a long life, and most do not enjoy one. The rapid widening of the boundaries of music research heightens the importance of preserving those ephemera that are still at hand.[42] Such sometimes scruffy brochures, catalogs, programs, scrapbooks, and announcements, along with almanacs, calendars, trade cards, indulgences, broadsides, ballads, directories, photographs, and the rest, help us piece together the past or, as a New York State report on conservation puts it, help us locate ourselves "in the stream of time."[43]

Ephemera bear most heavily on the social ambience of civilization, and they are mostly localia. Materials in that category can be gathered effectively without our having to hammer out elaborate collective acquisition agreements. The obligations are already delineated: we each need to collect those materials that document what has happened in our own region—and preserve them assiduously.

Handling ephemera in libraries is no frolic. Granted: the variety of shapes, sizes, and formats is endless, and the distribution of ephemera is infinitely haphazard. They

37 Another such survey may be circulated later this year by Lenore Coral covering large and expensive serials and microfilm sets.

38 RLG's Collection Management and Development Committee reports in *Operations Update*, Issue 51, September 1989, 17, that "twenty-two libraries have pooled tentative commitments to acquire specific chemistry titles for the next five years" and that CMD institutions will be following the same process for business and mathematics serials "later this year." And I will not here go into the long-range effects that cooperative agreements might have on the publishing industry!

39 As suggested by the very title of E. B. Sullivan's article on preserving campaign ephemera: "Hogwash, Snake Oil and the White House," *AB Bookman's Weekly*, 73 (1984), 2467–2468.

40 Alice D. Schreyer, "Permanence of Ephemera," *Printing History*, 4 (1982), 26–27.

41 Katherine F. Pantzer, "Ephemera in the *STC* Revision: A Housekeeper's View," *Printing History*, 4 (1982), 29.

42 Examples of their value are commonplace though apt to be overlooked. Mortality bills, for instance, ephemeral broadsides of the seventeenth century, now provide critical statistics, weekly and cumulative, for the years of the plague. A series of posters that announce concerts conducted by a famous composer put him at a different place at that time from where his biographies put him. Benny Goodman's daughter recently asked for any souvenirs, home movies, or documents related to her father's life for an archive at the Carnegie Hall Museum (reported in "Looking for Mr. Goodman," *Modern Maturity*, Aug.–Sept. 1989, 9).

43 New York (State). Document Conservation Advisory Council, *Our Memory at Risk: Preserving New York's Unique Research Resources* (Albany, N.Y.: State Education Department, 1988). Lane Jennings, in his "Why Books Will Survive," *The Futurist*, 17, no. 2 (April 1983), 11, thinks that "the trashiest, the corniest, the least skillful writings . . . are surrogate memories that reveal values and concerns of those who wrote and read them." It is these, he fears, the "less-famous works, including whole genre routinely dismissed by scholars and critics as trivial, that may be lost to the future."

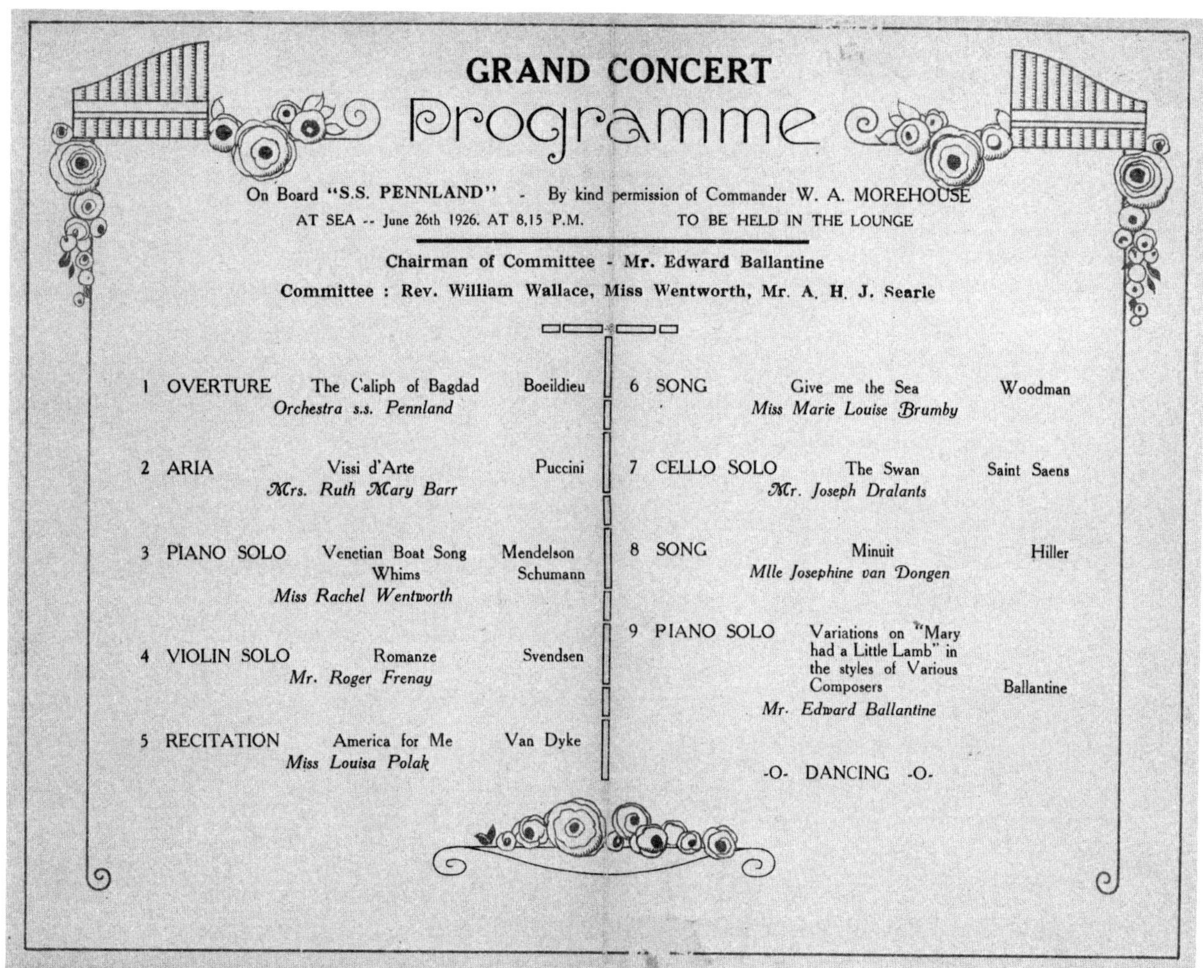

GRAND CONCERT

Programme

On Board "S.S. PENNLAND" - By kind permission of Commander W. A. MOREHOUSE

AT SEA -- June 26th 1926. AT 8.15 P.M. TO BE HELD IN THE LOUNGE

Chairman of Committee - Mr. Edward Ballantine

Committee : Rev. William Wallace, Miss Wentworth, Mr. A. H. J. Searle

1 OVERTURE The Caliph of Bagdad Boeildieu
Orchestra s.s. Pennland

2 ARIA Vissi d'Arte Puccini
Mrs. Ruth Mary Barr

3 PIANO SOLO Venetian Boat Song Mendelson
Whims Schumann
Miss Rachel Wentworth

4 VIOLIN SOLO Romanze Svendsen
Mr. Roger Frenay

5 RECITATION America for Me Van Dyke
Miss Louisa Polak

6 SONG Give me the Sea Woodman
Miss Marie Louise Brumby

7 CELLO SOLO The Swan Saint Saens
Mr. Joseph Dralants

8 SONG Minuit Hiller
Mlle Josephine van Dongen

9 PIANO SOLO Variations on "Mary had a Little Lamb" in the styles of Various Composers Ballantine
Mr. Edward Ballantine

-O- DANCING -O-

Concert programs, such as this example documenting a shipboard concert, are often regarded as ephemera.

frustrate conventional filing, binding, and shelving; many are surpassingly irksome to catalog or index. Nevertheless, libraries are the institutions that society depends on to "take the responsibility for preserving all the material that no one has a personal reason for storing."[44]

Fortunately, before long, it will be quick, easy, inexpensive, and probably routine to conserve most library materials in digital form on some optical medium. Robot scanners controlled by artificial intelligence programs will cache, and at the same time index, the ideas contained in documents. They may identify nuances and relationships, and even read between the lines. Second-generation, trainable optical character recognition (OCR) text readers are already available, with enhancements appearing frequently. Though not yet robotic, they scan virtually all fonts and type sizes, read half-tones and colors, recognize foreign diacritics, and treat pages of various dimensions. And they do so quickly. (Look what they do in the post office!)

The technology, however, has only recently attracted serious attention in library circles. That it has played no measurable role in retrospective conversion is unfortunate, for with some improvement it might reduce the costs of routine keyboarding. Neither was its use in preservation widely discussed until the 1988

44 Ithiel de Sola Pool, "Looking Down the Road of Technological Change," in *Crossroads, Proceedings of the First National Conference of the Library and Information Technology Association, September 17–21, 1983, Baltimore, Maryland*, ed. Michael Gorman (Chicago: ALA, 1984), pp. 16–22.

National Agricultural Library Conference on the application of scanning methodologies in libraries.[45] The conference papers leave little doubt that scanning and digital storage will soon prove superior to microfilming, especially if the aesthetic nature of documents is unimportant.[46] Scanning costs less, packs information into less space, permits image enhancement, resists wear and tear, and allows remote access and rapid delivery. In a few years, we are promised an integration of scanning "with the decision process of the human brain."[47]

If doubts remain about the conversion efficiency of scanners and the longevity of digital storage—doubts sufficient to deter headlong leaps into extensive application—it is nevertheless time to be planning for their imminent refinement. Technology rumbles ahead, and we are warned that we will be either part of the steamroller or part of the road.[48] Recent events give us hope that the latter is unlikely. RLG's Collection Management and Development Committee has established, as one of its 1990 goals, the completion of "an optical scanning assessment contract with the National Committee for Preservation and Access." Optical scanning pilot projects continue at LC, the National Archives, Syracuse University, and elsewhere.[49] And the International Association of Music Libraries Commission on Hofmeister XIX, whose goal is to find ways to digitize the contents of the Whistling-Hofmeister bibliographies from 1817 to 1900, announces that it will be evaluating new scanners in 1990.[50] The present imperfections and limitations appear to be minor and momentary, though a few individuals still harbor doubts.[51] University Microfilms has no immediate plans to convert its film backlog to a digital medium but has said that for high-demand items where quick retrieval is essential it will begin to move toward disc-based image systems linked with CD-ROM indexes.

Ironically, the digital age itself is generating increasing amounts of ephemera. Perhaps the greatest force for change that the library has ever encountered is the computer, not just because it promises a retrieval Elysium, but because it has had a drastic effect on what and how people write. Many writers whose loquacity used to be kept in check by the tedium of cut-and-paste have been seduced by the "insert" capability of personal computers. While the computer's editing capabilities nurture concision and cleaner prose, they often foster, too, the accidental loss of text. Although the ease of insertion should guarantee more voluminous drafts and sketches from composers and writers—provided that they deliberately save their

45 *Proceedings* . . . (Beltsville, Maryland: National Agriculture Library, 1989). Scanning technology, according to Leo H. Settler, Jr. in "The Library of Congress Pilot Project with Optiram, Ltd.," (pp. 17–23) is viewed by many as "perhaps the one means by which the international library community has a chance to convert its still-huge files of manual cataloging records into machine readable form within a reasonable time frame" (p. 23).

46 Clifford A. Lynch and Edwin B. Brownrigg assert that microfilms reduce access. Patrons do not like them. They are expensive to copy, which thwarts resource sharing. They also do not stand heavy use and have a limited lifetime. Digital images, on the other hand, do not wear out and can be copied or transmitted cheaply and at high speed. They are less vulnerable to environmental threats; many copies will exist because they are easy and inexpensive to copy. See "Conservation, Preservation, and Digitization," in *National Conference of the Association of College and Research Libraries*, 4th, 1986, Baltimore (Chicago: ALA, 1986), p. 226; appeared also in *College and Research Libraries*, 47 (1986), 379–382.

47 Robert M. Hayes's concluding address in the *Proceedings* (see note 45), p. 135.

48 "Once a new technology rolls over you, if you're not part of the steamroller, you're part of the road," in Brand, *Media Lab*, p. 9.

49 Annette Melville memorandum for Research Library Group Coordination, 14 August 1989: "Minutes of the CMDC Steering Committee," p. 7.

50 Efforts to date, as reported in *Fontes artis musicae*, 36 (1989), 18, have centered on the trainable Kurzweil machines.

51 John C. Mollinson expresses reservations in his "On the Preservation of Human- and Machine-Readable Records," *Information Technology and Libraries*, 7 (1988), 20: "Putting digital records into high density storage conserves space and markedly shortens access time, but is inimical to long-term archival preservation." This does not strike me as a problem that will exist for very long.

emendations electronically or on paper—the ease of erasure will undoubtedly cause inordinate losses. We can hope that e-mail and fax will bring a revival of correspondence, particularly among the gifted and learned. We should also expect mountains of texts from "computer forums" or "conferences," in diverse formats: prose, music notation, audio-visual. And we must devise systems to capture and preserve all of them. Otherwise we may be left to rely on participants' memories as a record of our history and creative activities.

Librarians who are comfortable with the present stage of the information revolution—in which computers and printed materials seem complementary and technology makes things go more smoothly in the library—may not be so happy in the next when, some say, electronics will replace Gutenberg's gift.[52] Science fiction confirms that the notion of a paperless society is widespread. It projects libraries that are totally electronic except for a residuum of elegant printed items and manuscripts retained principally for their physical attributes, their care entrusted to doddering old warders called librarians.[53] The advent of xerography prompted equally disagreeable and, as it turns out, incorrect predictions about the cataclysmic changes that were sure to follow. That its effects were far from devastating suggests that new modes of information transfer tend to be additive, not displacive; telephones did not replace mail, the phonograph live concerts, television the radio, the movies, or the book. And although we may be moving towards a society pervaded by image and sound, so far book publishing continues to expand at a giddy pace.[54]

Library collections in the future will inevitably and increasingly comprise digitized information, but the totally paperless society may in fact never arrive.[55] Electronic publishing may supplant printing but only for certain types of materials, because it faces many difficulties. The goals of those who advocate electronics conflict with those who advocate print. The enforcement of copyright and performing rights would be a nightmare, file security an oxymoron, and encryption a major new industry. Government support and its regulatory duties are nowhere near settlement.[56] And, on a more basic level, does anyone want to read the *New York Times* in the subway on a hand-held monitor? Nevertheless, the young industry expands rapidly, many firms rush to get into the act, and various study groups, like

[52] William Green, "The Information Revolution and the Future of Libraries: Towards a Paperless Future?" *Kentucky Libraries*, 48 (1984), 14–20.

[53] The idea of paperless libraries is usually associated with F. W. Lancaster and his much-discussed predictions arrayed in "The Future of the Library in the Age of Telecommunications," *Telecommunications and Libraries: A Primer*, by Donald W. King et al., (White Plains, N.Y.: Knowledge Industries Publications, 1981). See especially p. 147. A more balanced survey of the possibilities comes from D. I. Raitt, in "Look—No Paper! The Library of Tomorrow," *The Electronic Library*, 3 (1985), 276–289.

[54] Green, "The Information Revolution," 20; also John P. Dessauer's "More About Books and Electronics" in *Trends Update*, 3, no. 4 (April 1984), 2.

[55] Even so, as more publications appear in electronic form, preservation decisions will become increasingly problematic. Self-publication, ungoverned by publishing standards that serve as "gatekeepers," may result in "billions of pages of information that no one needs," or even more menacing, an unpublished deluge, unknown and unreachable. Efrem Sigel, "The Future of the Book," in *Books, Libraries and Electronics* (White Plains, N.Y.: Knowledge Industries Publications, 1982), pp. 14, 17.

[56] Edward Kurdyla, in a paper read at an AMIGOS workshop in Dallas in December 1987, debunks what he sees as several current myths of information technology. He does not believe that the prospects are bright for electronic publishing: projected 1990 earnings for the entire industry are estimated at merely one billion dollars, contrasted to the eighty billion dollars that IBM, alone, will earn. John W. Haeger's memo dated 26 June 1989 to the RLG Board of Governors lists other problems: electronic publishing is far from a mature industry; so far returns on investments have been small; "toe-in-the-water" approaches will not work; because they lack graphics, electronic journals are inferior to their print counterparts and are essentially "glorified bibliographic" files. Richard Dougherty and Wendy P. Lougee identify some of the same problems in their article "What Will Survive?" *Library Journal*, 110, no. 3 (1 February 1985), 41–44.

the Center for Electronically Published Research in Cambridge, Massachusetts, try to establish standards.[57] In Britain, work continues on a "knowledge warehouse" of digitized publications contributed by various publishers.[58]

Breakneck progress and technological advancements thrust new challenges into our agenda. We hear dread warnings about not letting the information revolution get ahead of us and exhortations to grasp control of the electronic gateways to information. Or else![59] Faint and infrequent, by comparison, are similar injunctions about our even more basic responsibility to acquire and preserve the collections that our patrons will expect to access through those gateways fifty years from now.

For the time being, we will all probably choose not to preserve much of what we regard as junk—with or without guilt. But because we each have our own definition of junk, fortunately, not everything will disappear. Someday soon, optical scanning will be as quick and easy as the act of discarding. In the interim, we can use microfilm and discard only that which we are assured someone else will preserve. Shared responsibilities for resource acquisition will help meet the current information explosion, and optical scanning will help preserve a wider variety of older materials. Together, cooperation and technology make it likely that our colleagues in the next millenium will enjoy rich and comprehensive collections. We may not manage to save everything, but we have a better chance to succeed than did our forebears.

57 In an Associated Press release dated 25 June 1989, Peter Coy theorized that a knowledge economy will remake society and shift the balance of global power, and that the connection between knowledge and money ("knowledge will *be* money") is already widening the gap between rich and poor.

58 See John Martyn, "The Knowledge Warehouse and Library Users," *Journal of Documentation*, 45 (1989), 49–58; Michael Buckingham, "The Knowledge Warehouse: Technical Issues," *Electronic Library*, 6 (1988), 6–9; and R. Williamson, "The Knowledge Warehouse: Legal and Commercial Issues," *Electronic Library*, 6 (1988), 10–16.

59 According to Clyde Hendrick in "The University Library in the Twenty-First Century," *College and Research Libraries*, 47 (1986), 125, librarians will become managers of knowledge. "Teaching people how to use information resources and helping increase their information-seeking skills" will be their principal task, states Charles Forrest in his "Technological Conversion: A Brief Review," in *TechTrends*, 33, no. 6 (Nov./Dec. 1988), 2–12. And James M. Kusack in "Librarians and the Information Age: Is Reconciliation Possible?" *Bulletin of the American Society for Information Science*, 14 (Feb./Mar. 1988), 29, insists that "Libraries and library service should not be left to technocrats or commercial entrepreneurs without our traditions and philosophies of service." Nina W. Matheson in "The Academic Library Nexus," *College and Research Libraries*, 45 (1984), 207–213, voices fears, however, that libraries may adapt too slowly and thus lose control of electronic information delivery systems. The same concerns surface in Gordon B. Neavill's "Electronic Publishing, Libraries, and the Survival of Information," *Library Resources and Technical Services*, 28 (1984), 76–89; and in S. D. Neill's "Libraries in the Year 2010," *The Futurist*, 15 (1981), 47–51.

Questions and Discussion Part 1

Stephen Graubard, Chair

SOMMER: It's wonderful to imagine that we can preserve our cultural heritage with all of these methods, but we know they cost money and we are not infinitely gifted. So I will be an advocate for something that I call "stuff-in-a-box." Anyone who has ever worked in a large library knows what stuff-in-a-box is. For years I worked in a crowded area, and under my desk there was a big box that I kept bumping into but didn't want to open (although I didn't throw it away). It was labeled "Otterström Collection." The collection is still in the box. Christoph Wolff will inform us further on about an extraordinary stuff-in-a-box discovery that has just been made. If we can't afford to do all the other things we are supposed to do, let us at least keep the boxes.

Stephen R. Graubard is professor of history at Brown University and editor since 1961 of *Daedalus: Journal of the American Academy of Arts and Sciences*. Among the publications he has recently edited are *In Search of Canada* and *The Future of Opera*.

MICHAEL OCHS (Harvard University): In considering what not to preserve, two specific examples at Harvard of what Suki Sommer just coined stuff-in-a-box come to mind. One was in fact a large cardboard box, containing compositions by a recently deceased Harvard graduate of the 1920s who lived the life of a recluse, holding various odd jobs. He was, however, an accomplished pianist, and he composed some thirty or forty works, most for piano, some for orchestra, that looked somewhat interesting. The question of what to do with the collection answers itself: it's only one box, it's music by a Harvard graduate, it's the only copy in existence, so of course we'll keep it. There was also another box, containing material that came to the library sometime in the 1950s. In this case, a Harvard alumnus had died in Vienna in an accident. There were no survivors or relatives, so the U.S. Embassy took over the man's few possessions. Among them was a pile of music—compositions and exercises—that they felt they shouldn't just throw away, so they packed it all up and sent it off to Harvard with a letter explaining the circumstances. The box has been sitting in one storage place or another since 1953, and I hoped this panel would tell us what to do about it.

COOVER: Most of us at this meeting have piles of such material sitting around in our libraries. It's in the way, it takes up valuable space, and we don't have time to take care of it the way we ought to. Probably we are all guilt-smitten and do not throw it away. Much of it is local music history, and we don't dare—and shouldn't—discard it. It's not unheard of for someone to get a master's thesis out of material like that and catalog it for us at the same time.

WILLIAM COSCARELLI (University of Georgia): Our stuff-in-a-box episode at Georgia developed out of a letter from Kiev in the Soviet Union asking for a copy of the only surviving manuscript of George Antheil's *Jazz Sonata*. The letter, addressed to the music school, was directed to the dean, who sent it to the jazz band director, who forwarded it to me. I took it to our rare books department, which, it turned out, did indeed have the Antheil work, and also a piano work of Bohuslav Martinů. The manuscripts were included among the papers of a little-known musician, Carol Robinson. One of the musicologists on our faculty started digging into this collection and began gathering enough material for a journal article, which has since grown into a book. Robinson was apparently involved in the New York premiere of Antheil's *Ballet mécanique*, took part in first performances of Charles Ives's violin and piano sonatas, and met Martinů in Europe. We learned all these things from a seemingly unimportant collection of stuff-in-a-box that provides a window into the cultural history of the 1920s and 30s. Such serendipitous discoveries can have wonderful results: we can see a whole project grow from a brief inquiry and suddenly get an entirely different perspective on history. We are now trying to obtain more stuff-in-a-box related to Carol Robinson: piano compositions, letters, other writings.

SAMUEL: I'm sure that scholars would be happy if librarians would all be pack rats and save everything that comes to us. We would catalog it all, so it would be ready for a scholar to come along and mine it or reject it. But it's a great financial burden on an institution to catalog and preserve such material, and we really have to draw the line somewhere.

FREDERICK HEUTTE (University of Maryland): Some years ago, my library launched a program to preserve band music. (If there's anything more American than that, I don't know what it is.) I approached Bob Hoe, a businessman who is known to music librarians through his record series, "The Heritage of the March." We were hoping to get his collection of band music scores. He told me that most of his music had come from libraries that were throwing it out because band music did not have any status. We have to turn ourselves around, go out from this room like apostles, and proclaim that we are interested in what we may once have called junk but whose value we now understand.

HAMM: We have to take the position—musicologists and librarians alike—that everything should be preserved. Consider all of these examples of "this box contained this" and "that box contained that." So the issue is how do we cope. The only practical way it can work is to have regional collections, where different libraries preserve different things. Preserve everything, and get it in the right place. Then the question becomes, how do we get it in the right place? I come from a part of the country where a profusion of flea markets and yard sales is a way of life. New Englanders periodically put what they have but no longer want out on their front lawns, and people come and buy. If they don't buy, then things get put back in the garage or the barn until the next sale. This way, eventually, a lot of stuff finds its way to the right place. My own collection of LP records grows every year because I buy a hundred or two hundred that I want, and there they are: located. What about a grand-scale flea market as part of the MLA meeting every year? Every library loads its boxes onto a truck . . .

Q: Perhaps we should have consortia with reciprocal arrangements. That is, we know from *Resources of American Music History*[1] and other sources who is collecting what, or at least who owns what materials. But wouldn't it be useful to announce in *Notes* or by some other means when a library has something that perhaps might find a more appropriate home in another library—both who has materials to give away and who is collecting?

WOLFGANG FREITAG (Harvard University): Visual arts librarians do not have the stuff-in-a-box problem because we can send such material to the Archives of American Art, a bureau of the Smithsonian Institution. Maybe what the music library profession needs is a central archival collecting point that would absorb material that no institution wished to preserve.

CHRISTOPHER MILLIS (Hobart & William Smith College): A psychology professor came to class one day and asked his students to write down what was furthest from their minds. Will our descendants eighty years from now be astonished by what we aren't thinking about? What about the material that isn't being saved today?

EPSTEIN: I'm not sure anyone knows what isn't being saved, because what one library doesn't collect, another library may. Years and years ago, when I was working on a master's thesis, I looked in vain for the catalog of a Chicago publisher who was put out of business as a result of the great fire of 1871. Recently I found out that the Grosvenor Library in Buffalo holds a catalog issued by the successor to the firm; thus communication today is much better than it was in the 1940s. We now have computerized networks. Although it's quite possible that our great-grandchildren may not find a specific work in the near environs, somewhere in the country it may be preserved and they will be able to gain access to it.

GERALDINE OSTROVE (Library of Congress): The 1989 meeting in Oxford of the International Association of Music Libraries included several presentations alerting us to the importance of identifying music materials that are parts of special collections; much still needs to be done toward locating such materials. On Jim Coover's concern regarding discards at the Library of Congress: many of the discarded items represented in the LC statistics are duplicates. Of course, the Music Division always keeps one exemplar of every music copyright deposit.

THOMSON MOORE (Princeton University): The *Boston Composers Project*[2] (*BCP*) lists works by Boston area composers, probably ninety-five percent of which are unpublished. How can our libraries make sure that contemporary works get into a library somewhere? It's hard enough collecting the modern scores that *are* published, but certainly there is plenty of music that we ought to have that is available only in manuscript.

Q: I have tried to find out about works by several composers in the *BCP* and was informed by the compiler, Linda Solow Blotner, that for two-thirds of the entries

[1] D. W. Krummel et al., *Resources of American Music History* (Urbana: University of Illinois Press, 1981).

[2] Boston Area Music Libraries, *The Boston Composers Project*, ed. Linda I. Solow et al. (Cambridge, Mass.: MIT Press, 1983).

there was no record of the location of the manuscript or the address of the composer or heir. So we have documentation for pieces but no easy way to find the original source material.

Carolyn Rabson (Oberlin College): There is a related problem of material that is not being collected, not through any decision of librarians, but because its original had been created in some kind of electronic medium—for example, sketches or preliminary compositions for which we have only the finished composition. As more and more composers use electronic media, they increasingly produce music in its finished version and erase their sketches. The same is true of valuable correspondence between musical figures that now takes place on electronic mail. This sort of material, which has always been of scholarly importance, will, with greater use of electronic media, simply disappear, so that librarians will no longer have to make such decisions.

Maurice Press (London): As a blind performer, I am very much interested in computer technology for disabled people. New technologies may frighten librarians who for years have been dealing primarily with print, but the new media make it possible for disabled people to actually use live-scale monitors, sound, synthetic speech, and on-line databases—in short, to gain access to the information they need. Let us herald the new technology and exploit it to the fullest.

James E. Cyphers (Massachusetts State Archives): Many of the issues raised at this session are ones the archival field has been involved with for years. We must think about cross-professional linkages, so that people in the archivist's camp and those in the music librarian's camp are not duplicating each other's efforts. My own responsibilities, for instance, have led me to work with RLIN and to explore the archival implications of the development of compact discs. From talking with the people in research and development, I've concluded that the durability of the data on compact discs will be a problem in the future.

Q: What about the future of our aural collections? LP's are on their way to obsolescence, reel-to-reel tapes are crumbling, and those dear 78s cannot be stored easily in a small library. These recordings are very important, but they are not easily taken care of or put on a computer disk.

Alejandro Planchart (University of California at Santa Barbara): Central storage of 78-rpm collections is already occurring among some California libraries. The library first tapes the records on cassettes that are kept for local use and then sends the 78s to a central storage facility in Southern California that is equipped with compact shelving. The trouble is, people begin to think that since the contents are on tape, they might as well get rid of the 78s.

Epstein: Libraries that cannot satisfactorily store older forms of recordings can offer them to one of the major sound archives that has appropriate facilities. Another possible solution to this problem was developed at the University of Wisconsin in Milwaukee. They received a comprehensive collection of 78-rpm jazz recordings but had no facilities for processing the collection properly or taking care of it. So they worked out a contract with the Institute for Jazz Studies at Rutgers University whereby the collection was transferred to Rutgers, but ownership remained with the University of Wisconsin in Milwaukee. Any time a recording is requested in Milwaukee, Rutgers immediately provides a tape copy. The arrangement satisfies the terms of the bequest, satisfies the responsibilities of both institutions, and allows the collection to reside where it will be used, not just kept indefinitely uncataloged and in the way.

RICHARD F. FRENCH (The Juilliard School): I support Alejandro Planchart's point about 78s. I hope that you won't throw them away. Perhaps you don't have to keep them all, but you must keep a recording of my favorite song, Cole Porter's "Love for Sale." But why do we need the 78 rather than the compact-disc version? Well, one reason (speaking as a musician, not as a librarian) is the need to understand a certain compositional principle. How long does a piece have to be? If we ask a Mahler scholar, we get one answer; if we ask a medievalist who is interested in Machaut, we get another answer. Cole Porter, however, illustrates the skill with which a composer can get in and out in three minutes. Students today would not understand the problem unless they knew that there was something—a 78-rpm record—that lasted only three minutes. So I implore you not to lose that aspect.

Cole Porter's "Love for Sale." (New York, late January 1931.)

HAMM: There is another reason for keeping the 78. Music is now being studied in context—as part of the musical life—as opposed to its study as object, so it's important to know what people heard when they played those 78s. And it's not only a matter of keeping the 78s, it's also a matter of keeping the machines they were played on. When we listen to music from the 1930s in my course on American popular music, we hear the old discs on a wind-up machine from the period because that's the way the music was heard, not digitally remastered and with all of its character taken away. This controversy has come up with new Elvis Presley recordings; they don't sound the way they did to people who heard Presley records when they came out.

SOMMER: I still defend those people here who should not be saving things. I spent twenty-five years in the Research Division of the New York Public Library, where I wanted to get one of everything and save it forever. I now administer a quarter-of-a-million-item circulating collection at the same institution that consists entirely of commercially-issued material, and when something wears out, we throw it out. We feel comfortable doing so because we know that there is a place upstairs in the research library where, if we have any doubts, we can say, "Do you want this? If not, then you throw it out." In response to Charles Hamm's suggestion: many research libraries run the equivalent of yard sales, and librarians derive double satisfaction, first in knowing that the materials are being recycled, and second, in using the proceeds from such sales to acquire even more for their own collections.

The Scholar and the Music Librarian

H. Colin Slim

As president of the American Musicological Society (AMS), let me begin by describing the role that the Society plays in the lives of American music librarians. First, it has sustained an active publishing program. The late musicologist, librarian, and longtime treasurer of the AMS, Otto Albrecht, used to call its publications "jams"—referring to the Society's journal by its initials—and "jellies"—referring to the Society's less regular publications. "Jellies" began in 1947 with the second volume of Johannes Ockeghem's complete works. (We pray only that the third and final volume will appear in print before the five-hundredth anniversary of its composer's death is celebrated in 1997; even so, publication of the three volumes has already exceeded the time it took to publish all forty-seven volumes of the first Bach complete edition!) The Society also publishes those indispensable lists of doctoral and master's theses that Helen Hewitt began in 1952 (under the joint sponsorship of the Music Teachers' National Association), and that Cecil Adkins with Alis Dickinson diligently continued in 1971 and expanded to international scope in 1977 (aided by the International Musicological Society, or IMS).[1] Joined by the Colonial Society of Massachusetts, the AMS has published the *opera omnia* of William Billings, a project *Notes* aptly saluted as "a landmark in musicological service to music in the United States."[2] In collaboration with the Sonneck Society, the AMS will soon be publishing a series of later American music (MUSA). Among the possibilities are the complete works of Duke Ellington, the organ music of Fats Waller, marches by John Philip Sousa, songs by Louis Moreau Gottschalk, and *Rhapsody in Blue* by George Gershwin. Also, the Society has, since 1965, aided scholarly presses in India, Denmark, France, and the United States in publishing a number of distinguished works.

H. Colin Slim is professor of music at the University of California, Irvine, and past president of the American Musicological Society. His scholarly editions of Renaissance and Baroque music include Alessandro Scarlatti's opera, *Massimo Puppieno*, and *A Gift of Madrigals and Motets*, for which he won the Otto Kinkeldey Award of the AMS in 1973.

Second, the AMS supports significant bibliographical projects. With the Music Library Association, the Society sponsors a committee on RISM, the International Repertory of Music Sources, chaired alternately every three years by a member of each organization. One of its major projects is the RISM-U.S. Manuscript Inventory, housed at Harvard and directed by John Howard. For the past ten years the AMS has contributed to the American operation of RILM, the International Repertory of Music Literature, whose U.S. office Lenore Coral directs at Cornell. The AMS also has a representative on the U.S. RILM Board, the redoubtable Sam Pogue.

Third, certain AMS members known primarily as scholar-teachers have made major contributions to library science: for example, Howard Mayer Brown, Daniel Heartz, and Mary Lewis to bibliography, and Kern Holoman, Jan LaRue, and

1 *International Index of Dissertations and Musicological Works in Progress* (Philadelphia: AMS, 1952–).

2 Deane L. Root, review of William Billings, *The Complete Works*, vol.1, ed. Karl Kroeger, *Notes*, 40 (1983), 147.

H. Wiley Hitchcock to thematic catalogs. I might even mention my own study of the Herwart Music Library in the final volume of *Annales musicologiques*.[3] Another noteworthy example is H. Robert Cohen, who, as co-chair and general editor, established RIPM, the International Repertory of the Musical Press, sponsored jointly by the IMS and the International Association of Music Libraries (IAML). (RIPM thus joins its parent organization, RISM, and its older siblings RILM and RIdIM, the International Repertory of Musical Iconography, as the fourth R of modern music bibliography.)

Fourth, members of the AMS who serve primarily as music librarians have made enduring contributions to music scholarship. A selective list of such librarian-scholars would include: Harold Samuel, James Pruett, Lenore Coral, Hans Lenneberg, Dena Epstein, Donald Krummel, Mary Davidson, and, in particular, Michael Ochs, current editor of *Notes*, an indispensable tool for librarians and music scholars.

Moreover, the union of music librarian and musicologist is time-honored. Otto Kinkeldey, long associated with the New York Public Library and with the Cornell Music Library, was described by Donald Grout in *The New Grove* as "the founder of American musicology."[4] Oscar Sonneck, at the Library of Congress in the early years of this century, was surely the founder of serious musicological study of American music.[5] In the generation separating Kinkeldey and Sonneck from ours, Vincent Duckles splendidly continued the tradition. He amassed such an outstanding cache of books and music for the University of California at Berkeley that its riches are still being assessed; his scholarship contributed crucial knowledge to the study of early seventeenth-century English song; and his book *Music Reference and Research Materials*, now updated by Michael Keller, continues, along with Jim Pruett's *Research Guide to Musicology*, to set standards for librarians and for new musicology students.[6] While less numerous, the breed is not yet extinct. In this generation, for example, John Roberts quickly proved his expertise as a music librarian at the University of Pennsylvania while he also staked out an international reputation as a Handel scholar. It is safe to assume that Roberts, now at the University of California at Berkeley, will attain that special margin of excellence that characterized the achievements of Kinkeldey, Sonneck, and Duckles.

Before they assumed their second careers as librarians, these giants of the past were trained as scholars. If we wish to replicate such near mythic figures, then we had better improve and augment the education for music librarianship. For just as we must train an army of library technicians, so must we educate an elite corps of generals who are experienced and above all knowledgeable enough to determine wisely what occupies the increasingly restricted space on our library shelves. Let me also plead for the continuation of scholarship among music librarians through the support of enlightened administrations, understanding department heads, and such generous endowments as the one we are honoring at this symposium.

3 H. Colin Slim, "The Music Library of the Augsburg Patrician, Hans Heinrich Herwart (1520–1583)," *Annales musicologiques*, 7 (1964–1977), 67–109.

4 Donald Jay Grout, "Kinkeldey, Otto," in *The New Grove Dictionary of Music and Musicians*, 10: 68.

5 As chronicled by Gillian B. Anderson in "Putting the Experience of the World at the Nation's Command: Music at the Library of Congress, 1800–1917," *Journal of the American Musicological Society*, 42 (1989), 108–149.

6 Vincent Duckles and Michael A. Keller, *Music Reference and Research Materials: An Annotated Bibliography*, 4th, rev. ed. (New York: Schirmer Books, 1989); James Pruett and Thomas P. Slavens, *Research Guide to Musicology* (Chicago: American Library Association, 1985).

Obviously, it is too early to predict the impact on the profession of this singular generosity. Will the establishment of the first United States chair in music librarianship spawn similar developments across the country, just as the first chair of musicology did at Cornell in 1930? Will it allow greater freedom for its incumbents to pursue their own goals in librarianship and in research? Will it increase the present relatively small number of scholar-librarians? How might it affect the music library of this particular department of music, surely already one of the nation's best in respect to the depth and breadth of its collections? What is likely to be its effect on other music librarians employed elsewhere? Although such questions cannot be answered now, some future symposium held here in a decade or so will surely want to try.

Although the title of this paper implies a dialogue, I will now add a *dramatis personae* and describe a trialogue between librarians, musicologists, and art historians.

The trialogue opens with an apology to Iain Fenlon and James Haar, who invited me to read the typescript of their recent book, *The Italian Madrigal in the Early Sixteenth Century*, shortly before its publication.[7] Knowing my interest in Renaissance musical inscriptions, they wanted suggestions for illustrative materials about the madrigal before 1550. As they correctly note, pictorial examples of the early madrigal are surprisingly few.[8] When Fenlon and Haar made their request, however, I had forgotten about the earliest known example; even worse, it turns out that four years before I had used it to illustrate an article in *Early Music*.[9]

This *lapsus memoriae* endured until early this year when Barry Brook, a cofounder of RIdIM, forwarded a letter he had received in late February from the venerable London auction house of Christie, Manson & Woods. Christie's letter included two photographs of a painting depicting a young man holding a sheet of music (figure 1), a preliminary catalog description, and a request to Brook "for anything you can tell us about the music depicted in the man's hand."[10]

We are told that a picture is worth a thousand words: indeed, Christie's photograph quickly recalled the 1985 article I had written for *Early Music*. At that time, my knowledge of the painting came mostly from its reproduction in a German art periodical of 1910, after which the painting went to a Munich dealer and then disappeared entirely from view until turning up at Christie's some seven decades later.[11] Providentially, both the Epstein Photo Archive in the Regenstein Library at the University of Chicago and the Witt Reference Library of the Courtauld

7 Iain Fenlon and James Haar, *The Italian Madrigal in the Early Sixteenth Century: Sources and Interpretation* (Cambridge: Cambridge University Press, 1988).

8 Fenlon and Haar's frontispiece is a painting attributed there (and elsewhere) to Giovanni Cariani and dated ca. 1540. Attribution, date, and their statement (p. 326) about its musical notation deserve some comments. In Rodolfo Pallucchini and Francesco Rossi, *Giovanni Cariani* (Bergamo: Silvana Editoriale, 1983), pp. 26 and 88, note 9, Pallucchini rejects the painting as Cariani's; and although Rossi (p. 274) believes it might be authentic, he would date it some two decades earlier. Moreover, the music is not "undecipherable," just unidentified; see H. Colin Slim, "Musical Inscriptions in Paintings by Caravaggio and His Followers," in *Music and Context: Essays for John M. Ward*, ed. Anne Dhu Shapiro (Cambridge, Mass.: Harvard University, Department of Music, 1985), p. 260, "the same piece [is copied] onto facing pages."

9 H. Colin Slim, "Giovanni Girolamo Savoldo's *Portrait of a Man with a Recorder*," *Early Music*, 13 (1985), 403–404 and plate 5.

10 From Charles Beddington, Old Master Picture Department, Christie's, dated 15 February 1989.

11 See Wilhelm Schmidt, "Gemälde aus der Sammlung Röhrer," *Monatshefte für Kunstwissenschaft*, 3 (1910), 141–142, plate 29, no. 2; Hermann Voss, "Italienische Gemälde des 16. und 17. Jahrhunderts in der Galerie des Kunsthistorischen Hofmuseums zu Wien," *Zeitschrift für bildende Kunst*, n.s. 23, 47 (1912), 42–44, plate 4; and Voss, *Die Malerei der Spätrenaissance in Rom und Florenz* (Berlin: G. Grote, 1920), 1: 244.

Figure 1. Francesco Salviati (1510–1563) or Jacopino del Conte 1510–1598): Portrait of a Young Man, *dated 1540.*

Institute at the University of London held old, but decent enough photographs from which in 1981 music and poem could be transcribed.

Half a dozen madrigals by different composers set to this same poem and published between 1551 and 1591 are listed in the first-line index of François Lesure and Claudio Sartori's revision of Emil Vogel's still-essential bibliography of Italian secular music.[12] Comparing the music's transcription against prints of those works in the British Library, the Royal College of Music, the Bavarian State Library, and

[12] Emil Vogel et al., *Bibliografia della musica italiana vocale profana dal 1500 al 1700* (Pomezia: Staderini, 1977), 3: 499, s.v. "S'altra fiamma." Essential here is also the first-line index in Harry B. Lincoln, *The Italian Madrigal and Related Repertories: Indexes to Printed Collections, 1500–1600* (New Haven: Yale University Press, 1988), p. 877, referring to Bellasio's madrigal (cited note 13, below) in RISM 1590[18], p. 16, with thematic incipits on p. 86. Though not listed in Lincoln, it also appears in RISM 1587[6].

later in the Isham Memorial Library's fabulous microfilm holdings, eliminated all but one possible print.[13] It was likely, then, that the picture's music appeared in just that print, albeit—for the first time in my experience—one not held on film in the Isham Library. Two years later at the National Library in Florence I was able to compare my transcription against the only complete copy of Giovanni Animuccia's second book of five-voiced madrigals and to confirm that the painting bore the top voice of Animuccia's madrigal, "S'altra fiamma giamai m'arse, madonna, il core" ("If ever another flame burned my heart, my lady").[14] In publishing his second book of madrigals at Rome in 1551, Animuccia dedicated it to the sixteen-year-old literary prodigy, Alfonso Cambi (1535–1570), who came from a wealthy Florentine business family in Naples.[15] Animuccia called these madrigals his "second efforts" ("seconde fatiche mie").

From 1910 until 1963, art historians read the date at the bottom of the painting as 1547,[16] the same year that Animuccia published his first book of madrigals at Venice,[17] and not long after he left his native Florence permanently for Rome. Without access to the picture there was no certainty that art historians were correct about the 1547 date or whether, as it seemed from the Epstein and Witt photographs, the painter had really signed it 1540. Either possibility would help to date the picture's madrigal. Either date also meant that this madrigal was already written and, as we shall soon see, circulating even before Animuccia published his first book of madrigals, to say nothing of his second book. With the painting out of limbo, Christie's eyes, mine, and now yours can verify the date as 1540.[18] Animuccia thus composed the madrigal some eleven years before printing it in his second madrigal book. And since he wrote it at least seven years before his first book was published, the picture also disproves Animuccia's own claim that book one represents "first flowers" ("i primi fiori"). Probably all the madrigals in his first and second books belong to his early manhood in Florence, a period when Duke Cosimo I de' Medici was tightening his grip on Tuscany and causing many an artist and musician to consider self-exile. Two poems by A. F. Grazzini (1503–1584) from the

13 Eliminated were: Antonio Barré, *Madrigali a quattro voci . . . Libro primo* (Rome, 1552), p. 25; Paolo Bellasio, *Madrigali a3. a4. a5. a6. a7. & a8. voci* (Venice, 1591), p. 4 (see note 12, above); Francesco Manara, *Il primo libro di madrigali a quattro voci* (Venice, 1555), p. 17; Raimondo Vettore, *Madrigali a quattro voci . . . Libro primo* (Venice, 1560), p. 2; and Annibale Zoilo, *Libro secondo de madrigali a quattro et a cinque voci* (Rome, 1563), p. 22.

14 Giovanni Animuccia, *Il secondo libro de i madrigali a cinque voci* (Rome, 1551), p. 20. The entire madrigal text reads as follows:

S'altra fiamma gia mai
m'arse, madonna', il core
che quella che per voi m'acces' Amore,
o se per altra donna unqua provai
[Gli amorosi tormenti]
Crescha in voi il ghiaccio;
in me le faci ardenti;
Né trov' il cor merce de danni suoi;
Sia mi crudel il ciel, più cruda voi.

If ever another flame
Burned my heart, my lady,
Like that which Love has lit [in me] for you,
Or if I ever tried for another woman
[The amorous torments],
In you would increase the ice
[But] in me the burning torches;
Neither does my heart find respite from your injuries:
If the heavens be cruel to me, you are yet harsher.

15 See Claudio Mutini, "Cambi, Alfonso," in *Dizionario biografico degli italiani* (Rome: Istituto della Enciclopedia Italiana, 1974), 17: 91–92.

16 See note 11, above, and Iris Hofmeister Cheney, "Francesco Salviati (1510–1563)" (Ph.D. diss., New York University, 1963), repr. (Ann Arbor: [University Microfilms?], 1973), 2: 487.

17 See Vogel et al., *Bibliografia,* 1: 59, no. 86, and its dedication: "i primi fiori che alla mia tenera primavera ne è stato concesso mandar fiori."

18 Charles Beddington of Christie's: "The last figure of the date was practically illegible but on stylistic grounds we tended towards the assumption that it is a 'o'," (letter of 19 July 1989).

late 1530s link Animuccia to Florentine literary and musical circles.[19] Grazzini addresses one poem to "Giovanni Animuccia musico," bizarrely titling it: "In praise of spinach" ("In lode degli Spinaci"). Grazzini addresses the other one that mentions Animuccia to the composer's coeval, Lorenzo degli Organi (1519-1544).[20]

Since Animuccia's madrigals probably come out of Cosimo's Florence, they require more scrutiny. Although a study of them by Jaroslav Mracek, cited in the 1977 *International Index of Doctoral Dissertations,*[21] never surfaced, its mere listing discouraged at least one Ph.D. candidate. Lewis Lockwood's article about Animuccia in *The New Grove* concentrates almost exclusively on Animuccia's production of sacred music at Rome between 1551 and his death there in 1571.[22] Alfred Einstein, in *The Italian Madrigal*, does not mention Animuccia's second print.[23] Citing Animuccia only once, Fenlon and Haar almost imply that he did most of his madrigal composing at Rome.[24]

The picture's significance is that it tells us that Animuccia was, so to speak, one of the last of the early Florentine madrigalists. The sheet of music depicted in the painting has folds as if it were a letter. Fenlon and Haar cite several manuscripts comprising sheets of different sizes, wherein folds in the sheet and in one case, even an address, testify to music circulating as letters or within letters.[25] This picture is the first that visually documents the practice of the circulating madrigal. Identification of the words and music points to a thoroughly love-stricken young man.

Helpful as this painting is in delineating the composition period of Animuccia's madrigals and in documenting a contemporary mode of transmission, it will neverthess trouble art historians and musicologists. If the painter really is Francesco Salviati (1510–1563), to whom many art historians have attributed the portrait since 1912, and as Christie's preliminary catalog entry asserted, (figure 2) there is a problem. For, in mid-June of 1539, Salviati left Florence for Bologna and Venice and did not return to the Arno until 1543.[26] Because Salviati lived in Venice throughout 1540, unless he postdated or predated this portrait, the madrigal had reached Venice by 1540.

Although a 1910 attribution of this painting to Pontormo was quickly found unacceptable by art historians, one to Salviati found general favor until 1963 when Iris Cheney, in her dissertation on Salviati, objected: "There is a quality of brutality in the portrait which is closer to an artist like Jacopino del Conte than it is to Salviati."[27] In offering the picture again for sale in July, Christie's discarded their initial attribution to Salviati and opted for Jacopino del Conte (1510–1598;

[19] Antonfrancesco Grazzini (Il Lasca), *Le rime burlesche,* ed. Carlo Verzone (Florence: G. C. Sansoni, 1882), pp. 566–569: Capitolo 34 (In lode degli Spinaci) and pp. 593–595: Capitolo 42 (Al M. Lorenzo degli Organi), lines 19 and 49.

[20] See Frank A. D'Accone, "Alessandro Coppini and Bartolomeo degli Organi—two Florentine composers of the Renaissance," *Analecta musicologica,* 4 (1967), p. 49, who shows he was Bartolomeo's son, succeeding Corteccia as organist at the Baptistry in 1540. This document appears in D'Accone, "The Musical Chapels at the Florentine Cathedral and Baptistry during the First Half of the 16th Century," *Journal of the American Musicological Society,* 24 (1971), 45. Neither D'Accone nor Mario Fabbri, "La vita e l'ignota opera-prima di Francesco Corteccia musicista italiano del Rinascimento," *Chigiana,* 22 (1965), 197, note 40, who gives Lorenzo's birth date as 1515, cite Grazzini's poem and three others (*Rime,* pp. 106, 590, and 596) addressed to him.

[21] P. 86. Mracek kindly informs me that his "research about the madrigals is not complete and has not been published," (letter of 12 September 1989).

[22] Lewis Lockwood, "Animuccia, Giovanni," in *The New Grove Dictionary of Music and Musicians,* 1: 437–438.

[23] Alfred Einstein, *The Italian Madrigal* (Princeton: Princeton University Press, 1949); Animuccia is discussed in vol. 1, pp. 289–291.

[24] Fenlon and Haar, *The Italian Madrigal,* p. 86.

[25] Ibid., pp. 120–121; further, see Slim, "Savoldo's *Portrait,*" p. 406, note 40.

[26] See Cheney, "Francesco Salviati's North Italian Journey," *The Art Bulletin,* 45 (1963), 337–338, 341, note 30, 342, and 347; and Wolfgang Stechow, "Salviati," in Ulrich Thieme and Frederick Becker, *Allgemeines Lexikon der bildenden Künstler* (Leipzig: E. A. Seeman, 1935), 29: 365–367.

[27] See note 16, above.

Salviati

Portrait of a young man, bust length, wearing a black cap and doublet, and holding a sheet of music

dated 1540, on panel

23 x 19.5/8in. (58.5 x 50cm.)

SOLD BY ORDER OF THE TRUSTEES

89

Jacopino del Conte (1510-1598)

Portrait of a young man, bust length, wearing a black cap and doublet, and holding a sheet of music

dated 154(0?), on panel
23 × 19⅝in. (58.5 × 50cm.)

PROVENANCE:
Röhrer Collection, Munich, by 1910
with Julius Bohler, Munich

LITERATURE:
W. Schmidt, *Gemälde aus der Sammlung Röhrer*, Monatshefte für Kunstwissenschaft, III, 1910, p. 141, and p. 142, pl. 29, fig. 2, as Pontormo
H. Voss, *Italienische Gemälde des 16. and 17. Jahrhunderts in der Galerie des Kunsthistorischen Hofmuseums zu Wien*, Zeitschrift für Bildende Kunst, new ser.23, XLVII, 1912, pp. 42-4 and pl. 4, as Francesco Salviati
H. Voss, *Die Malerei der Spätrenaissance in Rom und Florenz*, 1920, I, p. 244, as Francesco Salviati
H. C. Slim, *Giovanni Girolamo Savoldo's 'Portrait of a Man with a Recorder'*, Early Music, vol. 13, no. 3, Aug. 1985, pp. 403-4 and 406, and fig. 5, as Francesco Salviati

Professor Colin Slim identifies the music as the opening nine breves of the *cantus* part to 'S'altra fiamma giamai m'arse, madonna, il core', a madrigal composed by the Florentine Giovanni Animuccia (c. 1500-1571); this was not published until 1551, in Animuccia's 'Il secondo libro dei madrigali a cinque voci', which suggests that either the piece was known in Florentine musical circles some years before its publication, or that it was received by the artist from the composer himself. 'By revealing the madrigal's amorous text and depicting folds in the sheet of music, the artist suggests that the young man either has just received from a lady friend or is about to send to her this musical message' (Slim, *op. cit.*, p. 404)

For the attribution, compare, for instance, the 'Portrait of a Young Man' in the John G. Johnson Collection at Philadelphia (*Catalogue of Italian Paintings*, 1966, p. 24 and illus. p. 201) and the 'Portrait of a Man' in the Gemäldegalerie, Berlin (*Catalogue of Paintings 13th-18th Century*, 1978, p. 114, illus.)

£60,000-80,000

Figure 2 (above). Preliminary catalog description, February 1989.

Figure 3 (below). Final catalog description, 7 July 1989.

figure 3).[28] Like Salviati, del Conte was a native Florentine. He also left that city in 1534 and traveled to Rome, where he remained.[29] So, if del Conte painted the portrait, then Animuccia's madrigal was circulating in Rome in 1540, for there is no record of Animuccia having gone to Rome that early.

Wilhelm Schmidt, the first art historian to discuss the painting, guessed that the music is the opening of a madrigal and wondered if the figure portrayed was a singer or, more likely, the madrigal's composer; he suggested that identifying the madrigal might help identify the sitter.[30] No other art historian addressed any of these musicological problems.

Might this portrait, then, be of Animuccia? Animuccia's birthdate is unknown. Einstein supposed that he was younger than his fellow citizen, the composer Francesco Corteccia, who we know was born in 1502. With traditional British certainty and equal lack of documentation, the *New Oxford History* furnishes an unequivocal date of 1505;[31] Lockwood and others now estimate his birth at about

28 *Important Old Master Pictures . . . which will be sold . . . Friday 7 July 1989* (London, 1989), lot 89, pp. 120–121 with color plate. The attribution made (apparently independently of Cheney's) by comparing paintings in Berlin and Philadelphia seems compelling, though Cheney might deny the comparison to the Philadelphia portrait (see next note, Cheney, p. 39, note 51).

29 See Cheney, "Notes on Jacopino del Conte," *The Art Bulletin*, 52 (1970), 34; and Thieme and Becker, *Lexikon* (1912), 7: 330, s.v. "Conte."

30 See note 11, above.

31 Henry Coates and Gerald Abraham, "Minor Masters of the *A Cappella* Style," in *The Age of Humanism 1540–1630*, ed. Gerald Abraham, vol. 4, *The New Oxford History of Music* (London: Oxford University Press, 1968), p. 363.

Figure 4. Eighteenth-century portrait of Giovanni Animuccia.

1500,[32] and two Italian encyclopedias opt for about 1514.[33] Obviously we need to search Florentine archives. Animuccia might well have been close in age to the Lorenzo degli Organi born in 1519 and mentioned with him in Grazzini's poem. The subject of the portrait is arguably closer to twenty than to thirty, thus making his birthdate around 1520—an estimate for Animuccia's birth that Lockwood gave earlier when editing his Norton score of Palestrina.[34] Even if Animuccia had been born as late as 1520, he could still have written "S'altra fiamma" in time for it to have been painted in 1540. Evidence abounds that composers write music at such an age. In his first book of madrigals, Animuccia characterizes 1547 as "my tender spring." Now "Mia tenera primavera" is fine for a man then around twenty-seven but unsuitable for an ancient of forty-seven. Indirect evidence of a birthdate around 1520 might also derive from the scarcity of any of his music before 1550[35]—save for his first book of madrigals and the madrigal in this painting.

Finally, we might ignore Lowinsky's warning (since he often did so himself) that "it is only with trepidation . . . that a music historian proceeds on the path that art historians fear to tread."[36] We could compare Christie's picture with an eighteenth-century portrait of Animuccia now in Bologna in which he is perhaps fifty or sixty (figure 4).[37] Our path will be much shorter than the harrowing ones Lowinsky took

32 See note 22, above; and Liliana Pannella, "Animuccia, Giovanni," in *Dizionario biografico degli italiani,* (Rome: Istituto della Enciclopedia Italiana, 1964), 3: 328–331.

33 *Enciclopedia dalla musica Ricordi* (Milan: Ricordi, 1963), vol. 1, s.v. "Animuccia"; and Maria Antonella Balsano, "Animuccia, Giovanni," in *Dizionario enciclopedico universale della musica e dei musicisti,* pt. 2 (Turin: UTET, 1985), 1: 107.

34 Giovanni Pierluigi da Palestrina, *Pope Marcellus Mass,* ed. Lewis Lockwood (New York: Norton, 1972), p. 23, note 1.

35 See Charles Hamm and Herbert Kellman, *Census-Catalogue of Manuscript Sources of Polyphonic Music 1400–1550.* 5 vols. (Neuhausen-Stuttgart: Hänssler Verlag, 1979–88).

36 Edward E. Lowinsky, "Problems in Adrian Willaert's Iconography," in *Aspects of Medieval and Renaissance Music: A Birthday Offering to Gustave Reese,* ed. Jan LaRue (New York: Norton, 1966), p. 588.

37 The Bologna Portrait is in the Civico Museo Bibliografico Musicale; see Georg Kinsky, *Geschichte der Musik in Bildern* (Leipzig: Breitkopf und Härtel, 1929), p. 102, plate 4 (detail); Franco Abbiati, *Storia della musica* (Milan: Garzanti, 1939), 1: 503 (rev., Milan: Garzanti, 1967), 1: 433; and Howard E. Smither, *A History of the Oratorio* (Chapel Hill: University of North Carolina Press, 1977), 1: 54, fig. II-7. On Padre Martini's collection of portraits at Bologna (still unstudied), see Edward E. Lowinsky, "Problems," pp. 579–582.

Example 1 (above). Giovanni Animuccia, "S'Altra fiamma," from his Il secondo libro de i madrigali a cinque voci *(Rome, 1551), p. 20.*

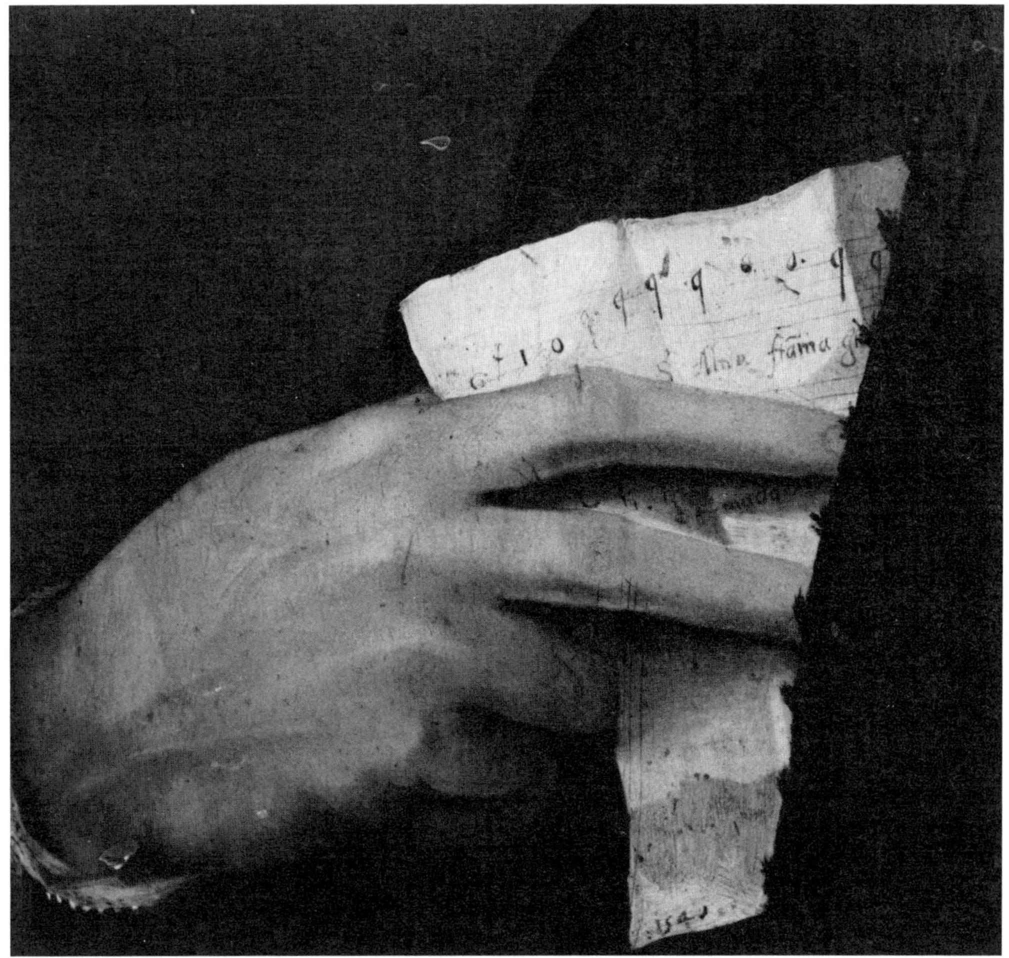

Figure 5 (left). Portrait of a Young Man, *detail.*

because beyond the ear, "which does not change with age,"[38] there is little other resemblance in the two pictures.

Even in the mere snippet of music that the painter allows us to see, there are several differences in both music and text from the print (example 1) of eleven years later. Although the picture condenses the print's three repeated E's into one dotted E in the fourth bar, the painter, unlike the music printer, does not repeat the first line of the poem (figure 5). The musical variant in the picture probably did not

[38] Lowinsky, "Problems," p. 585, quoting the late John Maxon.

result from painterly carelessness, since it makes such good musical sense. Clearly the painter did not present the first phrase at all until, free of the impediment of the subject's index finger, it could be visible. Be this as it may, repeating that first line of text with its sustained E results in a superior declamation for these opening bars in the painted version. Is then the picture closer to the madrigal as the composer conceived it than the 1551 print? The question is unanswerable because we have no notion whether Animuccia supervised the printing. Nor is there any evidence for a degree of intimacy between the painter and the subject, whoever they were. However, were we to hypothesize the subject as the young Animuccia himself, then we would have a nice explanation for these differences.

Without more evidence, and to paraphrase lyrics from *Oklahoma*, "I've gone about as fer as I can go." I have provided some new data, but left several new problems. If Christie's July sale catalog benefited from this research, it was not sufficient to fetch the reserve set for the painting, for it remains unsold. Our trialogue shows that scholarship "is constructed to be superseded, and [that] its most brilliant insights become building blocks for structures which no one could have foreseen."[39] Though I claim no "brilliant insights" and not yet any "structures," a few building blocks are now in place.

Let us finish by considering the support system and the underpinnings of this research, for it represents a microcosm of humanistic study. Indispensable (as a glance through the footnotes shows) was an array of titles that cuts across many sections of the Library of Congress classification system and that encompasses a broad selection of materials: ephemera, photographs, bibliographies, dissertations, manuscripts, journal and encyclopedia articles, scores, early editions, microfilms, and books. Dr. Johnson's famous claim that a person "will take over half a library to write a book"[40] surely assumes one library in one place. Even this little study required unpublished primary sources located in London, Munich, Florence, and Cambridge, Massachusetts. The need for large collections of microfilms is self-evident, although a facsimile edition of one of the sources is in the process of publication at Garland.[41] At least as important for finding Animuccia's birthdate are other primary sources not consulted, a task that could consume weeks in Florentine archives. Since rare books are certainly housed elsewhere than in European and Ivy League libraries, it required several phone calls and a four-hour drive through the smog to the Elmer Belt Library at UCLA, only to discover that Poccianti's 1589 catalogue on Florentine writers was not helpful.[42]

Very few libraries, one exception being that of the J. Paul Getty Museum in Santa Monica, California, had reproductions of the photographs in London's Witt Library. Much more is needed to make visual resources more widely available and accessible, regardless of where such collections are housed, and music librarians need to

39 Naomi Bliven, review of *The Last Tiffany: A Biography of Dorothy Tiffany Burlingham*, by Michael John Burlingham, *The New Yorker* (31 July 1989) 84, where "scholarship" is "science."

40 James Boswell, *Life of Johnson* (London, 1791), 6 April 1775.

41 Francesco Manara, *Il primo libro di madrigali a quattro voci* (Venice, 1555), an edition soon to appear as vol. 17 in the Garland series, Sixteenth-Century Madrigal, ed. Jessie Ann Owens, whom I thank.

42 Michaele Poccianti, *Catalogus scriptorum Florentinorum omnis generis* (Florence, 1589), pp. 101–102.

devise ways to control and index the visual materials relevant for our discipline. To some extent the iconographical sections of RILM reflect current work in this field, as exemplified by Howard Brown's monumental survey, "A Corpus of Trecento Pictures with Musical Subject Matter," currently appearing in *Imago Musicae*.[43] A master index is badly needed, however, similar to those in the RIdIM surveys of visual-musical resources in seven American museums.[44]

Timely ordering, followed by prompt cataloging, processing, and shelving, provide impatient scholars the necessary access to books recently published. The importance for my research of, for example, Harry Lincoln's recent work, *The Italian Madrigal*, with its thematic and other indexes, cannot be too strongly stressed.[45] (May his stunning achievement, made possible by computer technology, inspire similar Herculean efforts in others.)

Furthermore, strong reference collections must be in place, covering not only our discipline but sister disciplines such as literature and art history, and general areas such as national biography. Valuable periodicals now long out of print must be procured and preserved. Praise be to University Microfilms for making United States dissertations available, and to the reprint industry for republishing valuable reference works and periodicals.

Remote book storage causes real problems for scholars. Three weeks elapsed before the book with Grazzini's poem for Animuccia (about spinach) arrived from the University of California's Northern Regional Library Facility. The UC-Irvine Library nonetheless recently banished its complete run of the *Rivista musicale italiana* to exile in UC's southern storage facility, despite the presence of three scholars at Irvine who study Italian music. Happily, the *Rivista* quickly returned to our shelves. Writing not so long ago in *Notes*, Rey Longyear observed: "techniques of 'scientific library management' applicable to science and technology cannot be fairly applied to the humanities." His sound advice bears repeating: "Musicologists . . . should be given a voice in determining . . . storage, filming, and disposal policies [not only] for the journals in their own fields but for the humanistic journals."[46] Otherwise we harried scholars must hope that electronic optical scanning—which, in any case, may soon be essential for books and music stored remotely—will overcome increasing difficulties not only with ready access but also with rapidly deteriorating paper. Clearly, some major step forward will have to be taken, and scholars turn to new technologies and to music librarians. In a masterly essay, Charles Osburn identifies what he calls a "scholarly communication system."[47] He names scholars and librarians as its essential components, the former as initiators and the latter as eventual recipients (i.e., through publication). Osburn cogently argues that "librarianship has consistently opened the portals of opportunity for scholarly communication and advanced the system to more sophisticated levels." He laments the

43 Howard Mayer Brown, "Catalogus: A Corpus of Trecento Pictures with Musical Subject Matter, Part I," *Imago Musicae*, 1–3 (1984–86).

44 *RIdIM/RCMI Inventory of Music Iconography*, ed. Terence Ford (New York: Research Center for Musical Iconography, 1987–).

45 Lincoln, *The Italian Madrigal*.

46 Rey M. Longyear, "Article Citations and 'Obsolescence' in Musicological Journals," *Notes*, 33 (1977), 570–571. I thank William Prizer for this reference.

47 Charles B. Osburn, "The Structuring of the Scholarly Commmunication System," *College and Research Libraries*, 50 (1989), 277–286. I am obliged to John Roberts for drawing this essay to my attention.

present overload in communication, likening it to noise that has grown to a "deafening cacophony." Around the scholarly communication system, though, a kind of Star Wars is at work: "The library is the protective shield" because "selectivity is the underlying principle of libarianship." Selectivity depends upon knowledge. Here scholars can and must help educate music librarians in their formative years and advise them later when they have been promoted to the rank of general. It goes without saying, of course, that we musicologists and our students constantly learn from librarians. The synergy inherent in the "scholarly communication system" guarantees that librarians and scholars will always participate in that discourse.

The Publisher and the Music Librarian

Leo F. Balk

For over a decade—fourteen or fifteen years to be exact—Garland Publishing has sought to reproduce multi-volume facsimile editions of little-known or unavailable musical works in order to make source materials for the study of music more widely available. This is an eccentric kind of publishing, but it has nonetheless become an important part of our firm's profile. Garland as a whole consists of four divisions. The one for which I am responsible includes music as part of a larger facsimile program that embraces architecture, history, and literature. In these other fields we publish books similar to those that we issue in music. For example, we are publishing facsimiles of F. Scott Fitzgerald's manuscripts at Princeton University and of Walter Gropius's architectural drawings from the Busch-Reisinger Museum at Harvard University. Music has never accounted for more than ten percent of our annual sales. We also publish anthologies of reprinted scholarly articles in various fields, along with numerous recent dissertations. Our second major division is reference. The reference list focuses on one-volume encyclopedias, bibliographies, and information guides. These two divisions comprise Garland's core businesses and account for seventy percent of all sales. The remaining thirty percent comes from the law and textbook divisions. With the two core businesses—reprints, facsimiles, and dissertations on the one hand and the reference division on the other—Garland caters almost exclusively to a library market. Indeed, most of our books go to academic research libraries throughout the world, making librarians our major customers. Garland pursues this market to a degree that is unusual in publishing. This is the background for my observations about music librarianship.

Leo F. Balk is vice-president of Garland Publishing, Inc.

The music market is unique in a number of ways. The nature of the material makes it more international than the market in any other field. Linguistic boundaries are not as great a barrier as they are in other markets. This is true not just for scores, but also for scholarly material. Essentially the same books can be sold in North America, Europe, or Japan since the audience for academic music books is more conversant with foreign languages than that for parallel disciplines. Although music is a vast and diffuse field, the library market is actually very small: only about five hundred academic research libraries in the world have significant music collections. Many libraries have books about music in their collections but very few of them regularly purchase large quantities of music and books about music. I suspect that the people attending this symposium represent a substantial portion of the North American music library market.

Music librarianship requires specialized knowledge in a way that librarianship in literature or science does not. Indeed, it has been my experience that people who do not read music and know little about it are more baffled by musical scores or books about music than they are by materials in foreign languages. In addition to the specialized knowledge that comes from training in the discipline, a librarian needs pragmatism to decide how best to allocate resources. In addressing an audience of music librarians, the publisher finds a knowledgeable and discriminating clientele. Music librarians are often, by virtue of their specialized training, able to represent the scholar's perspective to the publisher. Most music librarians have the independent authority to make purchases, although they do act on faculty recommendations and in some cases report administratively to the faculty. In the course of developing comprehensive collections, they balance faculty interests; a library that caters only to the faculty's immediate needs will be lopsided. Our marketing approach reflects this situation. In other fields—such as literature or history—marketing by direct mail and by telephone is targeted to reach primarily faculty and secondarily librarians. We expect faculty to bring pressure on librarians to make decisions about the information we have sent to the librarians. Music marketing, however, can be directed primarily to librarians.

As a result music librarians hold a unique position in relation to publishers. The combination of knowledge, authority to make decisions, and financial power gives them a control of the market that is not evident in other disciplines, with the possible exception of art history. The financial power of music librarians is strengthened by their generally sizable budgets, wielded within a small, cohesive community. These factors position music librarians to work directly with book dealers and publishers in matters of policy: to exert editorial control and to shape sales and distribution practices.

Librarians exercise this authority in a number of ways. They have a voice through their professional journals and the reviews they publish. *Notes* by and large maintains a good review policy, one that mandates timely reviews. A review that appears years after a book is published is of no use to a publisher and is unlikely to affect the firm's policies. Reviews that appear quickly serve readers as well as publishers. Furthermore, reviews are among the best forms of publicity known: there is a saying in publishing that bad reviews sell more books than no reviews. If an entire publishing program got a very bad reception, however, it would be abandoned. We in the publishing world read reviews and pay attention to them. I always scan the reviews in *Notes*, for example, as I do in journals for other fields. My intent is not so much to find a review that praises the brilliance of the author or that finds fault with numerous details of the execution but to read reviews of various kinds of books. I want to see what is praised as useful so that I can do something similar in a different field. I also want to find out what topics interest libraries. All this information helps an editor plan an acquisitions policy.

Although publishers pay attention to reviews, I sometimes wonder if librarians do. A *Notes* review a number of years ago of one of our books was so negative that the review editor called me in advance and read large sections of it over the telephone. It concluded by suggesting that any library that had already bought the book should either remove it from the shelves or put a sign on it warning readers away from it. The lessons we learned from that book were to pursue no further projects with the author and to be more careful with books in that category (it was a biographical dictionary). Nevertheless, we have managed to sell 766 copies of the book and to realize an adequate financial return on our investment. The business manager is not unhappy with it.

Librarians can advise publishers about the feasibility of potential programs. But I can also think of at least one major issue on which Garland regretted having ignored the advice of music librarians. About five years ago, when we were aggressively planning to expand our music program, I asked many librarians about projects we were undertaking. Though no one ever criticized the projects, many said that we were planning too much. We nonetheless expanded our program to the point that for three consecutive years we published over eighty expensive facsimile volumes per year. To be sure, other forces were working against us in the market at that time, but it is perfectly accurate to say that we had begun to compete with ourselves. We simply published more books than any library could purchase in any given year. Sales fell off dramatically, and the program ran a significant loss until we reduced it to fewer than fifty volumes per year. Some may tell us that this is still too many, but we are now on a firmer financial footing.

I have been largely describing the purely commercial effects that librarians can have on publishers, especially in a field as small as music. Librarians should recognize and use this power: they should make their needs and wishes known, suggest new directions to publishers, and urge them to pull back from directions that pose problems. When they have done so, librarians have helped define our list. For example, in response to support from librarians we pushed forward with the composer resource manuals at a time when the project was encountering difficulties. We are now working on a major new effort in ethnomusicology that was strongly endorsed by librarians. We have also been urged to pursue popular music, although I fear that we have not yet succeeded on that count. We consider this direct editorial advice to be important and very useful.

All the points made thus far concern the librarian as consumer. But the librarian also functions as a conserver, and in that role other collaborative relationships are possible. A few such cooperative arrangements we have had with major libraries exemplify such collaborations.

The British Library has adopted an open-door policy regarding the publication of reprints and facsimiles of the manuscripts and printed editions in its collections. This policy has influenced the nature and the number of the music series we have published. *The London Pianoforte School*, *Renaissance Music in Facsimile*, and *English Song* are all heavily based on British Library material. In all three cases I encouraged the editors to consider British Library holdings while planning the sets. The cooperation of certain Italian libraries also shaped the contents of *Renaissance Music.*

Librarians may have a number of motives for undertaking such cooperative publishing projects. One is surely the desire to make their collections more widely available. Another is a concern about preservation. Facsimile publications give the library a new copy and also an archival microfilm, thus reducing the number of times a fragile manuscript or rare edition needs to be consulted.

Garland's collaboration with libraries and archives has been most extensive in the field of architecture. In some cases, the impetus for a project has come from a librarian, but always the organization, planning, and devlopment of the project have required collaborative efforts between the librarians and Garland. As an example, let me tell you about our Walter Gropius Archive. When Garland first approached the Busch-Reisinger Museum about their Gropius Archive, the drawings were entirely uncataloged and no photographic record of them existed. The Museum was willing to work with us on publishing a catalog. Garland advanced the funds for the project and engaged an editor to work on it with the Museum. In addition, we arranged for the complete photography of the collection. The Museum receives both microfilm copies and glossy prints of all the drawings. The creation of the microfilm and the prints was both indispensable for cataloging and crucial for conservation. When the illustrated catalog is published, it will serve to emphasize the importance of the collection and to open Gropius's work to scholars.

A similar project is under way with the Museum of Modern Art and its vast collection of Mies van der Rohe drawings. The Gropius collection amounts to just over three thousand drawings, but the Mies collection contains over twenty thousand. Two years ago we published a catalog of the European work; we are now working on the American output. The Museum has benefited from the creation of a photographic record of the archive and the impetus to complete the catalog of the collection. While this catalog was being prepared, several thousand new drawings were discovered among the Museum's own collections and elsewhere in architects' offices in New York. The Museum could have done all this work itself, but Garland acted as a catalyst and as a source of financial support.

We are also working with the Burnham Library of the Art Institute of Chicago to publish its card-file index to architectural periodicals. The wider distribution of the index serves scholars, earns a royalty for the library, and eliminates the necessity of maintaining 100,000 note cards. Although the library could have done the work itself, the publication would probably not have occurred without Garland.

Over the years we have maintained contact with the Frank Lloyd Wright Foundation in Taliesin West. We thus knew that the archivist there had spent many years cataloging the complete correspondence of Frank Lloyd Wright. And we learned that the Getty Center in Santa Monica was interested in working with Taliesin to compile and publish this catalog. Garland was able to step in, act as publisher, and help produce the catalog. In this way we have helped both institutions achieve their own aims. The interests of publishers and libraries can coincide, and such collaboration can further the goals of both. Though Garland has discussed other possible ideas with Taliesin staff, to our great disappointment, further collaboration has not been possible. So I think it is also safe to say that the goals of libraries and publishers are not necessarily the same.

Returning to music, we have been negotiating with the Enoch Pratt Library in Baltimore to publish the song index to its voluminous sheet music collection. The main difficulty has been in developing a workable formula for mutual publisher and library funding. I believe we have now advanced to the point of signing a contract. We hope that together Pratt and Garland will be able to complete the project.

These are a few ways in which librarians can work with publishers. Although none of the examples mentioned thus far has taken the librarian outside the traditional job description to the role of author, over the years librarians have also written or compiled information for books that we have published. Their bibliographical expertise is particularly useful regarding reference books. This expertise combined with musicological training tends to make music librarians excellent authors as well as music editors. Even so, librarians have usually left the role of author to members of the teaching faculty, which is unfortunate because librarians can bring to scholarship a unique combination of pragmatism, scholarly knowledge, and bibliographical expertise. So while a nine-to-five, five-day-a-week schedule does not leave much energy and time for scholarship, writing books and editing music is another avenue open to librarians that is welcomed by publishers.

Librarians acting as consumers, conservers, or authors can have a significant impact on the direction and shape of a publisher's work. Music librarians are particularly well placed by the strength of their financial power and scholarly knowledge. The financial power comes from the control that individual librarians have over their budgets and also from the relatively small size of the academic music library market. The position of the librarian vis-à-vis the publisher is further enhanced by the library's collections: collaborative publishing efforts can achieve a number of mutually beneficial results. If anything, American music librarians should feel that they hold positions of strength in relation to academic publishers. Both sides can only benefit from greater dialogue.

The Ethnomusicology Challenge

Bruno Nettl

Bruno Nettl is professor of music and anthropology, University of Illinois, and former president of the Society for Ethnomusicology. His most recent book is *Blackfoot Musical Thought: Comparative Perspectives*.

Among the fields of music, ethnomusicology is in some respects the least bookish; it is, after all, concerned mainly with music that lives in aural tradition. The title assigned for this paper, "The Ethnomusicology Challenge," poses most interesting questions. What does this field, that has very little in the way of books and scores, provide by way of a *challenge* to the now highly technologized and sophisticated field of music librarianship? (By rough estimate, for instance, the ethnomusicological holdings in my local music library account for a mere five percent of its total contents.) Or, how can a highly culture-specific profession such as Euro-American librarianship do anything at all with a field that virtually has no cultural home? In other words, should music librarians even be thinking about any of this?

Although overstated, this last question is justified, at least if we look at the relationships among areas of music-oriented scholarship in the last few decades. And yet, one of the things I noticed quickly upon entering academic life was that people associated with libraries tended to have a noticeable interest in the "odd musics"—those that comprise the folk/ethnic/non-Western/popular/vernacular continuum. The substantial energy that the Library of Congress devoted to the Archive of Folk Song along with the comprehensive bibliography of Asian musics that Richard Waterman, William Lichtenwanger, and others published in *Notes* forty years ago are illustrative. Possibly the psychological mold of those whose job it was to preserve (and justify) American music of all sorts was similar to that of the ethnomusicologists of earlier times. In the 1950s and early 1960s, many music librarians and ethnomusicologists—there were not all that many of either ilk—felt a close association, if for no other reason than that both saw themselves as benchwarmers in the game of musical scholarship.

The association has not really grown, but it still exists, possibly in changed form. In order to explore this newer relationship, I will consider three questions: (1) What would ethnomusicologists like librarians to do for them? (2) What would librarians like ethnomusicologists to do? And (3) How can the contemplation of libraries as cultural institutions contribute to an ethnomusicologist's understanding of music's relationship to the other domains of culture? All three questions focus on a central problem of ethnomusicology: how to study a culture and its music with the approaches and tools of another culture.

First, what indeed would ethnomusicologists like librarians to do for them? When one enters a library and consults its catalog, one expects an even-handed approach to the library's contents. But a hierarchy of musics quickly becomes evident: the seeker of Western art music is well served by the detail and sophistication of descriptive cataloging, classification, and subject cataloging, whereas the seeker of material in folk and non-Western music can hardly get started. Ethnocentrism in music cataloging may be difficult to change, since many librarians enter the field having been trained in Western art music. And yet it would be helpful to work at establishing a more neutral approach, one that recognizes the diversity of world cultures and also gives the various domains of our culture more equal treatment.

The second thing ethnomusicologists would like does not concern the management of libraries, but rather, a particular expertise that librarians can provide to ethnomusicological researchers. Ethnomusicologists have widely adopted ways of thinking about music, in particular Alan Merriam's three-part model, that consists of sound, behavior, and concepts or ideas about music.[1] But although there are many ways of taking apart the "sound" portion of the model—laying out a culture's stylistic elements or parameters according to the style of Alan Lomax or Erich M. von Hornbostel, or classifying tunes in the manner of Samuel P. Bayard or Béla Bartók, for example—we have little guidance for inventorying and describing the system of ideas about music in the world's cultures. To be sure, we can use the approach of each culture for its own ethnomusicology, but we also need a way of translating one culture to another, a way of facilitating comparative study. If librarians are experts in the classification of knowledge and its verbal expression, they ought to be able to help us. However, can the style of thinking that led to the Dewey and Library of Congress classification schemes, or the LC subject headings, provide leadership?

A third item concerns ethnomusicological archives, which are perhaps the most significant repositories of unique ethnomusicological data. Except for LC's Archive of Folk Song, such archives for a long time existed quite independently of libraries, and the staffs of the archives did not regard themselves as members of the library profession. Ordinary professors often served as archivist-librarians. In the last twenty years, the situation has changed substantially. Trained archivists now care for the large collections of field recordings that are major resources for study and research in such institutions as Indiana University, UCLA, the universities of Illinois and Washington, and more recently Harvard University, among others. The relatively modest use of ethnomusicological archives by researchers—an observation of mine that has met with some disagreement—can be attributed to the absence of a comprehensive network of catalogs. Locating particular types of items—American Indian Ghost Dance songs, or a list of recordings of the Raga Sankarbharanam, for example—requires approaches to many archives. Other types of materials—books or perhaps commercial recordings—can be found by using national bibliographies and interlibrary loan, provided the bibliographic tools in the home library are adequate.

One is tempted to say, "Archives of the world, unite, you have nothing to lose but your idiosyncracies"; indeed a union catalog of ethnomusicological field collections would facilitate research and reference work. Such a project was undertaken, in the early days of field recording, by George Herzog in a compendium, *Research in Primitive and Folk Music in the United States*.[2] Computers ought to make a successor to that publication possible, although the task is daunting. Many problems remain,

[1] Alan P. Merriam, *The Anthropology of Music* (Evanston: Northwestern University Press, 1964), pp. 32–33.

[2] ACLS Bulletin no. 24 (Washington, D.C., 1936).

in spite of technology. There is no standardization, particularly if we rely solely on a culture's own designations, regarding what to list (e.g., recordists, ethnic groups, genres, instruments) and how (i.e., under what term, or form of name).

Furthermore, the idea that a complete list of archival holdings could actually be compiled strains our credulity. There was a time when indexing tunes seemed appropriate enough, as evidenced by the LC *Check-List of Folk Songs* and the *National Tune Index*.[3] To be sure, such activity requires either a rather definite idea of what constitutes a tune and its variant, or faith in the process of transcription. In a set of cultures in which only recordings exist, and in which the labeling of units of musical thought is problematic, indexing tunes is even more difficult. In spite of these challenges, there are many ways in which ethnomusicological archives could cooperate.

A related problem concerns the cataloging of commercial recordings with their enormously varied origins and purposes. The care that goes into the cataloging of Western art music has never been approached in cataloging for non-Western and folk music. People say it can't be done. But perhaps the use of one example, the concept of composer, can help to convince otherwise. For Western art music, the principal approach is the composer, so that one seeks music by looking under Ludwig van Beethoven, Johann Sebastian Bach, or Stephen Sondheim. But composers are equally important, it turns out, in the way South Indian society thinks about its classical music. South Indian musicians will quickly tell the American musician that they, too, have their "trinity" of great composers: Tyagaraja, the greatest (often compared to Beethoven), Muttuswami Dikshitar, and Syama Sastri, who lived in the first half of the nineteenth century. Although the music of their songs has largely been transmitted aurally, the attributions appear solid. The concerts have printed programs, and composers' names appear on recordings. Indeed, there are LP records consisting entirely of songs by one composer. Yet most record library catalogs fail to list any entries under Tyagaraja. For the music of India, entries may be found under performers, as this music is said to be largely improvised—correctly so for much, but certainly by far not all of it. Indian musicians think our librarians are patronizing them. On the other hand, in the case of North American Indian music, the twentieth century has produced important and well-known individual performers and singing groups, but their names are usually not available in catalogs.

Solutions are complex. One may conclude that cataloging with the use of Western concepts is at best "etic," the anthropological shorthand for the outsider's view, and advocate the "emic" approach, in which each culture's own taxonomy of music is central. If an American, turning on the radio and hearing lush harmonies, says immediately "it's Brahms," a Madras resident, hearing a particular pentatonic scale, will say "it's Raga Mohana." Consequently, Indian music ought to be classified and cataloged with main entry under Raga. Ethnocentrics may object, "that's like looking up pieces under C-sharp minor": but no, it is the Indian's main approach. By using such reasoning, however, we could relegate the performer, who sometimes composes along the way and sometimes reproduces or just elaborates, to a secondary role in the catalog.

3 Library of Congress, *Check-List of Recorded Songs in the English Language in the Archives of American Folk Song to July, 1940* (Washington, 1942); Carolyn Rabson and Kate Van Winkle Keller, eds., *The National Tune Index* (microfiche; New York: University Music Editions, 1980).

After that list of tall orders, librarians ought to be allowed to articulate what they would like ethnomusicologists to do for them. There is much, to be sure, but let me suggest two possible areas of contribution. One is creating a definitive listing of the world's cultures, genres, instruments, and musical categories. I will not elaborate on this ideal contribution, but want instead to mention a second, longstanding desire: better reference sources. Some thirty years ago, I read a paper for the Midwest Chapter of the Music Library Association, suggesting that various reference tools for ethnomusicology were needed. The discussant for the session was Richard Waterman, who—uncharacteristically for a discussant—said that I was absolutely right, but that such tools (encyclopedias, anthologies, vocabularies) could not be produced in a properly comprehensive way. In the strictest sense he has largely been proven right. Realizing now that it is all more difficult than Waterman said, even though there are also far more of us to address the task, I do not want to push for such projects. The production of reference books has nonetheless improved greatly since that time. To mention a few key sources, we have *The New Grove Handbook of Ethnomusicology* and *The New Grove Handbook of World Music*, the forthcoming Garland *Encyclopedia of World Music*, Barry Brook's universal music history, the "*Organogrove*," and more.[4] When these works are all completed, we will have covered many aspects of ethnomusicology and enabled librarians to get authoritative information to their patrons more easily than before.

Finally, let me try to integrate the music library as cultural phenomenon into the substance of ethnomusicology as discipline. I must confess that my interest in music libraries has moved from the practical to the ethnographic as I have become increasingly interested in interpreting Western academic musical culture by applying approaches developed for the study of cultures foreign to the investigator. One of the current paradigmatic procedures in ethnomusicology is to extract authentic cultural values and principles from certain institutions central to a musical culture. These institutions might be what anthropologists and folklorists call "cultural performances," a technical term denoting events such as the central powwows of American Indian Plains societies, or concerts in traditional schools and other teaching establishments, or even the dissemination of musical recordings in record stores. For Western academic musical culture such institutions would include schools, concerts, and of course libraries.

I have touched upon the way music libraries use the academic set of Western music hierarchies and taxonomies to establish their system of operation. The hierarchy is implicit everywhere: the subject heading "music," for example, refers to Western art music, the music one performs in tuxedo. All other musics, including early music, are specifically designated—and for that matter, performed in different dress: blazers for big-band jazz, tie-dyed T-shirts for rock, Renaissance costumes for medieval music. (You can't tell the players without their colors and uniforms.) In America, as in most societies, segments of society—social and economic classes, age groups, ethnic groups—all draw cultural boundaries in part by their special association with different musics. The music library is a way for

4 Helen Meyers, ed., *The New Grove Handbook of Ethnomusicology* (London: Macmillan, in press); Helen Meyers, ed., *The New Grove Handbook of World Music* (London: Macmillan, forthcoming); Barry S. Brook, ed., *Universal Music History* (in preparation); James Porter and Timothy Rice, eds., *Encyclopedia of World Music* (New York: Garland, to be published in 1993); Stanley Sadie, ed., *The New Grove Dictionary of Musical Instruments* (London: Macmillan, 1987.)

these groups, via their musics, to meet, although the Western bias can make for a non-egalitarian meeting.

Librarians make value judgments by acquiring materials on the basis of their quality as well as the quality of the art with which the materials deal. At the same time, they try hard to be evenhanded, balancing patrons' requests and charges by governing boards with the demands of present and future curricula, thus applying the principles of democracy to an institution for the dissemination of knowledge. Looking at the music library ethnographically, we can see it as an institution that mediates—as do certain other institutions such as athletics—among the conflicting values of society. It seems to be torn between three values: selectivity, or deciding what is best and keeping the other rascals out; comprehensiveness, or giving all patrons the kind of music they want and in the quantity desired; and traditional education, or uplifting the unwashed and sweeping them into the Western academic tradition. In practice, a library maintains all three values simultaneously, manipulating them in any particular situation. Doing so hardly seems worthy of criticism. Although ethnographers try to identify the guiding principles that maintain a culture, they as often find it necessary to describe the conflicts among these values, so that it might be better, though admittedly different, to use these conflicts as units of cultural description. From an ethnographic perspective, then, the music library is one of the institutions that mediates among the musics of American communities. Just as various musics correspond to the ethnic and social units in a nation, the library is a microcosm of larger institutions that mediate among the segments of culture and society.

If there is a challenge from ethnomusicology to music librarianship, it now has less to do with acquiring materials and writing reference books, and more to do with sensitivity to the intercultural nature of music and to the role of music in society. But in the long run, ethnomusicologists—as anthropological students of musical life—might actually be interested in libraries primarily to ascertain why they do what they do, and how they fit into their own culture.

Scholar-Librarian? Librarian-Scholar?

James W. Pruett

"Scholar-Librarian? Librarian-Scholar?" "Chicken-Egg? Egg-Chicken?" The two-term theme I have been given for variations rightly ought to begin with some definitions, for whether we are scholars or librarians—mutants coming from some fortuitous strand of ancient DNA—we all aim for clarity in language.

What better place to begin than with the book that scholars and librarians keep closest to hand, the dictionary. Closest to hand—fortunately for our subject—are the unabridged *Random House Dictionary* and the unabridged *Webster's Third New International Dictionary*. In the former, the word "librarian" is defined in three senses: (1) a person trained in library science and engaged in library service; (2) an officer in charge of a library; (3) a person who is in charge of any specialized body of literature, *as a collection of musical scores* [emphases in these definitions added]. In one of Webster's definitions, the nod towards musicians continues: a librarian is "one whose special task is the management of any body of literature (*as the musical scores for an orchestra*)." Among the definitions for "library" in the Random House are: "a collection of any materials for study and enjoyment, as films, *musical recordings*, maps, etc.," and "a public body organizing and maintaining such an establishment: *the Library of Congress*." Webster's primary meaning for library is: "a room, a section or series of sections of a building, or a building itself given over to books, manuscripts, *musical scores*, or other literature and sometimes artistic materials (as paintings or *musical recordings*) usu. kept in some convenient order for use but not for sale," or "a collection of books, manuscripts kept (as in a library) for study or reading or a collection of paintings, *musical scores, musical recordings*, photographs, maps, or films kept for convenient use, study or enjoyment." (Happily neither dictionary calls a library a "learning center.")

James W. Pruett is chief of the Library of Congress's Music Division, professor of music *emeritus* at the University of North Carolina, and former president of the Music Library Association. He is the author, with Thomas P. Slavens, of *Research Guide to Musicology*.

The Random House dictionary describes a "scholar" as "a learned or erudite person esp. one who has profound knowledge of a particular subject." Webster's also finds in scholars the qualities of originality, creativity, and achievement. The related term, "scholarly," is characterized as: "of, like, or befitting a scholar; scholarly habits," and "having the qualities of a scholar: a scholarly person." Webster's offers an illustrative quotation (by Ronald Storrs) for "scholarly" that is particularly appealing: "having the manner and appearance of a scholar (never academic—still less pedantic—but always scholarly) with the effect of profound learning ever so lightly worn."

All these definitions are useful in clarifying the two terms of our theme. Furthermore, they imply such characteristics as seriousness of purpose, learning, and dignity; and they reflect as well the high calling to which scholars and librarians have responded. Librarians and scholars share many attributes, principally a love of books and respect for the learning and ideas that books contain. They share curiosity of mind. They ask questions, the main one usually being, "Why?" Though the differences between scholars and librarians could be listed, they would largely reflect the ways in which the working lives of the two groups are routinely conducted, not fundamental approaches or attitudes towards learning, or towards the collections in the libraries that both groups inhabit. Let us, instead, reflect on the responsibilities and qualities that may be considered essential for music librarians today, especially those whose work brings them into contact with students, including scholars (in the best sense, we all are forever students, whether librarians, or scholars, or both).

Librarians are gatherers and organizers, in much the same way, perhaps, that Ptolemy II was a gatherer and organizer for the library at Alexandria. Librarians are clearly driven, perhaps by primordial instinct, to gather the stuff that makes up a library and to make that stuff coherent and useful. They seem compelled to organize it, to impose rational order upon it, to systematize it, to service it, and yes, to catalog it.

Not too long ago—although it seems as though it was in olden times—collection building was relatively simple; and I emphasize the word "relatively." Books, scores, recordings on disc or tape, and microfilms were the mainstays of most collections, with manuscripts and other archival materials often housed in the larger libraries. Traditional printing technologies restrained the outflow from publishers and thus the inflow to music libraries. Technological innovations of the last two or three decades have so changed and so enriched the process of developing collections that, given enough money, it would be possible today to build a brand new major research music library. There is very little that is not potentially available on microfilm or microfiche, through xerography or other facsimile process, in reprint editions, on optical discs, or on CD-ROM. Fortunately, original sources—that is, principally manuscript and archival sources—will remain the treasure troves that they are today; even in this age of facsimiles they will surely continue to offer unique ties to the past, not just as information, but as artifacts that give immediacy to history.

Scholarly music librarians—is that the right phrase?—have a set of challenges to face, whether they are developing large or small collections. They must select judiciously and in keeping with the aims and needs of their libraries; they must be knowledgeable about old and new music and music literature; they must be able to judge dross from gold and fad from substance. The last achievement is easier said than done, for we have all found that yesterday's trash is today's treasure, at least in someone's eyes.

It seems that today's music librarians—especially but not exclusively those in research libraries—must be aware of a serious debate among humanists. It is an argument partly galvanized by statements from Allan Bloom, author of *The Closing of the American Mind,*[1] and William Bennett, first while he was head of the National Endowment for the Humanities, later as Secretary of Education, and following that, as the so-called "drug czar." They, among others, urge a return to a more classical canon of teaching, learning, and research. They generally disparage scholarly work and attitudes that are non-value-oriented and that tend more towards popular culture and sociological considerations. Many humanists are concerned about polarizing this debate into a leftist/rightist, liberal/conservative

[1] New York: Simon and Schuster, 1987.

dichotomy; taken too far in either direction, the controversy can lead to a serious misunderstanding by the public about the central values that humanists tend to have in common.

The concerns and interests of humanist scholars and librarians—indeed, of most intellectuals—are constantly broadening. The legacy and influence of "relevance" from the 1960s and 1970s may be stronger than we realize: societies and associations nowadays function as more than mere forums for scholarship. Committees on minorities are commonplace. The Council of the American Musicological Society, for example, considers such matters as how its Committee on Outreach can become more involved with media and public educational institutions.

How do such public debates affect music librarians? Should we participate in them and, if so, how? What effect should they have on the way we build collections? Several responses seem appropriate. First we need to know the substance and the nuances of the arguments, and we must in turn make sure that the governing bodies of libraries understand the implications for our collections. We need to repeat to all that a library's mission is always evolving and dynamic, and that the need for resources is constant. We must remind ourselves and others that the collection development we engage in today will yield the materials for future scholarship, provided the collections are preserved in some way. When Gottfried Leibniz was librarian at the Herzog August Bibliothek at Wolfenbüttel from 1690 to 1716, and when Gottfried Lessing was appointed to the same post in 1770, they acted as have countless others, as scholarly librarians interested in ideas and research: they gathered and organized, selected and preserved, and so must we. Although our library problems are surely more pressing and complex, and although we have an incredibly larger universe of materials from which to select, the overall obligation is constant. We must exercise judgments as fully informed as possible; those judgments will depend in great part on our being keenly aware of present needs and on anticipating, insofar as possible, the needs of the next generations of scholars.

Such judgment in any library invokes a system of values: we acquire and preserve materials that are useful artistically or intellectually, or both. Even when operating under the powerful influence of a changing system of social and intellectual values, we must keep the purposes of our individual institutions clearly in mind and—be sure that we tend our own gardens.

In more practical terms, what does this "gathering" require? It means carefully defining and knowing our readers or constituencies, those persons who rightfully expect a collection that will both answer their questions and enrich their lives. It requires melding a program of acquisitions for immediate and projected needs. It is based on knowing, among the plethora of available materials, what is or might be the most desirable for one's library—or, in economically realistic terms, the most necessary.

Each speaker at this symposium brings a set of experiences and a viewpoint; and each of us is or has been associated with an institution whose aims and purposes differ from those of other institutions. My gathering responsibilities at present are discharged in one of the world's largest and most complex libraries. Having spent a number of years at a medium-sized university blessed with both distinguished university and music libraries, I find it simultaneously fascinating and frustrating to observe how the collections of the Library of Congress have been and are being developed. The resources for research and discovery at the Library are extraordinary, and the problems of collection development are at one and the same time minor and overwhelming. A mountain of material comes automatically, offering many opportunitites for enriching the collections, but much can be missed if great care is not taken.

In the coming decades, music research doubtless will increasingly reflect a broader world view. Though traditional historical musicology will always remain of great importance, Western scholars will surely devote more attention to the art and traditional musics of the world, and the disciplined research that has distinguished Western musical scholarship will find a niche in the musical research of non-Western scholars. How those future scholars will develop research tools, analytical methods, and descriptive language is uncertain. Several institutions in this country have made special efforts to support research in music that lies outside the European high art tradition. The Library of Congress, partly through serendipity and partly through design, already has the nucleus of a great collection in ethnomusicology. (Bruno Nettl's excellent analysis of the collections a few years ago bears this out.) On a global basis, the Music Division of LC is acquiring as comprehensive a collection of publications of and about music as possible, regardless of language or format. Because the Library is equipped to attempt such a program, setting it in motion will be comparatively easy, but guaranteeing success will be more troublesome and will require considerable monitoring.

If our predictions are correct, the Library of Congress will be able, in conjunction with other institutions in this country, to meet the needs of researchers much more completely. If, on the other hand, we are only partly right, we shall still be ahead, and little will have been lost. In this game the odds are with us.

So, gathering and organizing are honorable pursuits, and music librarians may be the noblest practitioners. But what about service and education, the larger communities of librarians and scholars, and the world of libraries as institutions? It is at least interesting and perhaps significant that the term "school of library *service*" appears to be more out of fashion than in, and that it has a faintly quaint, archaic quality when it is encountered. "Library *science*," coupled with "information science," seems more current, more modish, and may actually be more apt for us today. Education in graduate schools that not merely train but educate future librarians has undergone a genuine revolution, mainly because of technology. New technology affords enormous control over the materials in our libraries. If the 1970s were the founding decade of the library network, then the 1980s have seen the rise of a new generation of librarians and scholars who are uniquely qualified to test the full resources of the computer. This generation of young librarians must challenge the old standards of cataloging, for example, and provide simpler but better ways of controlling, analyzing, and describing what we now call information or data. More important, these new librarians will surely design more effective ways of delivering the service that librarians will always have to supply. The card catalog—clearly moribund if not yet completely dead—was relatively easy to explain to readers (if not always to reference librarians themselves, who had to interpret the arcana supplied by brilliant, but sometimes unrestrained, subject catalogers). The growing challenges of new technology—supernetworking, proliferating commercial and in-house databases, and innovations such as hypertext and CD-ROMS—are already putting a premium on technological facility and skills, particularly for instructing users both within and outside our collections. But as we move further into whatever "brave new world" lies before us, let us not permit the word "librarian" to be replaced by a term as devalued as "interfacer."

There is a concern, however, about the new curricula appearing in graduate schools, and not just in schools of library science. New technologies have insinuated themselves so easily, so quickly, and so beguilingly, because they give the individual a sense of power and control over information that is just plain fascinating at almost any level of expertise. My concern is that the technocrats may win, that they may boil out of curricula the basic love of books and learning that led most of us to the professional lives we relish. There remains little truth to the old accusation that musicologists do not enjoy music or go to concerts; let it be true that librarians always read books and not just look at computer screens.

The concern may be groundless: curricula still offer histories of books, printing, and libraries, and surely most young music librarians and scholars are still enthusiastic about the bases and origins of their professions. But in a society where great value is placed on seeking the "new and improved," there is an inherent danger that the "new" is oftentimes merely the "novel." Generally speaking, then, in creating new systems, music librarians young and old must guard against relying on premises thought but not proven valid, or on programs that have not, in modern jargon, been debugged. Any novel systems, whether of bibliographic and information control, of financial management, of administration, of beliefs regarding the functions of libraries within society, require the most critical appraisals from those who teach and from those who practice the profession of librarianship. We must always be vigilant that the technical specialist does not replace the reader librarian, the thoughtful librarian, the *scholarly librarian.*

The rubric of this symposium, "Music Librarianship in America," underscores one of the symposium's themes: that music librarians have a special obligation and responsibility for music in the United States. Without listing lacunae in American musical studies, nor putting particular charges to American music librarians, I shall make some observations.

The intellectual and methodological schism between scholars who study European traditions and those who study American traditions is narrowing, in spite of the historical necessity to create the Sonneck Society for the study of American Music. As this beneficial trend proceeds of its own momentum, scholars will more clearly define ways to interpret, evaluate, and attach values to the various musics in the United States, past and present. Music librarians will always have the unique opportunity to gather and preserve not only the music of America's past, but also the diverse local and regional musics of the present. A colleague has a favorite story to illuminate my point. If, at the Library of Congress, we were faced with an impending disaster, what would we save in the Music Division: the manuscripts of Brahms and Beethoven? the Stradivariuses? the Dayton Miller Collection of flutes?" The answer is, we would save the several million pieces of American sheet music held as copyright deposits. Other libraries have European manuscripts and instruments, but the Library of Congress has a very large piece of irreplaceable American history. And dozens of other music libraries in the United States have already gathered or should gather additional pieces of American musical history that must be preserved. Almost every institution has a role; the effort is a collective one.

Music librarians bring to their work technical skills, learning, and—remembering those definitions—a scholarly attitude. It is not clear that we can or would even want to decide on the precedence of the words "scholar" and "librarian." We are, in fact, neither scholar-librarians nor librarian-scholars. We are—or should aspire to be—scholarly music librarians.

Questions and Discussion, Part 2

Christoph Wolff, Chair

Christoph Wolff is William Powell Mason Professor of Music, Curator of the Isham Memorial Library, and Acting Director of the University Library at Harvard University. He is the author, with Hans-Joachim Schulze, of the multi-volume *Bach Compendium: analytisch-bibliographisches Repertorium der Werke Johann Sebastian Bachs.*

WOLFF: Our topic, "Music Librarians and Music Scholarship," is as important as it is sensitive, and it's very good that not just this session but the entire symposium is largely devoted to this central aspect. Aren't we all, in fact, sitting in the same boat? Professional, organizational, even philosophical trends have unfortunately created some boundaries. As Harold Samuel pointed out, fewer and fewer musicologists attend Music Library Association meetings because those meetings have become concerned primarily with technical matters. There is also the arrogant scholar who looks down on the library as a service department. But sitting in the same boat means serving one another in the best possible way. Consider the universal phenomenon of stuff-in-a-box, as Suki Sommer referred to it earlier. There is ample opportunity for hands-on cooperation between librarians and scholars, especially in this area, as two recent examples will demonstrate. In April 1989 I was asked to survey the Philip Spitta estate in the university library of Łódź in Poland. The material had been sitting in boxes for forty-six years and had not been accessible to scholarship. I will not belabor the point here; the discoveries are described in the December 1989 issue of *Notes.*[1]

Closer to home and only one week before this symposium, Peter Wollny, a graduate student in musicology at Harvard, telephoned me at home to ask whether I knew a cantata, "Merk auf, mein Herz." I replied that I didn't, but I had seen a reference to it and an incipit of the music. It is listed in Wolfgang Schmieder's *Bach-Werk-Verzeichnis* under Anhang 163. Wollny, who is working on a Wilhelm Friedemann Bach project, informed me that the piece, which is identified in the Schmieder catalog and the Bach-Gesellschaft edition as lost, was here at Harvard. How did he locate the work, which does not show up in any Harvard catalog? It happened to have been among some stuff-in-a-box. The box contained uncataloged materials that came to the library from George Benson Weston, a Harvard professor of Italian language and literature, who left his music collection to the University in the 1950s. The collection contains very important materials, particularly some related to Wilhelm Friedemann Bach, and therefore Wollny had every reason to take a closer look at the papers. From a pile of late nineteenth-century transcriptions he pulled out some eighteenth-century manuscripts, among them a score and a complete set of parts for the eight-part Christmas motet, "Merk auf, mein Herz," by Johann Christoph Bach (1642–1703; figure 1). The manuscripts had never been described because they had not been accessible to scholarly investigation. We established quickly—in fact, in less than five minutes' time—that the copyist was

1 Christoph Wolff, "From Berlin to Łódź: The Spitta Collection Resurfaces," *Notes,* 46 (1989), 311–327.

Figure 1. First page of Johann Christoph Bach's Merk auf, mein Herz, *in a manuscript score by Johann Christoph Altnikol, a copyist for J. S. Bach.*

Johann Christoph Altnikol, J. S. Bach's principal copyist in the 1740s and later his son-in-law, and that the paper is the same as that used for the second half of the score of Bach's *B-minor Mass* and for some other Bach pieces. It could then be readily determined that these were performing materials used in Leipzig by the Thomaner Choir in the mid-1740s, and that the piece was actually part of the Altbachisches Archiv, a collection of music by Bach's ancestors in which the composer became particularly interested during that time.

So, what do we learn from this? Stuff-in-a-box is useful to musicologists only if librarians keep it in the first place, and then only if we know of its existence. At the same time, librarians need scholars to help identify the stuff-in-a-box. We are indeed sitting in the same boat.

LEONARD BURKAT (Danbury, Conn.): When I was a librarian at the Boston Public Library, it was common knowledge that Professor Weston had a number of music manuscripts by members of the Bach family, including obscure works, not well cataloged, of Wilhelm Friedemann Bach. I cannot imagine how that box of music from Weston's collection could have gotten into the hands of any librarian in any library who knew anything about Weston without being opened and carefully examined upon receipt, even if the library couldn't afford to process the contents and make them available. I wonder if there is a reason, if not an excuse, that the box just sat there.

OCHS: While I don't know the answer, I can guess: this material came to Harvard at a time when there was no *music* librarian—there were just *general* librarians, and they could not deal with it properly and adequately. This incident proves how urgently we need music librarians in our libraries.

PRUETT: Coming from the Library of Congress, I am a bit reluctant to comment on unopened boxes! As I have told many people since joining that institution, the magnitude of the problem is simply enormous: we keep discovering stuff in boxes, not only in the buildings on Capitol Hill, but also in various warehouses that we have. I would, however, make one slight plea to those who discover great treasures in boxes, that they temper their reactions and not readily assume that the material discovered has been scandalously neglected by ignorant library staff. Although such may be the case, there are very good reasons in many instances why things have stayed in boxes.

ALEJANDRO PLANCHART (University of California at Santa Barbara): Since we are continuing our discussion of boxes, I will relate one story from south of the border. In 1925 when the Escuela Superior de Música in Caracas was being remodeled, a trunk that had been sitting in a space underneath a staircase was moved and opened. The trunk had apparently been sitting there since 1800—the Escuela had been in the same building since the eighteenth century. In that trunk was found what is now the entire surviving corpus of Venezuelan colonial music, including the Mass of José Ángel Lamas and all the music we have of Cayetano Carreño—Masses and motets. It had literally been hidden there, apparently during the War of Independence, by blocking and plastering the stairs. When the plaster was removed during the remodeling, the trunk was found. So there are reasons that things like this happen.

A different issue is the one raised by Professor Slim and exemplified by the loss of this painting for seventy-odd years. We desperately need to encourage auction houses and those who cater to private collectors (who tend to be very secretive) to do very careful cataloging. And unless auction houses and private collectors make materials available to responsible scholarship for a certain amount of time, we will constantly be saddled with the problem of primary source materials remaining improperly identified and inaccessible to scholars. One of the most painful cases involved a private collection that contained the central sources of old Roman chant at Santa Cecilia, to which scholars were denied access with the excuse that the material was about to appear in facsimile. Completion of the facsimile edition took over a quarter of a century. In the meantime, however, thanks to John Connolly, who managed to get a bootleg microfilm, a number of people could have access. One mission of music librarians should be to preach to private collectors on the morality of denying access to crucial information to responsible scholarship. Paul Henry Lang, in a 1950s editorial, castigates an unknown New York collector who had refused access to a Mozart autograph for work on the *Neue Mozart Ausgabe*.[2] That sort of practice is still very much with us. It is an area in which music librarians, and librarians in general, can have a positive effect in creating a different cultural atmosphere.

MAURICE PRESS (London): I am not utterly convinced by Leo Balk that publishers have as a real goal getting information to musicologists. Doesn't profit come first?

BALK: In planning publishing projects we have to consider their usefulness, and if there is some financial gain to be derived, then they are worth doing. If projects are not well received they aren't done again. The world doesn't lose if it doesn't buy our books because it doesn't want them—we do.

PRUETT: We all need to recognize the enormous sums of money it takes to develop the technology that will give us instant access either to bibliographies or to the texts themselves. There are experiments going on all over the country, none of them cheap. We also need to be aware that by recording images of materials—either digitally or in other ways—we often destroy the materials. As in brittle book microfilming projects, we may be able to see an item only one more time before it is filmed. But we must not underestimate the enormous amounts of time and money that these digital representations are going to cost us. Writing in 1965, J. C. R. Licklider speculated that the library of tomorrow would be contained entirely within a single building, with all knowledge represented there.[3] I'm not sure, however, that such panaceas will allow us to relinquish our grasp on paper.

FRENCH: Regarding the futuristic scenario just described, have librarians at LC ever talked with members of Congress about that, and possibly presented it as an argument for diverting some funds from the Defense Department's Star Wars program? Librarians may play a more critical role in the national policy than we realize.

2 [For another instance of a collector being chastised for withholding music material see "E. H. Fellowes in Pursuit of Morley's Aires," *Notes*, 45 (1989), 882, n. 2. —Ed.]

3 J. C. R. Licklider, *Libraries of the Future* (Cambridge: M.I.T. Press, 1965).

PRUETT: If we could have just one-half of one-half of one-half of one-half percent of the Star Wars budget, the Library of Congress would be in good shape! "American Memory" is a project that concretely supports promising technologies. It has been the subject of considerable debate within the Library of Congress, where a great deal of energy has been devoted to defining it. In music, it attempts to record in digital or other format great quantities of information that reside in—or are represented by—musical documents, organized by genre and in other ways. The Library is now undertaking the preservation work and cataloging that must be done before these documents can be recorded on optical disk or in whatever format is employed. It is a grand plan, though we aren't quite sure at this point where it is going to lead us.

Q: Bruno Nettl mentioned a need and a desire for a union catalog of archival collections related to ethnomusicology. Can the RLIN Archives and Manuscript Control file (AMC) fulfill that potential? Should the file be enhanced to meet the need?

NETTL: It is certainly a start, but cataloging should provide access at a deeper level. For example, scholars should be able to pull together all recordings of Raga Sankarbharanam from South India or of a particular mode in Persian music without having to travel to UCLA, Indiana, and Michigan. Cataloging at such a level would make the AMC file, or any catalog, particularly useful.

PETER HIGHAM (Mount Allison University): I cannot speak for other archives, but I do know that the folklore and language archive at the Memorial University of Newfoundland, which has extensive music holdings, is putting data into the RLIN database, at least on an experimental basis.

D. W. KRUMMEL (University of Illinois): To the ethnomusicologist, what is the value of the notated artifact in the library in relation to the recorded artifact?

NETTL: A visitor to the Ethnomusicology Archive at Illinois, seeing our several hundred boxes of tapes, remarked, "What good is all this if the tapes haven't been transcribed?" The answer is, we can do an awful lot without transcribing them, and if we had only the transcriptions there are many things we could do, but there are many things we could not do without the recordings. Transcribing for archival purposes is not particularly valuable. Ethnomusicologists have concluded that there is not a homology between a recording and a transcription, that a transcription never has everything. People transcribe in order to solve certain problems. The resulting transcription exists as an analytical tool that follows the recording. Nevertheless, transcriptions by earlier scholars may be of enormous interest, and if we study the transcriptions by, for example, Béla Bartók, we learn a great deal that we would not learn simply from the recordings.

KRUMMEL: It seems that the transcript, the score, serves a special purpose in Western music, namely a promotional one. Other people can perform the music from the score, so that its function differs from the function it serves for non-Western music.

NETTL: Yes; with some major exceptions (European and European-derived folk music, for example), people do not perform music from transcriptions. But it is also falsely assumed by many that non-Western societies lack notation systems.

Several do have them, though they may be used rather differently from ours. But certainly in a music library, transcriptions of non-Western music would not play the role that a collection of scores and parts would. We wouldn't take them out to play them: they serve as teaching and research devices. Despite my statement that ethnomusicology may be the least bookish discipline, in certain ways it is the most bookish.

PATRICK MAXFIELD (New England Conservatory): At the New England Conservatory, Third Stream has existed as a department since Gunther Schuller's era there. As the head of the department he taught all his students the uses of Western and non-Western music, not by printed sources, but by archival recordings, or modern digitally-encoded archival records. Whatever the music—Greek, folk, classical—he didn't want students to look at the notes, he wanted them to hear it and perform it, in much the same way students in ethnomusicology do. And that's how people learn. Students in India learn music in a similar way, by hearing the master perform it and then taking over from there. The same thing is true of the two klezmer bands that have come out of the Boston area. They learn their music not from printed sources but from old 78-rpm recordings. They listen to it over and over, play it, and then elaborate on it. So it is important that librarians keep these old recordings to preserve an oral tradition.

Q: There seems to be a driving force in Western culture to record, preserve, and collect our cultural heritage. What points of contact are there between our culture and those that seem to have less of an interest in collecting, or a different way of doing so?

NETTL: The trend in Western society to preserve its culture is significant. Why don't other societies do the same thing? To some extent they do. It is partly a matter of technology; in certain societies writing did not develop until recently. American Indian peoples have become enormously interested in recording their musical heritage—even to the extent of including things that may be questionable, in order to get a certain amount of bulk. In the case of some Asian societies, record-keeping in written form has played an important role, but apparently it didn't occur to people in those societies that musical data was something that one could adequately record in writing—that doing so would benefit anybody—so they didn't do it very much. Then, however, the influx of Western culture through political and economic pressures caused a good many societies in the world to develop a certain self-hatred, a feeling that their cultures were not really worth very much and that they had to change and become Westernized. I learned something about this process in (of all places) Australia, where I met with a group of Australian aboriginal people who had moved to Adelaide and who were spending some time in a social welfare center. They complained that they had forgotten their traditional heritage. They wanted me there because they had heard that I knew something about American Indian cultures and they had heard that American Indians had been more successful in reviving their heritage. The aborigines had clearly learned that their culture was something not worthwhile—something to be denigrated—and they had therefore replaced it in their lives with Anglo-Australian culture. Then much later they wanted it back. Now almost everywhere in the world there is great interest in maintaining and preserving things. One example is the establishment in India of an ethnomusicological archive where recordings are being collected with great energy and devotion under the influence of American archivists.

Q: James Pruett did not mention the teaching that scholars usually do. By and large, librarians are not considered faculty, yet they play the role of teacher. There is a prejudice that will have to be overcome. One job interviewer, after a long look at a candidate's curriculum vitae, asked, "Do you want to be a librarian or do you want to be a teacher?" The two are not mutually exclusive; in fact, one goes hand-in-hand with the other.

PRUETT: Of course, informal teaching goes on every day in almost any librarian's life. Music librarians also play an integral role in formal teaching, both at their own departments or schools and at neighboring institutions.

WOLFF: As we have seen, the relationship between musical scholarship and music librarianship is an essential and productive one, and there is room for further development. With the establishment of an endowment for the music librarianship here at Harvard, at least at this institution the relationship will be one in perpetuity. The prospect is both a blessing and a challenge.

Singing The Body Eclectic: Immigrant Cultural Resources in America's Music Libraries

D. W. Krummel

Our European ancestors no doubt sang for joy once they got past Ellis Island. At least we have been proud to believe this. What they sang, and why, and how, we do not really know, for this evidence is badly documented. Although the inadequacy of the extant evidence causes scholars by nature to lament, in matters of political import it also encourages guilt and anger. The subject of immigrant cultural resources can also suggest a different agenda: an effort to determine what American music libraries are and are not, could be or can never be, want to be but may be helpless to be.

In a sense the strengths of America's music libraries were achieved largely at the neglect of all but two of its immigrant communities. The melting pot (or more appropriately, the cooking pot) in America's music libraries contains a stew with ingredients from around the world, but prepared by English cooks following German recipes. The result has been very nourishing, and rather tasty—especially for today's variously cosmopolitan or yuppie palates. Comparing the diet of a hundred years ago, our music libraries could give thanks; the years have left them perhaps a bit overweight, but far from senile, in fact still very healthy.

D. W. Krummel is professor of library and information science and of music at the University of Illinois and former president of the Music Library Association. His most recent books are *Music Printing and Publishing*, co-edited with Stanley Sadie, and *Bibliographical Handbook of American Music*.

A prevalent English character to music libraries should be expected, considering the character of America's library community in general. The landmark founding of the Boston Public Library reflected the Public Library Act of 1850 in Great Britain. It did so of course by fortunate default, since there was no other model anywhere at the time. The institution's notable donor was Joshua Bates, a Boston merchant longtime resident in London. Later library service in the United States, especially to scholars, found its models in three distinctive English institutions: the superb *Präzensbibliothek* that Sir Anthony Panizzi was building at the British Museum; the fine circulating collection at the London Library fostered by Thomas Carlyle; and the Bodleian Library, the fragrant odors of which were later to transport George Santayana's Last Pilgrim into his world of pathos and duty, or love and war. Francis James Child was discovering a world of humanity in the British ballad. Sustaining the viability of these elements in the interrelated worlds of music and commerce was England's rich tradition of antiquarian book dealers and collectors, which inspired a deep sense of veneration for the bibliogaphical icon.

The tradition of American libraries is distinctly British, but with a strong admiration for things German. Harvard University's first great special treasure was Cristoph Daniel Ebeling's collection of Americana, acquired in Germany in 1818.

It was brought to the attention of Harvard authorities by Joseph Green Cogswell, who later served briefly as Harvard librarian and, subsequently, as the first head of the Astor Library. His aspirations for Harvard were stimulated by his experience at the Göttingen University Library. Also influenced at Göttingen was George Ticknor, the first of a lineage of students at Göttingen that later included Child. Harvard built Gore Hall as her library between 1838 and 1841; one look at a picture of it (figure 1) makes one wonder how anyone could possibly imagine it to come from any time other than the period when Albert became Victoria's consort.

Did this Anglo-Germanic library world then actually contribute to the Germanic character of America's musical orientation? The case is thin. At most one might suggest that the world of libraries and books tolerated music because it was a sign of culture, and loved it because it was German. Clearly German music was vigorous and hearty enough to take care of itself. One needs no reminders of the German domination beginning just before the great immigrations of the late nineteenth century—through conductors like Theodore Thomas, followed by Boston's lineage of George Henschel, Wilhelm Gericke, Arthur Nikisch, Emil Paur, and Carl Muck; by impresarios like Oscar Hammerstein and Florenz Ziegfeld; by music publishers with names like Theodore Presser, Carl Fischer, Gustav Schirmer, and Arthur P. Schmidt; and editors like Theodore Baker, an American who had acquired German academic credentials with a dissertation on Amerindian music. Baker's successors, cast in a similar mold but holding more traditional scholarly credentials, were also the heroic founders of American music librarianship, Oscar Sonneck and Otto Kinkeldey.

As for the other national traditions, some today will argue that they were all mothered by late eighteenth-century sentimental romanticism, and fathered by the slightly younger national states that emerged over the nineteenth century. In the early years, their study was fostered by scholars (notable among them being Bishop Percy in England and the Grimm brothers in Germany). From such roots sprang the cultural stereotypes that we remember more colorfully than we might wish. They often define the current text: however unfortunate, these stereotypes embody what ethnic music has come to mean in America today.

Powerful among the promoters of the stereotypes, of course, was a music publishing industry that found nationalistic sentiments a useful means to sell copies. The traditions of the fake-Irish, the phony-Dutch, and the coon-song African-American owe much to the exploitations of American music publishers. European music publishers were more genteel in appreciating the opportunities: Simrock, thanks to its superstar composer Johannes Brahms, persuaded Antonín Dvořák to join its flock; Peters caught Edvard Grieg on the way up; while Breitkopf & Härtel did very well indeed with Jean Sibelius. Among later publishers, Universal Edition in Vienna was to build a gloriously cosmopolitan catalog on the slightly more rebellious spirits of Leoš Janáček, Alois Hába, Karol Szymanowski, Béla Bartók, and Zoltán Kodály.

In the United States, meanwhile, when one surveys the stunning Moravian music archives at Bethlehem, Pennsylvania, and Winston-Salem, North Carolina, that were begun in colonial times, one finds many umlauts but few haceks. This is no surprise, since common wisdom holds that in Europe around 1750 the Mannheim rocket-launchers came mostly from Bohemia. By 1850, most of Europe's concert music was dominated by a musical empire with its composers in Vienna, its pub-

Figure 1. Gore Hall, home of the Harvard College Library, 1841-1913.

lishers in Leipzig, and its politics in Berlin. The immigrants came from lands whose institutions—publishers, conservatories, and concert life—strived bravely to maintain an independence, before affiliating themselves with the stronger German interests. It was clear that the best talent would eventually be lured to Germany in search of an international reputation. In time the dominant music aesthetic of all of Europe, appropriate to the notions of German master composers, became "composerly." America's immigrants really had no choice but to sing a German tune; the best they could do was to sing it with delightful arrogance—and in their own language. If my several odd examples seem mischievous, we have only to blame what is sometimes known as the Power of Music.[1]

Scandinavian immigrant music is less than memorable for its Hardanger fiddles or Viking cellos. The giants in the earth seem instead to have preferred to worship God through "Fairest Lord Jesus" by F. Melius Christiansen, with contrary voice leadings reminiscent more of Jean Sibelius's *Finlandia*, done up in a Fred Waring choral style so as to sound very much like Brahms. From my own teenage years in southwestern Michigan I recall the regular Saturday night "Polish hops" with Bert Novak's orchestra out of South Bend. Never mind that the Novaks probably came from the wrong side of the Tatra Mountains: at least South Bend was known for the Poles who masqueraded as the fighting Irish. Furthermore, Bert's last number was always that pre–Archie Bunker answer, not to Brahms in this case but to Johann Strauss, "The Beer Barrel Polka."

One also recalls Antonín Dvořák's visit to Spillville, Iowa. Brief and sad perhaps, although he was probably there in part because his music sounded so much like

[1] In comments on the papers at this session, Oscar Handlin warned about oversimplifying categories. The ethnic categories do reflect those discussed in the *Harvard Encyclopedia of American Ethnic Groups*, ed. Stephan Thernstrom (Cambridge, Mass.: Harvard University Press, 1980), although these are themselves evolving conceptions that reflect changing conditions of geography, language, religion, and culture. Whether musical ethnicity is more of a commercial artifact than other forms of ethnicity is interesting to study, if partly because the evidence itself is unclear.

Brahms. Next came Dvořák's brief dealings with Jeanette Thurber and the Institute of Musical Art in New York. The episode may conjure a relationship rather like that between Otis B. Driftwood and Mrs. Claypool in the Marx Brothers' film *A Night at the Opera*. Less than fair no doubt: better to see in the event a model for Charles Seeger's later conception of "The Folkness of the Nonfolk and the Nonfolkness of the Folk."[2]

Meanwhile, were any of the immigrants really served at the public library? Yes, in a few celebrated instances where general materials are concerned, but one finds little evidence of any music. Revisionist historians tell us that it was the Irish who drove Justin Winsor out of the Boston Public Library in 1877 and sent him packing across the Charles to the more genteel atmosphere of Harvard. This may indeed have been what happened, although it should also be noted that the library's recently published catalog reports five times as many subject headings for English music as for Irish, twice as many for Jewish, and about as many for Spanish. (So much for Library of Congress subject headings, of course, although in this instance one must wonder that they may be telling us something.) Several public libraries earned special respect for their provision of service to ethnic communities: Cleveland and St. Louis in general, and various units of the New York Public Library, such as the Aguilar branch for the Jewish community. The Cleveland Public Library program no doubt further encouraged one of its trustees, the attorney John Griswold White, to assemble the fine collection of *Völkerkunde*, including folksongs, that it today justly treasures. As evidence of a concern for music in any of the institutions, this is the most conspicuous instance I know of.[3] The other libraries are famous for their services through books. Often in the early twentieth century, book collections were assembled as part of what came to be known as "Americanization programs." To my knowledge, music was never mobilized to serve the cause. It was irrelevant, or it was hopeless. Which one? Publicly the former, privately, the latter perhaps.

One may reasonably go one step further and argue that a neglect of immigrant music in American libraries is a natural state of affairs. The immigrant communities themselves required what cultural anthropologists today refer to as "barriers"—devices that enabled the local unit to sustain and justify itself by excluding outside influences. Music can function powerfully as a barrier: the community maintained its identity through its affection for music that society in general would be quick to damn, as "awful stuff that doesn't sound the least bit like Brahms." The nuances of the musical style itself, much like the patois of its native speakers, contributed significantly to preserving the sense of community. Scores and other music library materials were irrelevant, not so much because the redneck ethnics were necessarily illiterate but rather because their music was too important to belong in the library. Thus, instead of the electric, our libraries today have inherited the eclectic; instead of the grin on the Cheshire cat, we end up with the cat on our doorsteps.

2 Charles Seeger, "The Folkness of the Nonfolk versus the Nonfolkness of the Folk," in *Folklore and Society: Essays in Honor of Benjamin A. Botkin*, ed. Bruce Jackson (Hatboro, Penn.: Folklore Associates, 1966), pp. 1–9; also published with revisions in Seeger's collected *Studies in Musicology, 1935–75* (Berkeley and Los Angeles: University of California Press, 1977), pp. 335–343.

3 On hearing this paper, Susan Sommer recalled receiving at the Music Division of the New York Public Library a collection of Czech musical editions of Zdeněk Fibich, Josef Suk, and their contemporaries. The collection came from the NYPL's Yorktown Branch, which serves an area of New York that was long populated heavily by German-speaking immigrants. Other examples may be worth investigating; my assertion is based largely on the commonly known evidence.

The sense of local community thus falls largely outside the pale of the public library. More colorful and also more erratic are the attempts to document and serve the community in the name of the nation at large, specifically through folk music collecting at the Library of Congress. The founder of the Archive of Folk Song, Robert Winslow Gordon, came fresh out of Harvard classes on ballad scholarship taught by Child and George Lyman Kittredge. He was succeeded by John Lomax (also from Harvard, incidentally, albeit less plausibly), whose program later on reflected the fieldwork tradition of Cecil Sharp but was directed toward the music more than the words. Equally important was Lomax's dialectic, which revived an inspiration that Sharp was either unwilling or unable to advance—namely, the radical socialism of William Morris. The sympathies of these researchers for the Eastern European labor movements emerged with particular power over the Depression years. At the same time, however, their dreams also slowly evaporated, in deference to the rather different dreams of Harold Spivacke. Spivacke's values were more cosmopolitan, aristocratic, and scholarly than theirs. His credentials included hardened experience as a New York concert pianist; his doctoral work in Berlin was in the rigorous science of physics; he was also clearly a tough behind-the-scenes negotiator in New-Deal Washington. All of these strengths, and the benefit of a long career at the Library of Congress, were still not enough to allow him to establish an American version of the Berlin *Phonogrammarchiv* of his mentors, Carl Stumpf and Erich Moritz von Hornbostel. What he did achieve, however, was to shape an institution where it was discovered, through the recent discographic scholarship of Richard Spottswood in particular, what all of them seemed totally unaware of: that ethnic record producers had been there before any of these people, issuing Broadway show tunes, ancient ballads, and foreign-language favorites all sung and merchandised in a funky miscegenation of other foreign languages.[4]

One can find occasional survivals of the immigrant presence in America's music libraries: odd documentation of Finnish music in Hancock, Michigan; Chinese music in Fresno and Berkeley, California; Czech music in Wilbur, Nebraska; Japanese music in Seattle; a few Irish songs owned by Louisa May Alcott in Concord, Massachusetts; Tamburitzan music at Duquesne University in Pittsburgh; foreign-language hymnals and psalmbooks, printed here or abroad, wherever members of the congregation left them; sound archives wherever an ethnologist was at work.[5] There are also legends of lost artifacts—Russian balalaika music assembled at the turn of the century by Alan Grover Salmon; songbooks of the *Gesangverein* from Austin, Texas, which in 1853 found themselves, literally, up Onion Creek without a disaster plan;[6] the long lost marble bust of Hans Balatka from Milwaukee.

4 These materials were the subject of the American Folklife Center conference that led to the publication of Ethnic Recordings in America: A Neglected Heritage (Washington, D.C.: Library of Congress, 1982). See also Richard Keith Spottswood, *Ethnic Music on Records: A Discography of Ethnic Recordings Produced in the United States, 1894 to 1942* (Urbana: University of Illinois Press, 1990).

5 These examples are drawn from D. W. Krummel et al., *Resources of American Music History* (Urbana: University of Illinois Press, 1981). At the symposium at which this paper was delivered, Paul Mercer called my attention to a large collection of Armenian music recently acquired by the New York State Library. See also the section "Music of Immigrant Ethnic Communities" in my *Bibliographical Handbook of American Music* (Urbana: University Illinois Press, 1988), pp. 77–80.

6 Theodore Albrecht, "The Music Libraries of the German Singing Societies in Texas, 1850–1855." *Notes*, 31 (1975), 525.

Page from a 1928 conductor's score of Joseph M. Rumshinsky's Di Goldene Kale *(1924), a Yiddish musical. Shown is the opening number of act 2, "Mir zenen ale meidlach."*

In the larger terms of their value as primary source materials for historical scholarship, library resources are generally of three kinds: (1) The puny, consisting of odds and ends that leave us to wonder what intelligent questions we might ever ask; (2) the tantalizing, which offer rich prospects for questions that are provocative if rarely answerable; and (3) the profligate, which leave us secretly wishing that a good fire might have simplified our problems. Most of the collections I know about—even the celebrated ones—fall clearly in the first category; I know of none at all in the third. America's music libraries have come to be measured by classes "M2" and "M3" in the Library of Congress classification scheme—by their holdings of monuments of Germanic music scholarship devoted to master composers.[7]

7 Music publishing in the United States for special foreign-language purchasers is a topic for another lecture—probably leading mostly to the same conclusions proposed here. Protestant hymnals would no doubt fill most of the story. Among the few instances I know of extensive secular music publishing is that of sheet music for the Yiddish musical theater.

Meanwhile America's public library community itself, throughout the social upheavals of the late nineteenth and early twentieth centuries, remained serenely WASPish.[8] Melvil Dewey sensed rich and appropriate prospects for feminizing the library profession, although his recruits naturally came mostly from good New England stock. The adrenalous Dewey was inevitably drawn as well to notions of eugenics. He found little place for foreigners, and his profession followed his lead. A few Norwegians made a mark for themselves in Chicago after the founding of the Newberry Library, and later in Detroit; but immigrants rarely became librarians, at least through World War II. The profession was, if not outright anti-Semitic, at least a-Semitic. (The early exceptions include, significantly, two chiefs of the Music Division at the Library of Congress.)

By today, in contrast, anglophilia seems all too comfortably compatible with Beatlemania—an odd blending that defines the cosmopolitan as monolingual radical chic—but this is no place for an old-timer to lament the triumph of vulgarity. Better perhaps to consider the present-day immigrants, notably from Latin America and the Far East, and wonder how our music catalogers might ever distinguish their music from "New Age." The essential difference must clearly reflect on a concept of community: one music rationalized through its spirit of barriers, the other through giddy togetherness; one with the intent of challenging, the other with the effect of stupefying. Next we must of course wonder how such matters, truly important, might be usefully accommodated in any possible MARC (machine-readable cataloging) record field.

The United States has been proud of its diversity: all of mankind minus one person, regionalism, states' rights, community in the context of society, the *Gemeinschaft* in the larger environment of the *Gesellschaft*. If our country's libraries have been rather quick to serve the majority needs—in books and in music—they have done so for several reasons. The very mission of libraries is service. Fiscal responsibility, unless it is rationalized in terms of special outreach efforts, fosters the tyranny of the majority. Qualitative considerations may indeed often intrude; but when conceived in musical terms the result is a better collection of *Denkmäler* and *Gesamtausgaben*, or when conceived in bibliographical terms the result is rare books. Thus, in Chicago, the musical treasure of the city's notable Polish population is probably the personal papers of Ignace Paderewski. Chicago's inner-city groups are left to wonder what to do with it, while its atavistic Polish community plays bingo in the suburbs.

This paper has mentioned our host university rather often, not so much to suggest that Harvard should feel any anger or guilt for any specific neglect of our country's immigrant heritage, but rather with a larger current agenda in mind. An endowed chair for its music librarian recognizes a special challenge. Our country is unlikely ever again to be so richly infused with immigrants—unfortunately. Yet, even acknowledging the power of mass media, our musical life is unlikely ever to be so thoroughly homogenized as to form one single society, to the exclusion of various deviant communities—and in this case, we think, fortunately. Indeed, specialties seem to be proliferating, at a staggering rate. One has only to look at the

[8] Dee Garrison, *Apostles of Culture: The Public Librarian and American Society*, 1876–1920 (New York: The Free Press, 1979).

current music periodical shelf to recognize the Ellis Island of today, its huddled immigrants with wondrously strange exotic names like the *Jimmie Rodgers Memorial Association Newsletter*, the *Journal of the American Liszt Society*; the *Journal of Research in Singing and Applied Vocal Pedagogy*; *Diva*; *ClariNetwork*; for guitar the *Review* and *Magazine*; for opera, the *Guide*, *Journal*, *News*, *Quarterly*, and *Fanatic*. Each is written for a special community, in its own patois, and with other signals that announce, "if you love Brahms, we're not quite for you." Each journal exists in its distinctive physical medium so as to convey outreach, almost in a Madison-Avenue sense. At the same time, each journal also conveys a message that, with varying militancy, reflects a spirit of what earlier periods called "Balkanization."[9]

I should like to think that there is a lesson for the music library community to learn from its spotty encounters with immigrant music. It is appropriate that the endowed chair we are honoring should be designated as a librarian rather than a professor, since the proper role of the music library is complementary to that of its music faculty. A librarian's duty to faculty and students must be to recognize communties that no faculty or student body, however diverse, learned, and cosmopolitan, can possibly accommodate. In contrast, the music librarian's responsibility to the general library, equally unpopular, must be to plead the cause of one special community within the world of learning. Perhaps the basic point is that the appropriate title for the position we are celebrating should be neither that of professor nor librarian, but Richard F. French Music Alchemist.

[9] The dichotomy is nicely developed in Archie Green, "Hillbilly Music: Source and Symbol," *American Journal of Sociology*, 52 (1947), 293–308, a work that deserves to be better known than it is.

Collecting Native American Music

Don L. Roberts

Although my title is "Collecting Native American Music," I will be concerned primarily with the Native American cultures that reside in what is now the United States, thus excluding the extraordinary cultures that existed, and still exist, elsewhere in the Americas. It might be assumed that any such discussion would commence with an homage to Jesse Walter Fewkes. After all, it was just a century ago, on 18 March 1890, that Fewkes made the first ethnomusicological field recordings when he recorded a Passamaquoddy Indian in Calais, Maine. (And it is not inappropriate to point out that for decades these cylinders resided in the Peabody Museum at Harvard University.) However, to state that Fewkes was the first collector of Native American music would perpetuate an ethnocentric myth. Instead, it must be argued that Fewkes was several milennia too late to be dubbed the "first collector."

Don L. Roberts is head of the Music Library at Northwestern University and president of the Music Library Association.

According to *Webster's Third New International Dictionary of the English Language Unabridged* (1961), "collect" means "to bring together especially in accordance with a principle of selection" and "to include as a part of one's experience." Libraries and librarians are not mentioned in these definitions, appropriate omissions in terms of our topic, as I shall explain.

There are four broad categories of collectors of Native American music: (1) Native Americans; (2) non-Native American individuals—scholars, hobbyists, and other observers; (3) commercial enterprises—record and film companies; and (4) institutional entities—archives and libraries.

The first Native American collector was a singer who heard an interesting song performed by another singer. Not having, and certainly not needing, music staff paper and a pencil, the singer listened carefully to the song and committed it to memory. Retaining a complex song after only one hearing may seem like an extraordinary accomplishment, but it is a talent possessed by many present-day Native American singers and composers. Beginning forty thousand years ago, shortly after humans first crossed a land bridge from Siberia to North America, the collecting of songs by Native American musicians has continued through the centuries and is widely practiced today. Native Americans recognize a good singer's ability to compose and collect songs by referring to the singer as "packed full of songs" or as "having a big bag of songs." Singers often have large repertoires of several hundred songs and are constantly borrowing from one another. An interesting example of borrowing and collecting concerns a Hopi sacred *Katsina* song that was heard at a Hopi ceremony in Arizona by a singer from Santo Domingo Pueblo in New

Hopi flute ceremony at Oraibi, in an undated photograph by Jesse Walter Fewkes (Courtesy of the Peabody Museum, Harvard University)

Mexico. The song was subsequently incorporated into a ritual at Santo Domingo, where it was learned by another singer, who took it to San Juan Pueblo. At San Juan it became an *Okushare* (Turtle Dance) song, but since the San Juan community would not understand the Hopi and Keres (Santo Domingo) words, the song was translated into English—an extremely rare occurrence in sacred pueblo music. It was recorded by a member of the San Juan tribe, who gave me a copy of the tape, which I then presented to a singer from the Hopi/Tewa village of Hano. After many years and a circuitous journey of approximately seven hundred miles, the song ended up about eight miles from where it had originally been composed!

It has long been recognized that Native Americans with ethnomusicological training would make some of the best collectors of Native American music. Such scholars have the language competencies and the knowledge of the cultural, sociological, religious, and psychological patterns that are essential to the study of ethnic music. In the last few years, we have begun to see some excellent ethnomusicologists who are also Native Americans. The most prominent of these is Charlotte Heth, a Cherokee who is on the faculty at UCLA.

That some of the well-educated Native American collectors have not been academicians has not diminished the importance of their activities: the late Tony Garcia of San Juan Pueblo is an outstanding example. Garcia realized, in the late 1950s, that the complex musical repertoire of his village needed to be regularly documented.

He purchased a tape recorder and started recording several of his pueblo's prime singers. Garcia tapes are now considered major documents.

The most important collecting of Native American music is done by the Native Americans themselves. They regard songs as representing the vibrant core of their religion and culture. The songs and song texts serve as the centerpiece of the culturally vital ceremonial activities that provide some shelter from the outside world. Numerous Native Americans are now collecting songs. Some are singers and composers who use tape or video recorders to learn new songs. Others listen to songs to strengthen cultural awareness or for enjoyment. Songs recorded at pow-wows and ceremonies can be heard in Native American villages and on local car and truck stereos.

It is impossible to identify the first non-Native American collectors of Native American music. Although the Phoenicians, Vikings, Celts, and early Southwest Asians who explored the western hemisphere may have interested themselves in the music of the Native Americans, no surviving evidence documents any such interest.

About five hundred years ago, the Native Americans residing on one of the Caribbean islands "discovered" a group of people who were lost and trespassing. Rarely does anyone think about the tragic and traumatic implications that this discovery, by the Native Americans, was to have on their people and cultures. As we near the extremely misoriented festivities that are being organized for the 1992 quinquencentennial celebration of the European "discovery" of the Americas by Christopher Columbus, it is fitting to consider this other perspective. The following excerpt from the text of a song, "Christopher Columbus," recorded on Canyon Records (C-7121) by a Native American rock group called XIT (Crossing of the Tribes), is most telling:

Christopher Columbus
what have you done to us
Christopher Columbus
what have you done to us
they give you the credit
and the whole world's read it
I said we discovered you
I said we discovered you.

Christopher Columbus
your name makes me curious
Christopher Columbus
your name makes me curious
in 1492
you sailed the water blue
and we discovered you
I said we discovered you
I said we discovered you.[1]

Every American music library should acquire this recording, which is still available, and make its existence known to the library's clientele—especially to anyone who is concerned with American history or American music.

Most European conquerors or settlers had little interest in the Native Americans and their music. However, there are some useful early reports describing ceremonies and instruments. In 1496, Columbus commissioned a Catalonian cleric to write a description of the Taino people. This report, by Ramón Pane, mentions a two-keyed slit drum, two feet in diameter by four feet long, constructed from a hollowed-out tree trunk.[2] Pane's document may be the first evidence of organological research done in the Americas by non-Native Americans. The qualification "non-Native Americans" is important, because the elaborate musical instruments used

[1] Copyright by Canyon Records; reprinted by permission.

[2] Robert Stevenson, "Written Sources for Indian Music Until 1882," *Ethnomusicology*, 17 (1973), 1.

by Native Americans for centuries before the European conquest did not suddenly appear; rather, they evolved through a long period of experimentation, a process that can surely be considered research.

One of the earliest reliable transcriptions of Native American music was made by William Beresford in 1787.[3] The song he wrote down was encountered near the present site of Sitka, Alaska. Featuring a two-part heterophonic form in a style that is still common in that region today, Beresford's transcription reinforces strong evidence found elsewhere that many genres of Native American music have resisted change during the long period of dominance by foreign cultures. Transcriptions made in 1822 by the noted military explorer Stephen H. Long of a Sioux Dog Dance song and a Chippewa Scalp Dance song are similar to old songs still performed by the Sioux and Chippewas.[4] The relatively accurate transcriptions by Beresford and Long represent a considerable improvement over previous attempts to notate Native American music that forced the rough—that is, rough to non-Native ears—melodic and rhythmic patterns into molds acceptable to those accustomed to European-derived music.

The first serious study, *Über die Musik der Nordamerikanischen Wilden,* was published by Theodore Baker in 1882.[5] When this book was translated into English in 1976, its publisher, Frits Knuf, was about to translate *Wilden* as "savages." After a large outcry from various sources, the book was eventually printed with the title, *On the Music of the North American Indians.*[6] Baker's standards—yes, this is the Theodore Baker who gave us *Baker's Biographical Dictionary*—would not have pleased Nicolas Slonimsky, the present editor of *Baker's.* Although Baker did collect songs, at least one of his "transcriptions" came from a published source and was actually a tune written by a pale-face composer. Unfortunately it was this non-Native American melody that Edward MacDowell chose as a theme in his *Indian Suite.*

No consideration of the study of Native American music would be complete without mention of Jesse Walter Fewkes. His use of the phonograph opened the doors for the discipline of ethnomusicology, because musical performances could now be documented in a medium that allowed for repeated listenings. In the century since Fewkes' pioneering recordings, dozens of non-Native Americans have collected and studied Native American music. Since early transcriptions of recordings tended to present the melodies in the style of European art music—or even worse, as harmonized tunes—it was the recordings themselves that became most useful to scholars. The leading non-Native American collectors are Frances Densmore, Helen H. Roberts, George Herzog, Laura Boulton, Willard Rhodes, David McAllester, Odd Halseth, Alan Merriam, Bruno Nettl, Gertrude Kurath, William Powers, Charlotte Frisbie, and Thomas Vennum. The work of these collector/scholars is well documented elsewhere and will not be covered here.

The third category of collectors of Native American music are commercial record companies. The discs issued by the Library of Congress and recordings bearing the Folkways label have long been useful sources for ethnomusicological studies. The Library of Congress has taken an active collecting role, while Moe Asch, founder

[3] Robert Stevenson, "English Sources for Indian Music Until 1882," *Ethnomusicology,* 17 (1973), 408.

[4] Ibid., 421–422.

[5] Theodore Baker, *Über die Musik der Nordamerikanischen Wilden* (Leipzig: Breitkopf & Härtel, 1882).

[6] Theodore Baker, *On the Music of the North American Indians,* trans. Ann Buckley (Buren: F. Knuf, 1976).

of Folkways, collected more passively, often recording what was offered to him, with results of variable quality. Although Folkways and LC are the big names, the largest producer of Native American recordings is Canyon Records in Phoenix, Arizona. Canyon Records was founded in the early 1950s when Ray Boley of Canyon Films was impressed with the voice of Natay, a Navaho singer. Boley recorded Natay and issued a 78-rpm disc. Much to Boley's surprise, the record that he initially introduced to the non-Indian market had its biggest sales on the reservations. Indeed, the primary customers of the record companies specializing in Native American music continue to be Native Americans themselves, who repeatedly play the cassettes at home and in their vehicles. Boley's initial success encouraged him to expand his efforts to the point that Canyon Records now has a catalog of over two hundred in-print recordings of Native American music, ncluding country/western, pop, and rock, as well as traditional songs.

Native Americans have also been among those who have established record companies. One of the first Native-owned companies was Tom Tom, created in the late 1940s by Manuel Archuleta of San Juan Pueblo. Some of the songs on the Tom Tom discs are the only available recorded examples from one of the most conservative pueblos. The American Indian Soundchief label was founded in the late 1940s by Rev. Lynn Pauaghty, a Kiowa from Oklahoma who was a Methodist minister. At first Pauaghty recorded tribal church hymns, but he soon branched out to traditional songs. His records were geared to the Native American market, one that wanted the newest songs of a particular genre. Thus, instead of issuing "sampler" discs, according to the prevailing practice, Pauaghty's releases contain only one genre: all round-dance songs or all war-dance songs, for example. Indian House recordings, established by Tony and Ida Isaacs in 1966, followed Pauaghty's example by featuring a single genre on an individual disc or a two-record set. Indian House immediately established itself as the source of the finest recorded performances of Native American music. Ida was a Taos/San Juan native, and although Tony is a non-Native American, he has extensive experience singing with the Oklahoma Native Americans. Indian House's approach to recording is significant and unique. The singers are asked to arrange the songs in a proper sequence; these are then recorded without a break. The result documents, for example, the increasing excitement in the music as the song set progresses.

The fourth category of collectors of Native American music consists of libraries and archives. Music libraries in the United States have, for the most part, not done especially well collecting Native American recordings. Very few have any field recordings and their holdings of commercial recordings are generally sparse. Indian House reports that only two or three libraries have standing orders for the few new record releases they issue each year. Probably the majority of Native American recordings found in music libraries are on the New World Records label, discs that were originally distributed free of charge. Of the music libraries that do have major holdings, foremost is the Library of Congress which, in addition to its maintaining collections of both field and commercial materials, continues to issue distinguished recordings of Native American music. Another important collection may be found in the Fine Arts Library at the University of New Mexico.

The other major institutional collections of Native American music are found in archives that usually exist outside the purview of university library administrations. These institutions are generally better than libraries at collecting Native American Music. There are outstanding collections at the Archives of Traditional

Music at Indiana University, the Institute of Ethnomusicology Archive at UCLA, and the Lowie Museum of Anthropology at the University of California at Berkeley.

Another kind of important collection is the tribal archive. Various tribes have made a conscientious effort to document the music of their own cultures. A significant collection has resulted from a project in which medicine men on the Navajo reservation have been recording their ceremonies. Access to these recordings is restricted to young medicine men who want to learn the repertoire. Recording the ceremonies is crucial because the Navajo reservation is huge; contact between the various medicine men is minimal; and a good medicine man is expected to perform, perfectly and from memory, a ceremony that continues for four days and nights. The ceremony consists of music, sand paintings, and prayers, all of which must be perfectly executed. Any mistake means that the ceremony must be stopped and that the patient will not heal. Performing such a ceremony may be equated with conducting Richard Wagner's entire *Ring* cycle from memory. Thus, it is extremely important that some of the tribes are establishing their own archives.

Radio stations, particularly those that are located on or near reservations, also have archives of Native American materials. Station KGAK in Gallup, New Mexico, which can be heard while driving on Interstate 40 through the western part of the state, broadcasts almost exclusively in Navajo. (The commercials are marvelous, by the way: after listening to a Native American song, one may hear English words, such as "Gallup Chevrolet," in the middle of a Navajo language message because there are certain words that do not translate into Navajo.)

The subject of broadcasting and field materials leads to the question of who retains the copyright to the original field recordings in our collections. Is it the original singer? Is it the tribal unit? The answer to both those questions is yes. Furthermore, who should have access to these materials, particularly field recordings of private and/or sacred ceremonies? Librarians must be extremely sensitive to the needs of Native American cultures; and they must be conscientious in developing clear policies about use, an important issue for Native Americans, as the recent government decision to return bones and other tribal artifacts illustrates.

Dissemination, or returning Native American materials to their true owners, is one of the most valuable services a collector or a library can provide. The ultimate goal of those who collect and preserve Native American music should be to enable the Native American people to have full access to their historical and contemporary documents. A most rewarding experience for a collector or disseminator is for the disseminated documents to inspire the reintroduction of a ceremony. Archuleta, who created the Tom Tom record company, also made a number of recordings that were never issued commercially. I had the experience of taking these tapes back to one of the pueblos, playing them, and asking people to identify the songs. At one point one of the main singers exclaimed, "Oh, that's the going-in-the-middle dance." I remarked that they don't perform that. He replied, "Well, we used to. We remember the dance, but we have forgotten the songs." I am happy to report that through the dissemination of those tapes, which had been made some thirty years earlier, this particular ceremony was reintroduced at San Juan Pueblo.

The Federal Cylinder Project headquartered at the Library of Congress has probably disseminated more recordings than any other collector. By collecting cylinders from various Federal agencies and from other non-governmental institutions, the Library of Congress has amassed over six and one half thousand cylinders of Native American music. These cylinders have been transferred to tapes, which along with catalogs and supplementary materials have been returned to the tribes.

The proper collecting, preservation, and dissemination of Native American music is an extremely important endeavor. The collectors of Native American music, be they Native Americans, non-Native American scholars, hobbyists, institutions, or commercial enterprises, have been, are, and will be a critical force in documenting and preserving Native American music for conducting scholarly research, enhancing performances, raising cultural awareness, and providing pleasure. In the contemporary library world, preservation is a major component in any sensible collection management program. Preservation in the collection management context generally means that steps are taken to ensure that a physical object is available to and usable by future generations. However, preservation in the context of "Collecting Native American music" has a much broader meaning. Even more than the physical object it is necessary to preserve the cultural and spiritual elements embodied in it. The songs of the Native Americans are the essence of a people's existence, an expression of their religion, and a source of considerable inspiration, satisfaction, and enjoyment. Music librarians and other scholars must work together to ensure that Native American music is always properly collected, preserved, and disseminated.

Tracking Vernacular Music . . . Across the Great Divide

Richard Crawford

The Great Divide is a fact of American geography. Also called the Continental Divide, it is that stretch of high ground in the western United States on either side of which the river systems flow in opposite directions. It is both a boundary and a vantage point. It is borrowed here as a metaphor for history-writing for two reasons. First, it goes nicely with tracking, the muscular outdoor verb of my assigned title. Second, each of the historians to be discussed has, in effect, crossed over a divide, a boundary established by earlier historians, and presented a new image of what "the history of American music" means. (The problem of American musical historiography has been to define the range of the subject. And historians of American music have found it especially hard to agree on how to treat our various musical vernaculars.)

Richard Crawford is professor of music at the University of Michigan and former president of the American Musicological Society. His most recent book is *American Sacred Imprints, 1698–1810: A Bibliography*, with Allen P. Britton and Irving Lowens.

In recent years, writers have tended to concentrate more upon musical joinings and the breaking down of old barriers than upon boundaries, divides, and disjunctions. We are often told that the old categories, such as classical and popular music, or, to use H. Wiley Hitchcock's terms, "cultivated" and "vernacular" traditions, do not mean what they used to mean. But in fact, even if the categories are not exclusive, the differing musical values, venues, functions, and institutions in our society testify to divisions in the structure of our musical life. The very fact that American composers have been fond of playing with, crossing, and recrossing the territory between cultivated and vernacular testifies not to the arbitrariness of such boundaries but to their abiding presence. And then there's the "divide" between musicology and music librarianship: whatever the two trades share, the musicologist's emphasizes the ideal and theoretical while that of the librarian has its being in the real, practical world. If musicologists create images of music as part of human history, then librarians create environments in which those images can be encountered, studied, tested, and changed.

With this background in mind, I will review trends in American music history-writing since around 1930 and show how musicological tradition has treated vernacular music. Then I will suggest how the story of musicology's changing view might be of use to music librarians. Many will already recognize the implications of this view, but sometimes, someone else's idea of "where we are" and "how we got there" can shed new light on where we might want to go in the future.

John Tasker Howard wrote his history most of all to tell the story of American composers—the writers of sonatas, string quartets, symphonies, concertos, art songs, and operas.[1] Howard's predecessors—Frédéric Louis Ritter, W. S. B. Mathews, Louis Charles Elson, even Oscar Sonneck—had written to trace the establishment in America of a musical culture based chiefly on performances of European music. Although Howard was sympathetic to their efforts, he believed that earlier historians had failed to grasp, much less to explain and celebrate, how well American composers had mastered European forms. Howard's view of "our" American music is symbolized by the organization of his book into three parts: 1620–1800, "Euterpe in the Wilderness"; 1800–1860, "Euterpe Clears the Forest"; and 1860 to the Present, "Euterpe Builds Her American Home." The saga of American music as told by Howard lay in the struggle of the Old World muse to hack out a place for herself on American shores, triumphing over nature and poverty, indifference and ignorance. Historians of American music have tended to see themselves as representatives on behalf of losing (or lost) causes, advocates for the historically weak and disenfranchised. What seemed most fragile and needful of protection to Howard, writing in the late 1920s, was the impulse, chiefly of composers, to transplant music as a creative fine art, maintaining its Old World aesthetic integrity in a New World setting. Americans' ignorance of what American composers had achieved in the European tradition, Howard believed, was a form of cultural impoverishment.

American musical historiography, being an undeveloped field, has so far produced few axioms. One that is widely shared is that the publication of Gilbert Chase's *America's Music* in 1955 marks our historiographical Great Divide.[2] Chase wrote his history in the 1940s and early 1950s, driven, among other things, by the conviction that Howard's approach was much too limited and genteel. The most important American music, Chase announced, was that which differed most from European music. Inspired by the work of Charles Seeger, Chase had discovered that the wellsprings of American musical distinctiveness could be found especially among people low in the social order. Spirituals (black and white), the music of blackface minstrelsy, Anglo-American fiddle music and folksongs, shape-note hymnody, songs of American Indian tribes, ragtime, blues, early jazz—all genres whose musical worth Howard could not quite bring himself to believe in—were for Chase the heart of American musical achievement. In short, though he didn't use the term, Chase put the vernacular at the very center of his history. Americans risked cultural impoverishment, he believed, if they failed to recognize the beauty and worth of these musics. Where Howard had found "cultivated" fine-art music fragile and needful of his protection, Chase wrote to plead the case for "plain Americans," who had succeeded in making and maintaining musics rich in human substance if often rough and unpolished in manner.

Chase's belief that vernacular music-makers defined the heart of American music is familiar to most music librarians, among other reasons, because his image of the subject has had a profound impact on the contents of music libraries. In fact, Chase believed so fervently in the truth of his historiographical image that he wrenched history out of shape to dramatize it. The last chapter of his first edition of *America's Music* is devoted to Charles Ives, even though Ives had stopped composing some thirty-five years before Chase's book appeared. Chase's chronological license allowed him to treat Ives as American music's man of destiny: the amateur composer

1 John Tasker Howard, *Our American Music: Three Hundred Years of It* (New York: Crowell, 1931; 4th ed., 1965).

2 Gilbert Chase, *America's Music from the Pilgrims to the Present* (New York: McGraw-Hill, 1955; 3d rev. ed., 1987).

who brought together in one grand synthesis all that was most distinctive and vital in our musical past, no matter how scattered or apparently unrelated. On the one hand, Ives composed in European genres and accepted their challenge of craftsmanship and high seriousness. On the other, Ives's works drew heavily on techniques and melodic quotations borrowed from American vernaculars, including hymn tunes, patriotic and parlor songs, fiddle tunes, band music, and rags—the very vernaculars that Chase had brought to the fore in his historical account. Ives's fusing of "vernacular" and "cultivated" traditions created a hybrid music that was American to the core and that also, in Chase's view, showed an artistic strength beyond anything achieved by earlier American composers working within either tradition. Chase's message was clear: the United States is a democracy, and the cultivated composers most likely to grasp the national spirit and character are those whose music, in one way or another, incorporates American vernaculars.

Charles Hamm's view of the American vernacular was first set forth in a book on popular song, then summarized in a dictionary article, then integrated into a general history of American music,[3] and, more recently, elaborated in articles, speeches, and organizational activities on behalf of "popular music." To encounter Hamm's view is to cross another divide and to enter a world as different from Chase's as Chase's was from Howard's. Hamm's work contrasts so startlingly because his protective instincts as a historian are called into play not by the obscure, forgotten figures of our musical past who play so large a role in Howard's and Chase's accounts, but by the most famous American musicians: those who have composed and performed the music that Americans have most loved and paid money for, musicians whose popular success led historians to view them with mistrust. (Note, for example, that Chase, champion of "the vernacular" that we acknowledge him to be, in his first edition chose vernacular genres that either never had been or no longer were forces in the marketplace. In contrast, Tin Pan Alley, Broadway, and Hollywood, all major commercial venues of the 1940s and early 1950s, together with the denounced swing, are conspicuous by their low profile in Chase's account or their absence from it.) To borrow terms from economics, we might say that while Howard and Chase, in good musicological fashion, concentrate on the supply side—on the makers of the music and what they made and how—Hamm takes his cue from the demand side—from the preferences of singers, players, listeners, and other consumers.

The economic analogy is appropriate here. For Hamm's unabashed acceptance of the musical marketplace as a fact of American musical life, as a possible touchstone, even, of musical significance, leads us to recognize a fundamental assumption in earlier histories. Before Hamm, historians comfortably assumed that music whose chief aim was profit, success, or immediate results in the mass market was somehow not an integral part of the history of music. Or put in slightly different words, music tailored to the dictates of the mass market, which is governed by financial profit, is marked by traits of musical substance and structure (melody, rhythm, harmony, sound) that separate it from music worthy of scholarly study. Or, to put it even more tendentiously, the circumstances of commercial music's origin have, by definition, corrupted and debased it, so that it stands outside the

[3] Charles Hamm, *Yesterdays: Popular Song in America* (New York: Norton, 1979); "Popular Music, II–III," in *The New Grove Dictionary of Music and Musicians* (1980); *Music in the New World* (New York: Norton, 1983).

purview of serious scholars of the art. According to this assumption, the corrupting forces are evanescence and money. The commercial world's obsession with immediate popularity contradicts the academic world's belief that the power to endure beyond the moment is a truer measure of musical worth. As for money, it is thought to corrupt by its profusion, for in the world of commercial vernaculars, money exists in vast, undreamed-of quantities. Where commercial values reign true artistic values flee. Musical artistry, in other words, cannot stand up to the commercial demands of the marketplace, where the shoddy drives out the good. Therefore, artistic quality must be sought in genres uncorrupted by commerce.

I have put this assumption in terms that are probably more absolute than any working musicologist would endorse. But surely something like this belief lies behind earlier histories of American music and continues to be held today, even though it has been a decade now since Hamm invited Tin Pan Alley, country music, and rock 'n' roll into the mainstream of our music histories.

These trends have had a decided effect on libraries. To begin with, music librarians in America have followed collecting policies that for the most part parallel the historiographical path that leads from Howard to Chase to Hamm. By the time Chase's book appeared in the mid-1950s, American composers were no longer strangers to American music libraries, as Howard's book suggests they had been two decades earlier.

Similarly, by the late 1970s, when Hamm's major writings began to appear, academic music libraries were welcoming a growing stock of American vernacular music as defined by Chase. Projects like the collected works of Scott Joplin, the *Smithsonian Collection of Classic Jazz* (and other recording reissues in jazz and musical theatre), Oxford University Press's many books on jazz history and criticism, recordings from the Library of Congress's Archive of Folk Song and Moses Asch's Folkways label, and the large vernacular representation in the New World Records' 100-LP series—all of these ratified Chase's historiographical image of American music. And all were distributed and marketed with academic users in mind. The canon of American music had indeed broadened since the 1950s. From the library's perspective, a broader canon means more materials to collect. Music librarians know best how heavy that added burden has turned out to be. But libraries shouldered it without having to cross any Great Divide themselves. The acceptance of Chase's canon probably brought an expansion of books, recordings, journals, and scores proportional to the expansion of musicological materials as a whole. Moreover, such institutions as the Library of Congress, the Smithsonian Institution, university presses, and philanthropic foundations, already linked with the academic enterprise, were screening and disseminating these materials on our behalf. (Similar projects sanctioned by the academic community continue today: for example, the American Musicological Society's Music of the United States of America, or MUSA—our first national series of scholarly editions of American music—which will devote a healthy number of its forty volumes to vernacular musics, and the Jazz Masterworks Series, featuring transcriptions and editions, sponsored by the Smithsonian and Oberlin College.)

Perhaps recognizing the impact of Chase's view will help us appreciate the different challenge posed by Hamm's crossing of the Great Commercial Divide. For one thing, many of Chase's vernaculars were casualties of the past or survivors from it. Many of Hamm's are still very much alive in the present and, being mass-produced in huge numbers, deny scholars the historical distance and hindsight upon which we count so heavily. The vernaculars Chase selected were, by the time he wrote about them, no longer a potent force in the marketplace, if they ever had been. Many of Hamm's are still valuable commercial property, which means that academics must pay the going market price to obtain them, and our use is subject to the restrictions that copyrighted material enjoys. (A publishing scholar's enthusiam for quoting copyrighted song lyrics or tunes may be dampened by the cost of permission fees.)

The academic enterprise, in which I include both musicologists and librarians, is accustomed to receiving music through a collaborative process of screening: recognition by performers and scholars, authoritative editions, recordings, and integration into a historical framework in articles and books. Some American vernaculars have already passed or are now passing through that process. Ragtime comes to mind, especially Scott Joplin. Looking further back in history, the music of Stephen Foster has just become available in a complete critical edition, so we will have at hand more evidence for judging his place in the history of American music.

But let us take an example closer to our own time. Recently tributes poured in to Irving Berlin, dead at the age of 101. The passing of time has helped to transform him from a market-driven Tin Pan Alley tunesmith into a master of a "classic" genre of American song. This assessment, for me, has been helped along by reading Alec Wilder and Charles Hamm among others, by listening to recordings of Berlin songs by artists of his own day (Harry Richman, Ethel Waters, and Fred Astaire come to mind), by hearing his works sung by Joan Morris, and by spending some time with about twenty-five of Berlin's songs in an anthology I picked up a few years ago in England. But can we, as a community of musicologists and music librarians, really assess Irving Berlin as a figure in American music history and American culture? If so, how have we reached that understanding? What scholarly work lies behind the superlatives we have been laying so generously at his shrine? How would the academic community respond to a groundswell of interest in Berlin studies? Where would anybody go to test the claims of Berlin's greatness as a song composer? Who owns the complete works of Irving Berlin and would make them available for scholarly study and publication along with the songs of other composers with whom Berlin's work would have to be compared? Should we start demanding an Irving Berlin *Gesamtausgabe*?[4]

These last few questions strike us as naive, because we know the barriers in the music business that would have to fall to make Irving Berlin and his tradition accessible for musicological research. Few if any American music libraries own collections in which research on Berlin could be carried on, even though Berlin worked in a genre whose heyday ended some four decades ago.

The Berlin example illustrates a more pressing issue. Hamm's toughest challenge to the academic community is that we stop overlooking commercial pop musics of a more recent day: the music that permeates the urban landscape, that absorbs the musical energies of many of our children, students, and fellow citizens, that people around the globe have embraced, that is surely a powerful social force, and that maps out new chapters in the history of musical reception,

4 As a first step in that direction, Charles Hamm is now editing *The Complete Songs of Irving Berlin (1907–1914)* as a volume in the MUSA series.

Irving Berlin's first hit song (1911), through which he gained an international reputation

musical performance, musical aesthetics, and the forming of musical institutions, if not in the history of musical composition.

When, ten years ago, Hamm crossed the Great Divide that had shielded the academic enterprise from the bruising world of musical commerce, he exploded our idea of "the vernacular" beyond Chase's limits, and he layed it, like a noisy foundling child, on our doorstep. To the foundling's arrival, musicology has so far reacted chiefly with silence, as if no one were home. Librarians, whether out of inclination or duty, have not always had that option. I doubt that Robert Frost had music libraries in mind when he wrote in "Death of a Hired Man" that "home is the place where, when you have to go there, they have to take you in." But in my admittedly limited experience, it has been the libraries, if anywhere in musical academia, that have "taken in" the new commercial breed of American vernaculars. Of course, simply to open the door the tiniest crack is to introduce a set of new problems. Accepting a new breed into a library doesn't mean that one can cast out the older ones. Like children, collections don't shrink, they grow. And once in the door, they stop demanding your attention only in the direst of circumstances. At the same time, given the abundance and diversity of today's commercial vernaculars, the cost in money, time, energy, and space of collecting more than a small portion of them is prohibitive.

So how to choose? Surely, most music librarians have their own methods. Accepting a random donated sample? Buying what one personally happens to hear and like? Listening to what the students who work the desk have suggested over the years? Deciding to find and buy the recordings on some critic's list of "The One Hundred Rock Albums Everybody Must Own"? Attempting to collect certain artists? Acting on the advice of certain distributors? Or perhaps sticking with the network of university presses and archival recording projects that have begun to inch into certain corners of commercial pop? Some or all of the above? All seem reasonable enough in a field where, at least to my knowledge, no academically sanctioned screening process yet exists.

Of course, one of the things that has brought us into academic life in the first place is our inclination toward systematic procedures. Knowing we chose the right thing isn't enough for most of us if we are not sure why we made the choice. We want to repeat the right choice, again and again, and it is hard to trust instinct or chance over a rational system. For collecting vernacular musics, especially recent ones, I have one painfully obvious principle to suggest, and that is that librarians can meet Hamm's challenge by seeking a closer collaboration with what we might call private enterprise.

Students of American vernaculars such as jazz, bluegrass, and Broadway music, although they have found some helpful materials in academic libraries, have been quick to reach the limits of most such collections. Those who bring a scholar's sensibility to their work, who want to pursue their subject through the biographical, bibliographical, and discographical labyrinths that research requires, have done so chiefly by cultivating personal contacts with private collectors and gaining access to their collections. On almost any conceivable vernacular subject—the music of group X, or singer Y, or genre Z—scholarly expertise exists, even if it hasn't found its way into our libraries. People out there are gathering books, clipping articles, collecting commercial and bootleg records, often out of an evangelical attitude that makes many of them willing and eager to supply information, advice, paper copies, and tapes of the artists and genres that have kindled their passion. Music librarians who want to "track" vernacular music, whether through Chase's or Hamm's image of it, have succeeded by getting to know people, especially those in their local communities, who fit the collector's profile. The knowledge, enthusiasm, and expertise of such people should be encouraged and tapped by academics, their advice on collecting decisions sought (maybe even followed), and, in good time, the ultimate fate of their collections seriously discussed. Insofar as possible, they should have a chance to be in contact with students and scholars who share their interests and who seek the knowledge they possess.

All this talk about Great Divides and "tracking vernacular music" across them brings to mind the most compelling few sentences on American culture that I have encountered in recent years. The words are Ralph Ellison's, from a speech he gave at West Point in 1969:

> I felt that there was a great deal about the nature of American experience which was not understood by most Americans. I felt also that the *diversity* of the total experience rendered much of it mysterious. And I felt that *because* so much of it which appeared unrelated was actually most intimately intertwined, it needed exploring. In fact, I believed that unless we continually explored the network of complex relationships which bind us together, we would continue being the *victims* of various inadequate conceptions of ourselves, both as individuals and as citizens of a nation of diverse peoples.[5]

We can see American music as an ever-broadening field. Its historical study at first centered solely on a consideration of our composers (Howard), then in addition on the place of distinctive vernacular expressions (Chase), and now, together with those two concerns, on the role of the commercial marketplace (Hamm). We will be able to use our historiographical "Great Divides" as vantage points for spotting the connectedness that Ellison invites us to seek.

[5] Ralph Ellison, *Going to the Territory* (New York: Random House, 1986), p. 42. Emphases added.

Furthering the Cause of American Music

Steven Ledbetter

"American Music" is a vast topic, and there are many ways of "furthering" its cause: through scholarship, collecting, organizing, analyzing (its materials and context), performing, recording, and publishing; in general—by disseminating both the music and information about it. Several speakers have dealt with various aspects of popular music and its genres; I will concentrate on certain areas of the "cultivated" tradition, the kind of music we play in tuxedos—as Bruno Nettl describes it—the music in which I have been most directly involved.

It is important first of all to recognize the role music librarians have already played in furthering the cause. To a large degree, music librarians, beginning with Oscar Sonneck, created the subdiscipline of American music. They have led the way by collecting material, organizing it, and informing the rest of us of its existence. From Oscar Sonneck's seminal work as bibliographer and historian to more recent contributions, such as Don Krummel's *Resources of American Music* and his *Bibliographical Handbook of American Music*,[1] and special resources like the *Boston Composers Project*,[2] we musicologists would be much the poorer without the devoted work of music librarians. They have sparked our interest and enabled our work through their own scholarship, their generous assistance to scholars, whether experienced researchers or neophytes, and in some cases by their dissemination of American musical works to suspected kindred spirits.

Steven Ledbetter is musicologist and program annotator, Boston Symphony Orchestra. Most recently he edited *Sennets and Tuckets: A Bernstein Celebration*.

Others at this symposium have considered the relationship between scholars and librarians; I will deal with the dichotomy between scholars and performers. One individual sometimes undertakes both scholarly and performing activities, but there is a fundamental difference between scholars and performers, particularly in the way they interact with a music library. Although scholars are generally knowledgeable about the organization and use of library materials, they are usually less experienced with or interested in any of the practical elements that are related to preparing and putting on musical performances. Performers, on the other hand, are almost always less familiar with the library—even wary of it, uncertain about how to proceed. To many performing musicians, "research" means looking in the card catalog (or its modern high-tech version) or possibly in *Grove's Dictionary*. Their primary concern is to find performing materials, and many musicians are interested in going beyond the canon—that rich but overworked standard repertory—but they want guidance in finding genres of music, specific pieces, and, especially, usable scores

[1] D. W. Krummel et al., *Resources of American Music History* (Urbana: University of Illinois Press, 1981); D. W. Krummel, *Bibliographical Handbook of American Music* (Urbana: University of Illinois Press, 1988).

[2] Boston Area Music Libraries, *The Boston Composers Project*, ed. Linda I. Solow et al. (Cambridge, Mass.: MIT Press, 1983).

and parts. To the performer, whether a scholar/performer or just one who wants to do a little "intimidating" research, the music librarian is the noble, generous-spirited soul who has assembled a rich horde of materials and who opens it up to others.

Performers tend to feel quite at home with stuff-in-a-box—to use Suki Sommer's coinage—if they can only find a way of gaining access to the box. (After all, most musicians sooner or later store considerable portions of their own working scores in boxes somewhere.) Sometimes, when the boxes are opened to performers, surprising things can happen as soundless materials come to life. Two areas of American music, albeit in the vernacular tradition of silent film music and Broadway musicals, have recently been the direct beneficiaries of "box-opening."

Silent films, of course, were never truly silent; they were always accompanied by music. The Library of Congress has a particularly rich collection of materials from the early film studios, especially from those that were located on the East Coast. Several scholars and librarians have been working to bring these materials under bibliographic control and to make them heard after years of silence. Martin Marks has surveyed most of the collection. Wayne Shirley has prepared performing parts from the unpublished manuscript of Victor Herbert's full-length score to the 1916 film, *Fall of a Nation*. What we discover upon hearing Herbert's Prelude to the film, which was intended to warn Americans of the possibility of foreign invasion, is a rhetorical style that was subsequently used in countless film melodramas. Unfortunately, the film itself has been lost. Gillian Anderson has been reconstructing and performing important musical scores to major films, among them D. W. Griffith's *Intolerance* and the silent version of *The Thief of Bagdad*, which starred Douglas Fairbanks. *Thief* was recently shown on public television with a highly touted score that turned out to be a cobbled-together version of excerpts from Nikolai Rimsky-Korsakov's *Sheherazade*, repeated ad nauseam and scarcely connected to the events on the screen. Given the choice, one naturally wants to hear the music that was conceived specifically for the images of the film.

Among the most publicized finds of recent years is the rich trove of materials found in a Secaucus warehouse—rather than in a well-ordered library—containing original orchestral parts for Broadway shows, among them many important works. The recent complete recording of *Show Boat* in John McGlinn's reconstructed score resulted from this discovery. Furthermore, the recording's success in both commercial and artistic terms has led to similar work on major shows of George Gershwin, which will include recordings as well as the publication of vocal scores and authentic orchestrations. For anyone interested in furthering the cause of American music, these events are indeed to be celebrated.

But the area of American music that I want most to discuss is that portion of the "cultivated tradition" that has long been known by such misleading designations as "The Boston Classicists" or "The Second New England School," terms that should be permanently retired from scholarly use.

About a century ago, when Frédéric Louis Ritter and Louis Charles Elson wrote their histories of American music,[3] the works of several Boston composers were considered the acme of American composition. Changes of taste and historical

3 Frédéric Louis Ritter, *Music in America* (New York: C. Scribner's Sons, 1883); Louis Charles Elson, *The History of American Music* (New York: Macmillan, 1904).

viewpoint reversed the situation: from not long after the First World War until sometime after the Second, these New England composers were virtually ignored. Their music was neither played nor recorded, and only a handful of single-minded people, mostly graduate students seeking topics available for dissertations, dealt with them at all. An entire series of such dissertations was directed by a theorist at the Eastman School of Music, who had his students analyze the harmonic techniques of each composer on the basis of available printed scores but failed to suggest any survey of the unpublished works, biographical study, or archival work on the composers' professional or institutional activities.

Gradually, however, these composers and their music are now regaining acceptance. Passage of time arouses curiosity about how the music sounds. Performers—including soloists, orchestra members and chamber music players—want to find something a little unusual and off-the-beaten-track, but not too "unpleasant" or "modern," for fear of frightening audiences. A good source for such repertory is American music of the pre-modernist period. As a result, more and more of this music is being recorded, allowing record buyers, concert-goers, and listeners to classical-music radio stations the opportunity to know the music of composers whose names, until recently, were unknown to them (that is, unless the radio station follows the devastating current trend of programming excerpted movements from larger works or the wallpaper music of nondescript Baroque trio sonatas, carefully avoiding anything with voice or chorus and anything that might arouse a response from the listener).

Performers no longer dismiss out of hand the music of John Knowles Paine, Arthur Foote, George Chadwick, Charles Martin Loeffler, Amy Marcy Beach, John Alden Carpenter, Frederick Shepherd Converse, Daniel Gregory Mason, Henry Hadley, and the like. They are willing to try the music and will often enough find something they enjoy playing and to which audiences respond favorably. Thus more and more performances of works by these composers are being heard.

In the late 1950s and early 1960s, Karl Krueger conducted various orchestras in a number of works by these older American composers. The performances were issued by the Society for the Preservation of the American Musical Heritage in a series of sound recordings called the Music-in-America Series. Unfortunately many of the works were drastically cut, seriously underrehearsed, and, obviously, recorded on a shoestring. But the recordings were exceedingly valuable because at the time they were all we had.

Times are changing for these composers, and in many places—from Boston to California to old Vienna to England and other unlikely venues. Last winter John Rockwell wrote a lead article for the music page of the *New York Times* Sunday edition that bore the headline "Paine and Chadwick Return to Favor."[4] Certainly if the *Times* says it, it must be so.

How did we ever reach such a watershed? The record companies have contributed greatly, two of them in particular. One is New World Records, with which most music librarians are familiar from the generous and richly varied series of recordings assembled and sent free to hundreds of libraries as part of the nation's bicentennial celebration. Among those records was one that I believe truly initiated the revival. Gunther Schuller "discovered" the *Mass in D* by the youthful John

4 *New York Times*, 15 January 1989, sec. H, p. 23.

Figure 1. John Knowles Paine's Mass in D *(published 1866).*

Knowles Paine (figure 1) and believed in it strongly enough to record it with the St. Louis Symphony Orchestra and Chorus. The recording demonstrated to anyone who heard it that a twenty-three-year old early American composer had fully mastered the techniques of the cultivated tradition and could express them in music of a remarkably wide expressive range. Schuller's commitment to Paine has continued to this day.

Around the time that these recordings were being released, I became actively interested in American music of this period (beyond simply listening to every new release from New World). For the Handel Society, an oratorio chorus that I was conducting at Dartmouth College, I wanted to find a major American work to program during the bicentennial season. Because I particularly relish works with a dramatic thrust, I began tracking down the manuscript score and parts of George Chadwick's lyric drama *Judith*, premiered at Worcester, Massachusetts, in 1901 (figure 2). After studying a reprint of the vocal score (in a Da Capo Press edition sponsored by the Music Library Association[5]), I decided that the work was well suited both to the occasion and to my chorus and soloists. Though I enjoyed working with Chadwick's piece, I had no intention of becoming a particular partisan of his. A year later, however, Rufus Hallmark invited me to talk about the Chadwick manuscripts at the New England Conservatory of Music for a Music Library Association session on the special resources of Boston-area music libraries. I had looked at only one Chadwick manuscript in my life, and that one was at the Library of Congress, but after a little arm twisting, I agreed to look at the Chadwick manuscripts at NEC. I discovered that the Conservatory's orchestra library owned the performing parts, not only of *Judith*, but of virtually every large-scale piece Chadwick had written. It seemed worthwhile to publicize this information, so I prepared a little handout that described the scores and parts and listed their respective locations. I thought that after the MLA meeting I would perhaps offer my paper for publication in *Notes,* but first I wanted to include just a bit more information about each piece. At the moment my little handout has reached book length and has taken on the format of a *catalogue raisonée.* It should be ready for publication in the near future.

What next directed my feet into the halls of American music was a professional move from Dartmouth to the Boston Symphony Orchestra, putting me only a block away from many of Chadwick's scores. The move also connected me to the institution where most of Chadwick's major works were premiered. In fact, Chadwick shares, with Walter Piston, the record for the most world premieres—eight apiece—with the BSO. More important, my move to Boston brought me into contact with a large number of highly talented musicians who were interested in finding new pieces to play. One day, violist Patricia McCarty, who was appearing on a vocal program that included the Brahms songs with viola obbligato, lamented the lack of other works with similar instrumentation. I suggested she look at a group of songs by Loeffler, a German immigrant who was assistant concertmaster of the BSO for twenty years, a popular figure in Boston's musical life, and a composer of great refinement. McCarty took the songs to her singer, D'Anna Fortunato, and pianist, Virginia Eskin, and before long they had planned an entire recording of Loeffler songs. The program was issued by the other record company that plays a part in this story, Northeastern Records, founded as a part of the Northeastern University Press in Boston. The company is now independent and—like all small classical record labels—is valiant and hopeful, but struggling to survive.

After that, things happened quickly. I was invited to review proposals for recordings on Northeastern, with special attention to music of New England origin, though the label has always ranged widely in its material. Upon hearing an interesting discussion of John Knowles Paine's unpublished violin sonata at an American Musicological Society meeting, I asked the BSO's concertmaster Joseph Silverstein, who had already recorded the Beach and Foote violin sonatas for New World, whether he would be interested in looking at the Paine work with the

[5] New York: Da Capo Press, 1972; originally published New York: G. Schirmer, 1901.

Figure 2. Page from the autograph of George W. Chadwick's Judith, *at the Library of Congress.*

possibility of recording it. After studying it, he was eager to record it. Coupled with two other unpublished works by Paine, the sonata became Northeastern's first release on compact disc. It received wide air play and the first pressing recently sold out. It also generated a large number of requests for a printed score, which John C. Schmidt is now editing for the series *Recent Researches in American Music.*[6]

Another BSO musician, flutist Fenwick Smith, is one of those performers who is not afraid of a library. He came to Northeastern Records with a carefully conceived proposal for a collection of all the chamber music by Arthur Foote that featured the flute. We eventually coupled the Foote works on a CD with Smith's performance of all of Copland's chamber music featuring the flute.

The BSO's choral director, John Oliver, also conducts his own group, the John Oliver Chorale, which has performed a wide range of American music from William Billings to Elliott Carter. When the Sonneck Society met in Boston in 1984, Oliver put together a choral program consisting entirely of turn-of-the-century New England music, with Ives's *The Celestial Country* as its main work and a half-dozen smaller pieces by other composers. Later he recorded the Ives for Northeastern, along with Loeffler's Psalm 137, an exquisite work for women's voices.

The biggest single project at Northeastern thus far began when the members of the Portland String Quartet were recording all of Walter Piston's quartets. I asked them if they had ever played Chadwick's Fourth String Quartet, the only one of five to have been commercially published. They had never heard of Chadwick, so I sent them the parts for the Fourth to play through and mentioned that manuscript material for four other string quartets and a published piano quintet were available. In very short order they called to say that if the others were as good as the Fourth, they wanted to play them all. Over several years, we recorded all six works, which were finally issued together just last winter. The set offers an opportunity to trace the development of a major American composer from his young days at the conservatory in Leipzig to his mature years later in Boston. Chadwick's personality is already clearly present in the First Quartet, one of his earliest surviving pieces. Moreover, the work uses familiar kinds of American music—hints of marches, hymn tunes, and dance melodies—even though it was composed in Leipzig in 1877.

For the last five years, I have had the special pleasure every summer of offering a lecture on older American orchestral music to the young conductors studying at Tanglewood. Not surprisingly, the majority are completely unaware of its existence (though this has begun to change). I try to tell them something about the tradition of American music—their own tradition, since most of them are Americans. Although I talk about the composers, I mostly play music—music they have never heard before. The reaction to Chadwick's Second Symphony, for example, is usually one of astonishment that it could have been written in Boston in 1883. The first year, one young conductor commented to me, "You know, when we play German music, we try to think 'German'; when we play French music, we try to think 'French'; it's wonderful to have some music that lets us be ourselves!"

I give the conductors a handlist of orchestral music by New England composers between 1875 and 1925 that includes timings and instrumentation, indicating which pieces can be borrowed from the Fleisher Collection at the Free Library of Philadelphia, which ones are still available for rental from a publisher (unfortunately, very few), and, in a few cases, where the manuscript materials are located. The results

[6] Published in John Knowles Paine, *Three Chamber Works for Piano and Strings*, ed. by John C. Schmidt (Madison, Wisc.: A-R Editions, 1991), 1-41.

have been wonderful: almost every year, at least one of the young Tanglewood conductors gets excited by a piece and ends up leading a performance with a local orchestra back home. They often send me tapes, especially of compositions that have never been recorded. In one case, Chadwick's 1890 Serenade for String Orchestra recently received its European premiere (by the American Music Ensemble Vienna, under the direction of Hobart Earle). Chadwick has developed a justified reputation as a composer especially gifted in the lighter moods, displaying a delightful musical wit and clever orchestration. But the string quartets and this Serenade also reveal a fine control in slower, more lyrical passages.

I also gave a copy of my handlist to Elizabeth Ostrow of New World Records. After perusing the several hundred pieces, she asked if I could recommend a few works that I knew were particularly deserving of being recorded. The result is that New World has now recorded both Paine's and Chadwick's second symphonies—works that Karl Krueger had recorded earlier for SPAMH, but with ill-conceived cuts. I still hope to hear a worthy recording of Horatio Parker's *Hora Novissima.*

The tide is turning. Indeed, perhaps it has already turned. More and more musicians are becoming interested in American music. Ten years ago I sometimes felt like a fanatic promoting all these composers whose works were of interest to no one. I rarely miss an opportunity to tell performers or ensembles that I have just the work they might be looking for—a string quartet, a piano trio, a sonata, an orchestral piece, a song, or whatever may be suitable. I don't push everything these composers wrote, but I am trying to get good pieces back into the repertory.

Music librarians should always be alert to making that crucial connection between performers who use their library and the music on their shelves. Some works need no special promotion: they can speak for themselves. But some valuable pieces are being overlooked, perhaps unjustifiably, and a nudge in the right direction may be all it takes. The expanded canon is, after all, already accepted. It has been said that teachers never know where their influence stops. The same can be said for music librarians who assist performers and scholars looking for material. With just a little healthy fanaticism about the materials in their collections, librarians can spark an interest that will have exciting repercussions for the musical community.

Questions and Discussion, Part 3

Oscar Handlin, Chair

Q: Regarding the divide between American vernacular music and that of the European immigrants, does Mr. Crawford think there is a connection between the sources from Europe and what has become the American vernacular?

CRAWFORD: For this paper, I stopped my consideration at national boundaries because someone else would be dealing with immigrant music. But certainly various immigrant musics have had a great impact on American vernacular music. Don Krummel mentioned the discography by Richard Spottswood that took many years of preparation and LC's *Ethnic Recordings in America*, a discography of all commercial recordings made by the various immigrant groups starting in the 1920s.[1] American music business executives discovered in the 1920s that recording the music of a given community gave them a powerful economic tool within that community—doing so was simply a good way to sell music. Our knowledge of the sources for many of these musics has until now been extremely sketchy. Spottswood's discography will be enormously helpful, and the LC publication allows us to see how rich this field is. But serious research requires a strong bibliographic-discographic base: that is another divide we have to cross. There is no question that this music is part of the larger picture, but studying it presents a serious challenge.

Oscar Handlin is Carl M. Loeb University Professor, *Emeritus*, and former Director of the University Library, Harvard University. Among his many books is *Liberty in America, 1600 to the Present*, written with Lilian Handlin.

Q: Over the past few years I have been particularly engaged in performing music of John Knowles Paine, in whose memory this hall is named. In looking for performance material, however, I was first appalled and then angered at its scarcity and its condition. A collected Paine edition supporting the American musical heritage would be of far more value than an edition of Johannes Ockeghem's works. On the subject of reservation life, my experience and knowledge are unfortunately limited to what I have gained from the novels of Tony Hillerman, but I am curious, especially in light of the Christopher Columbus song, to know whether Don Roberts thinks that white-faced, popular genres have indeed invaded the reservations. I am also curious about the extent to which songs in the traditional modes are still being created.

ROBERTS: The imported popular genres form a major component of Native American music today. This should not be surprising, because in addition to all the

[1] Richard Keith Spottswood, *Ethnic Music on Records: A Discography of Ethnic Recordings Produced in the United States, 1894 to 1942* (Urbana: Univerity of Illinois Press, 1990); *Ethnic Recordings in America: A Neglected Heritage* (Washington, D.C.: Library of Congress, 1982).

traditional forms, nearly every tribal unit has always had music for relaxation. Indeed, some of the ceremonies go on for four to six days and at their conclusion, the participants often hold round dances, which are purely social events and which serve to bring the practitioners and the active spectators back to the real world. So it is not unusual that in the realm of popular music Native Americans ventured from their own non-sacred music into some of the idioms that were around them. Some of the finest country-western groups in the country today are Navaho Indian groups. They perform in a completely secular context, portraying the old "boy meets girl" situation at the Saturday night dance. The performers are simply expressing the non-sacred aspects of their lives.

Q: What did Don Krummel mean when he spoke about immigrant music being too important for the libraries?

KRUMMEL: Just that all music must come to life, and it doesn't come to life in the library, it comes to life as sound.

Q: Can we assume any crack in the wall that the American musicological establishment has put up to keep out American and vernacular musics? We have seen years of confrontation between that establishment and scholars studying jazz, popular music, and other non-Western-classical genres. Do the musicologists here today represent a voice in the wilderness or is their view the prevailing one?

CRAWFORD: The American Musicological Society consists, like most other American scholarly groups today, of a diverse group of people displaying an extremely wide range of tastes and interests. A good part of the difficulty that American music has had in making its way into that framework has occurred simply through ignorance about, and lack of access to, many American things. There has been a divide—there is no question about that—but in the last ten or fifteen years the American Musicological Society has supported American projects, just as it continues to support projects of various other kinds. There is also another group, the Sonneck Society, that specializes entirely in American music, and many musicologists belong to both organizations. Our society is well represented, as are our interests as Americanists. There is no monolithic view of American music—at least not anymore.

A Performer's View: Libraries in My Life

Raphael Hillyer

It has been fifty-one years since my graduate student days at Harvard, where I studied music with Walter Piston, Tillman Merritt, Hugo Leichtentritt, and Edward Burlingame Hill, and mathematics with George Birkhoff. My contemporaries included Harold Shapero, Irving Fine, Elliot Forbes, Gib Sturges, Leonard Bernstein, Jesse Ehrlich, Jan LaRue, Henry Mishkin, Jonathan Schiller, William Austin, and, of course, Richard French. Archibald Davison, Woody Woodworth, and Donald Grout were very much in evidence. Being at Harvard changed my life's goals. As an undergraduate in a small New Hampshire town, I had been thinking of studying mathematics, but then, in a great university, surrounded by musicians, the choice was definitely music.

Raphael Hillyer is professor of music at Boston University and founding violist of the Juilliard String Quartet.

The music library at Harvard in 1936 was a modest room one floor above Paine Hall. We used the library frequently, not only to study musicology with the aid of *Denkmäler Deutscher Tonkunst*, Riemann's *Musik-Lexikon*, and *Grove's Dictionary of Music*, and counterpoint with Palestrina and Giovanni Gabrieli as guides, but as a room for performing chamber music written by Harvard faculty and students and by composers beyond Harvard's walls. Whether a new piece by Bernstein, an old one by Edward Ballantine, or some newly discovered Albert Roussel or Igor Stravinsky, all music excited and inspired us, and we were impatient to perform. The library here was our rallying point, Paine Hall the scene of frequent concerts by our group and by visiting artists. It may not be generally known that Béla Bartók and his wife, Dita, gave a four-hand piano recital right here in Paine Hall. Bartók took evident delight in stumping the Harvard audience when he asked them to identify some of his complex rhythms. No one could.

In those heady Harvard days, discovering music old and new, we didn't talk much about authenticity. I am not sure when it all started, but nowadays the word authenticity has a special ring. I recall hearing Ph.D. candidate Putnam Aldrich make a strong point about ornaments in the music of J. S. Bach; performing Bach cantatas with David Kimball, a superb young musician at Eliot House; playing Bach with Nadia Boulanger; and exploring all the Bach violin sonatas with the phenomenal harpsichordist Erwin Bodky, who seemed to know all of Bach from memory. We faithfully started all trills from the note above.

The authenticity movement can be said to have arrived on the day Dietrich Fischer-Dieskau spoke his famous five-word dictum at Yale, and I quote him, "The composer is always right." So to the libraries we turn—performers, scholars, students, teachers—trying to discover what it was the composer actually said that we are urged to embrace as right. It is common knowledge that eighteenth-century

John Ohl (left, facing camera) and other students in the Harvard Music Library about 1939, in a photograph by the music librarian, Marian Stewart Rumberger.

works have been edited almost beyond recognition by nineteenth-century editors. Finding the real composition behind the editions is reminiscent of Schliemann digging for the city of ancient Troy. The Bach Cello Suites, for example, appear in perhaps thirty different cello editions and a dozen viola editions. Knowledgeable musicians no longer read them at face value, because anyone can walk into a good library and find facsimiles of the old handwritten copies by Anna Magdalena Bach and Johann Peter Kellner, not to mention the venerable Bach Gesellschaft Edition and the new Bärenreiter *Ausgabe*. As teachers we can now guide our students to libraries that have the new scholarly editions and original sources, so that their knowledge and performance of a work ultimately flows from the composer rather than the editor.

The great singer and educator Phyllis Curtin recently pointed out that there are many opera editions, especially piano-vocal scores, that are full of interpolations and flagrant mistakes. Bach, Handel, and Mozart scholars have brought about many changes. Curtin recommends that singers check original sources in the library as a wise precaution against the conductor who might enjoy embarrassing a singer by pointing out mistakes. She would have singers study ornamentation and performance practice, even if current thinking turns out to be a temporary fad and styles revert back in thirty or forty years. Furthermore, she encourages independent study of books, from which singers can learn how and when to employ ornamentation as an integral part of a virtuosic gesture or as a device to intensify emotion. Finally, she urges students to visit the library often to search out new repertoire. A seemingly inexhaustible treasure of song exists, and student discoveries bring new delights for the teacher as well.

I have loved libraries as long as I can remember. I always liked the air of quiet you donned like a cloak as soon as you entered. The initial enchantment happened at Dartmouth College, where I grew up. The new Baker Library, built around 1930, offered free access to stacks, comfortable reading rooms, and a seeming infinity of choices. When I was studying Latin, I was drawn to the shelves of classics: the odes of Horace, *De Rerum Natura* of Lucretius, and the *Metamorphoses* of Ovid. Romantic Romans! I would rush to the library to watch José Clemente Orozco, the noted

Raphael Hillyer with the composer Michael Ippolitov-Ivanov in front of the Moscow Conservatory of Music, April, 1924.

Mexican painter, as he crouched on his scaffolding, creating his frescos of American myth and history on the white library walls.

At the time, I traveled a great deal with my parents. It was in the Moscow Conservatory Library, when I was nine, that I visited my first library abroad. My parents and I were guided by our new friend, the Russian composer Michael Michaelovich Ippolitov-Ivanov, then Director of the Moscow Conservatory. A bearded, kindly, grandfatherly figure, he had shown his affection for us—perhaps because in that year, 1923, a mere six after the Russian Revolution, when living conditions were so miserable and Russians so completely isolated from the outside world, we were the first foreigners to visit in years and were regarded as curiosities. Besides, in those days being an American abroad opened doors and hearts. Ippolitov-Ivanov also seemed to enjoy that this American youth was studying the violin. So here he was, this old friend of Peter Ilyich Tchaikovsky, guiding these starry-eyed New Englanders down the corridors of the library museum, opening one showcase after another filled with historic objects. He removed several to show us: one, he explained, a letter Tchaikovsky had written him; another, a framed miniature photo of Tchaikovsky with a dedication to him; then an old photo of the whole Tchaikovsky family, both parents with the composer and siblings as children; finally, he removed a manuscript page from a bulky music notebook—it was an early draft of Tchaikovsky's *Manfred Symphony*. Ippolitov-Ivanov handed these to me and my parents, saying, "these are for you as a souvenir of our friendship." Another example of the open generosity shown by our Soviet colleagues occurred when my Russian violin teacher, Sergei Korgueff, decided to leave Leningrad a few years later and come to Dartmouth as a professor. He brought with him a manuscript score of Alexander Glazunov's Violin Concerto and presented it to the Dartmouth Library.

Korgueff suggested I apply to the Curtis Institute of Music for further violin study. As a small-town boy, I was innocent of the musical facts of life. At Curtis, the facts hit with brutal force. I saw what real talent was. I saw what real work was. Encouraged to use the library, I discovered what a fine music library could mean to students eager to learn. Many a day we could be seen staggering under arms full of music to practice rooms, where we would sight-read by the hour, covering quantities of literature far beyond what our teachers could assign. I had been admitted on probation and had to prove I was a good student in order to stay on. In those years it was the custom for the Curtis faculty to take their students with them during the summer for continuing study at their summer homes in Camden, Maine. Josef Hofmann, Efrem Zimbalist, Léa Luboshutz, and the founder of Curtis, Mary Louise Curtis Bok herself, went to Maine with all their students. My teacher, Eddle Bachmann, was Hungarian and sugggested I go with him to Budapest for the summer to study. This idea my music-loving parents enthusiastically approved, and they decided to come too.

One day in Budapest, while we were exploring an antiquarian music shop, my father and I were shown a large collection of musical scores just then being offered for sale. It was made up of one thousand volumes of orchestral and chamber music scores. We noted that it was in perfect condition and included the main works in the literature, with the added fillip that the bindings were color-coded by composer (I recall Beethoven being light lavender). Mindful of Dartmouth's need to improve its music collection, my father wired the College and received approval to buy the entire collection. The Dartmouth Library thereby filled a gap, and future students at the College (I among them) benefited from being able to use these scores.

After leaving Harvard graduate school, our circle of young musicians continued to function, and it was a natural step for us to proceed to Tanglewood when it opened as a summer music school in 1940. The two summers at Tanglewood under Serge Koussevitsky, with teachers Eugene Lehner, Richard Burgin, Gregor Piatigorsky, and others, prepared me for chamber music and introduced me to the Boston Symphony Orchestra. Soon thereafter I was asked to join the BSO as a violinist.

For a number of years the Harvard Music Department had in residence the Stradivarius String Quartet. When a change in personnel took place, Eugene Lehner and I were asked to take the chairs of viola and second violin, respectively. Two experienced chamber musicians remained as the core of the group—Wolf Wolfinsohn as first violinist and Ivan D'Archambeau as cellist. Although by that time the quartet was no longer associated with Harvard, we retained Cambridge as our base. It was a revelation and an exalting experience to play with Lehner, the most poetically imaginative musician I had ever known. The quartet provided a much needed balance to the more impersonal music making in the BSO, and it prepared me for what was to come.

During this time of involvement with the BSO and the Stradivarius Quartet, I was as usual pursuing other interests, studies in pre-medical sciences and the Chinese language. I was attracted to the seemingly wild idea of taking an intensive course in the Cantonese dialect when I learned that the course would be taught by Yuen Ren Chao, a Renaissance man who was perhaps the most eminent linguist and teacher of his time (and, incidentally, the father of Harvard music professor Rulan Chao Pian). The course required total immersion—many hours daily of study and class work, which I pursued in the library of the Yenching Institute, the focus of Harvard's Far Eastern studies program. Thanks to the remarkable lectures and recordings prepared by Professor Chao, and to hard work on my part, I acquired quite a good Cantonese accent. It was a great learning experience, though I found little use for Cantonese in the BSO.

I had played in the BSO four and one-half years when I was called to help form the Juilliard String Quartet. Overnight I had to switch from violin to viola. The Juilliard study and concert activities required library as well as studio work. Since I was still a Cambridge resident, we scheduled our first rehearsals in Cambridge. With our early decision to learn all the quartets of Bartók and Arnold Schoenberg, we found it fortunate that the Harvard Music Library had several of the Bartók Quartets on record and all four Schoenbergs, which we had never heard. The Schoenberg recordings were of particular value because there were no commercial recordings in existence at the time. The works had been recorded privately by the Kolisch Quartet in the Hollywood sound studio of United Artists. I am sure no one at Harvard realizes to what an extent its music library helped Juilliard Quartet members in their earliest attempts to learn those works. In general, however, we did not care to listen to recordings of works we were studying. We preferred to explore each new work entirely on our own and develop our own voice and style.

In the years that followed, the Juilliard School's library became increasingly valuable to us, not only for its rich collection but for its role as an archive of the tape recordings made of our regular concerts given at the School throughout the years. Our concert tapes served as a unique study vehicle, enabling us to learn from our mistakes and to note our progress, if any. At the same time, we built our own library of chamber music—an informal library to be sure, but accessible in our own studio. It contained the entire classical repertoire plus Bartók, Schoenberg, Alban Berg, Anton Webern, and over one hundred new works given us by composers hoping for performances. These included quartets by Artur Schnabel, Edward Steuermann, Elliott Carter, William Schumann, Peter Mennin, Leon Kirchner, Irving Fine, Lukas Foss, Harold Shapero, and Glenn Gould. Gould, an aspiring composer as a young man, brought us his quartet. We read it in his presence and regretfully decided against performing it because it seemed excessively influenced by César Franck. Some years later we asked Gould if he would play the Bartók Quintet with us. He declined, saying "I'm not a Bartók fancier." We'll never know whether his rejection of our request was his answer to our rejection of his quartet.

Our concert tours in Europe permitted visits to important libraries. We had early on adopted Alfred Einstein's edition of the *Ten Celebrated Mozart Quartets* as our guide for study and performance, based as it was on the Mozart autographs and first editions. Consequently, when London appeared on our concert itinerary, that meant studying the Mozart autographs in the British Museum.

Then, in Budapest after one of our concerts that included Haydn's Opus 77, no. 1, the Hungarian musicologist Bence Szabolcsi invited me to his home for the next day. When I arrived to visit, Professor Szabolcsi had in his hands the manuscripts of Haydn's Opus 77, nos. 1 and 2 for me to study at my leisure. He had simply borrowed these treasures from the State Library. I have recently received as a gift a photocopy of both manuscripts. Haydn's feather-light pen strokes making up the notes suggest, perhaps, how the music should be played.

In Germany in the 1950s, one learned that many of the music manuscripts formerly held at the Prussian State Library in Berlin had been moved during the war to libraries in Marburg and Tübingen. On a special trip to these cities I was able to see autograph manuscripts of Bach's B-minor Mass and of masterworks by Handel, Beethoven, Schubert, and Wagner. In Bonn, Joseph Schmidt-Görg showed us as many manuscripts as we had time to examine in the Beethoven-Haus. Seeing Beethoven's thirteen different conclusions to the variation movement of the C#-minor Quartet leaves one with a totally new perspective on Beethoven's search for perfection.

In this country there have been visits to the Arnold Schoenberg Institute at the University of Southern California in Los Angeles, which houses the composer's own library and every possible book, manuscript, and recording related to Schoenberg, all available for scholarly research. Here in Harvard Yard we have the Houghton Library with its recent acquisition of the Rudolf Kolisch papers, providing authentic sources for the study of the Second Viennese School. We are fortunate in having numerous library research centers in this country at which twentieth-century music is featured.

It has been the custom in the United States during the past fifty years for some universities to engage string quartets as artists-in-residence. (It is unfortunate that this practice did not begin until after the dissolution of the original legendary Kolisch Quartet.) The ultimate residency in the United States is not at a college or university, however, but at a library—the Library of Congress in Washington, D.C., where the library's traditional repository function has been augmented. Here a quartet's joys and responsibilities coincide, resulting in the ideal situation for a musician. Four resident musicians are engaged to play on four well-matched and matchless Stradivari instruments, performing the greatest music in an acoustically ideal setting. What else can one ask for? If this atmosphere sounds too ethereal, let me mention that when we were in residence, Gertrude Clarke Whittall, the donor of the Strads, would on occasion call out to a fellow concert-goer, in a very loud voice and invariably at the moment of the quartet's upbeat, "Don't the boys look handsome tonight!" bringing everyone down to earth. It required a few treacherous seconds for the audience's laughter to subside and the proper mood to take over before the quartet would dare try another upbeat.

At the Library of Congress, we were encouraged to roam through the stacks in search of lesser-known or unknown works for possible performance. Thus works by Franz Krommer and other Bohemian composers, George Onslow, Johann Nepomuk Hummel, and Louis Spohr found their way into our studio and onto the stages, as did surprising discoveries like Schoenberg's Opus ½, then an unpublished youthful quartet written before his *Verklärte Nacht.*[1] The Library of

[1] Opus ½ has been published as *String Quartet in D Major, 1897*, ed. O. W. Neighbour (London:Faber Music, 1966).

Congress offers a special treat for both artists and audiences when, on concert night, it displays the manuscripts it owns of the works being performed, such as the Mendelssohn Octet, or the autographs of contemporary works commissioned by Elizabeth Sprague Coolidge or the Koussevitsky Foundation. Truly this library represents the pinnacle of musical art in the United States.

Some years ago, Edward Waters, chief of LC's Music Division, learned that I would be teaching at the Franz-Liszt-Hochschule für Musik in Weimar. He asked me to investigate for his book on Liszt certain pertinent documents in the institution's Library. The library staff were extremely cooperative in searching through their vast Liszt archive, and I was able to provide Waters with the desired information. Apart from the staff's efficiency and cooperation, what struck me was that their small talk seemed to consist of current gossip about Liszt's private life, expressed as if Liszt were still living down the street and still misbehaving.

The abundance of musical materials in the libraries of this country leaves us unprepared for the tragic scarcity of library facilities that we encounter in some foreign countries. Although it had already been ten years since the end of the cultural revolution when I taught at China's Beijing Central Conservatory, the destructive effects of that cataclysm were, for students and faculty alike, still a huge obstacle to study. Most of the library's recordings had been smashed by the Red Guards, much of the music destroyed, and because of limited funds, the Conservatory could replace very little. The library relied heavily on gifts from foreign visitors, who came mostly from the Soviet Union as guest teachers, bringing their music with them and leaving copies when they departed. It was strange to find Soviet editions of standard works we thought were printed exclusively by Schott, Peters, or Breitkopf. (So much for international copyright.) The music used by the students was so poorly photocopied it was hardly legible. Sad to say, it seems unlikely that this situation will improve any time soon.

I will close with a story about seeing my name in print, something we probably all aspire to at some time or another. I ought to be content in this respect, because a while ago I found out that a whole chapter was being written about me by Samuel Applebaum in his series on string players, "The Way They Play." I was not especially pleased when I saw the proofs of the chapter, but I cheered up at the thought that there would probably be good photographs. When the book arrived and I opened it to my chapter, I saw a fine photograph—of Dmitri Shostakovich—with the caption, "Raphael Hillyer as a young man." This mystery has never been explained to me. I just wonder whether somewhere in the vast Soviet Union there might be poetic justice in the form of a biography of Shostakovich showing a great picture of me with the caption, "Dmitri Shostakovich as a young man."

A Critic's View

David Hamilton

David Hamilton is a music critic, who also teaches at the Manhattan School of Music. He is the editor of *The Metropolitan Opera Encyclopedia.*

When preparing this talk, I thought back to my earliest encounters with music in an institution of higher learning. The first was a harmony class at Princeton, in a curious location known as the "Peking Room," at a very early hour of the morning. At the first session, Milton Babbitt—a member of today's panel—dumbfounded me and a number of my contemporaries by demonstrating a derivation of the tonal harmonic system from minimal assumptions. The necessity (indeed, even the desirability) of this exercise had never before occurred to us, but its elegance and power in clarifying the system's subtle asymmetries have never left my mind.

My second encounter took place a block or so farther to the west, in Clio Hall, a little neo-Greek temple that in 1952 housed the Princeton Music Department. There I discovered a circulating library of recordings, of a size and scope that—at least for the time—was staggering. It was a circulating library, for the simple reason that Princeton then had no private listening facilities. The opportunity it provided to engage with the enormous range of repertory then appearing on LP was as influential as anything in my Princeton education. Among the recordings that remain in my mind and ears from that time are the early discs of the Juilliard Quartet, of which Raphael Hillyer—another member of this panel—was then violist, and the first record of Schoenberg's Suite, op. 29, conducted by this session's chairman, Gunther Schuller. Through these encounters with recordings, my appetites for comparison, verbal description of music and performance, and evaluation first surfaced, so Princeton's record library was in a real sense the starting point of my vocation as a music critic.

Record libraries such as that one (of which I eventually became, for a time, the librarian) served several functions: (1) furnishing aural examples for faculty use in lectures and classes; (2) providing listening material for student assignments; (3) supporting independent research by students and faculty, notably the music majors' responsibility for learning the "canonical" repertory; and (4) providing service to the university community at large. Nor have these roles altered significantly over several decades, despite technological developments—the introduction of stereophonic sound, cassettes, compact discs, and video recordings—though student ownership of playback equipment, then relatively rare, has now become universal, and the continuing expansion of the recorded repertory has decisively undermined the "canon" of those earlier days.

Over the past five decades, our perspective on recordings has changed. In the 1940s, they primarily represented performances from the present and the recent past; earlier recordings were so much more primitive in sound that they had been relegated to the status of curios rather than substitutes for live performance. The advent of the LP didn't really change that—indeed, it produced newer recordings that were a much more suitable *ersatz*—and libraries continued to concentrate on collecting the latest product, discarding earlier ones as they wore out or could be replaced. Gradually, however, the memory bank that records represent has extended, now spanning virtually a century, and we can regard them in more complex ways.

This expanded perspective is reflected in the domain of discography, the audio equivalent of bibliography. Its early ventures were largely codifications of available and recent records—roughly equivalent to *Books in Print*. Historical (retrospective) discography grew by fits and starts, beginning with jazz and then with vocal music, the area of art music in which it first became clear that performance techniques and styles had changed radically over the period of audible history. Today, thanks to numerous researchers and to meticulous discographies devoted to label names and catalog and matrix numbers, many areas of recorded literature are at least canvassed, if not always fully indexed and documented. Among many examples, acoustic orchestral recordings, quickly forgotten after 1925, when the microphone brought astounding sonic improvements in registering large forces, were never adequately documented; a much-needed discography is now in progress (by Claude Arnold). Though many of such recordings are musically compromised by altered orchestrations, cuts, and time limitations, they nevertheless document important aspects of performance practice.

Parallel to the increasing quantity of recorded sound and the broadened bibliographic control, critical writing about recordings has changed its focus. For a long time, the prevalent—if unacknowledged—model was the "consumer report," aiming to establish the "best" recording of a work among the relatively few available for sale: Felix Weingartner or Arturo Toscanini or Bruno Walter conducting Beethoven's *Eroica* Symphony, Rosa Ponselle or Elisabeth Rethberg or Zinka Milanov singing "Ritorna vincitor" from Verdi's *Aida*, and so forth. Only examples from the present and recent past were considered. That model has gradually broken down, in part because it became unworkable: with literally dozens of versions of standard works current in the shops and many dozens more in libraries and archives, the task of discrimination and ranking far exceeds the appetites, even the capacities of rational beings. Record critics still evaluate newly recorded works, characterize new performances, and recognize obvious superiority in cases of limited competition—but forgive us for not even trying to rank the forty available recordings of Brahms's *Haydn Variations* or César Franck's Symphony in D minor.

In that respect, record critics are doubtless less helpful to music librarians than they once were. At the same time, our current concerns may suggest new directions for record libraries as well as for manufacturers. To that end, let us consider some of the things recordings can do for us. Most conspicuously, they can document the extraordinary changes in performance style during the present century. We need only think of Baroque performance practice, in which the progress of seven decades can be seen to have steadily shifted its destination. A dramatic illustration is offered by the opening of Bach's Brandenburg Concerto no. 5 in a selection of recordings—to be considered not as sources of pleasure nor criticized for their failure to match contemporary ideals, but as sources of information about past ideals and practices. The following performances are arranged not by recording date but by conductors' birth date:

Alfred Cortot (b. 1877, conductor & piano); Jacques Thibaud (violin), Roger Cortet (flute), Chamber Orchestra of the École Normale, Paris (HMV DB-1783; recorded late 1920s); M.M. ♩ = 100 (approximate tempo of opening measures);

Leopold Stokowski (b. 1882, conductor); Anshel Brusilow (violin), William Kincaid (flute), Fernando Valenti (harpsichord), Philadelphia Orchestra (Columbia MS-6313; recorded 1960); M.M. ♩ = 86;

Otto Klemperer (b. 1885, conductor); Henri Merckel (violin), Roger Cortet (flute), Marguerite Roesgen-Champion (harpsichord), Pro Musica Chamber Orchestra (Polydor 566.218/20; recorded 1946); M.M. ♩ = 92;

Edwin Fischer (b. 1886, conductor & piano); Manoug Parikian (violin), Gareth Morris (flute), Philharmonia Orchestra (HMV ALP-1084; recorded 1954); M.M. ♩ = 86;

Wilhelm Furtwängler (b. 1886, conductor & piano); Willi Boskovsky (violin), Josef Niedermayer (flute), Vienna Philharmonic Orchestra (Recital Records RR-515; recorded at concert, Salzburg, August 31, 1950); M.M. ♩ = 72;

Adolf Busch (b. 1891, conductor & violin); Marcel Moyse (flute), Rudolf Serkin (piano), Busch Chamber Players (British Columbia LX-445/6; recorded 1935); M.M. ♩ = 82;

Karl Münchinger (b. 1915, conductor); Reinhold Barchet (violin), André Pépin (flute), Germaine Vaucher-Clere (harpsichord), Stuttgart Chamber Orchestra (London LLP-222; recorded 1951); M.M. ♩ = 88;[1]

Nikolaus Harnoncourt (b. 1929, conductor); Alice Harnoncourt (violin), Leopold Stastny (flute), Georg Fischer (harpsichord), Concentus Musicus (Telefunken SAWT-9460-A; recorded 1964); M.M. ♩ = 84;

Reinhard Goebel (b. 1952, conductor & violin); Wilbert Hazelzet (flute), Andreas Staier (harpsichord), Musica Antiqua Köln (Deutsche Grammophon 423-116-2; recorded 1987); M.M. ♩ = 104.

Even a brief excerpt tells much: the tempo, its articulation at the cadence of the initial ritornello, the overall sonorous gestalt, and the treatment of the texture in the initial concertino passage. The earliest performances may be said to continue representing performance practices of the nineteenth century—especially (despite its late date and the presence of a harpsichord) the Stokowski recording, which sounds even slower than it is, thanks to the large sonority and the massive cadential ritard. For its day, the Cortot performance is remarkably fleet, though here too tempo is employed to inflect the cadence. Furtwängler's tempo is slowest of all, resulting in the effect of 2/4 rather than 4/4 measures and making the piece subjectively twice as long. However, the conductor's free reading of the cadenza in this performance is an enthralling document of an essentially Brahmsian understanding of Bach style. Already in the 1920s, a leaner, tauter approach was making its way (one might draw a compositional parallel in the progression from Max Reger to Paul Hindemith); Klemperer was one of its noted protagonists, though he recorded Bach only after World War II. (His Philharmonia recordings represent a still later stage in his own stylistic development.) Edwin Fischer and Adolf Busch epitomize intermediate stages, featuring the counterpoint lovingly "orchestrated" to underline motivic matters and, especially in Busch's performance, a chamber-music rather than a "conducted" ensemble. The early-1950s recording by Karl Münchinger and the Stuttgart Chamber Orchestra epitomizes the postwar "sewing-machine Baroque" style. With Harnoncourt's first recording, performance on

1 This recording was omitted from the tape used to illustrate the presentation.

Label of 78-rpm recording by Alfred Cortot of Bach's Brandenburg Concerto no. 5, 2d movement (1931), and compact disc containing Reinhard Goebel's performance of the concerto and two other works (1987), both reproduced actual size.

period instruments achieved consistent technical mastery, as well as an aesthetic outlook freshly conceived. Reinhold Goebel's Musica Antiqua Köln provides a sample of recent approaches—seemingly half again as fast as Harnoncourt, with much improvised ornamentation. Aside from a general speeding up of tempo (less pronounced, perhaps, than one might have expected) and slenderizing of texture, this series of examples nourishes the view that the postwar fascination with timbre as a constructive compositional element has been reflected in performance style as well.

Recordings can also remind us that not all change is progress. Recently I compiled an anthology of recordings from Verdi's *La Traviata*, performed by Metropolitan Opera singers from 1906 to the present (Metropolitan Opera Guild MET-505). These document a distinct hardening of the rhythmic arteries over the years, as well as a loss in dynamic variety and shading. In the older recordings, some of that light and shade was communicated by expressive devices that in recent years have been stigmatized as mannerisms, affectations, or liberties with the composer's wishes. The most famous example from *La Traviata* has long been Fernando de Lucia's early recording of Alfredo's "De' miei bollenti spiriti" (G&T 052129), with its long drawn-out diminuendos, sudden dynamic contrasts, metrical distensions, fermatas, unwritten ornaments, and the like. Since de Lucia did not sing this at the Met, his recording was out of scope for my anthology, but I found a similar, if less elaborate version by a less well-known tenor of a few years later, Fernando Carpi.

That Carpi recording also illustrates the historical value of recordings by forgotten performers. If we had only de Lucia's "De' miei bollenti spiriti" to illustrate that performance style, it might easily be dismissed as the whimsy of a spectacular eccentric. But the recordings of his run-of-the-mill contemporaries validate his centrality; they all share in that style. (And they and the Violettas and Germonts of the period make most modern *Traviata* performances sound driven, strenuous, and of limited expressivity.)

Historical recordings also enable us to deduce the unwritten axioms and practices of earlier performing styles. A splendid example is Will Crutchfield's systematic study of ornaments and cadenzas in Verdi recordings made by singers trained during the composer's lifetime, all the more valuable because it yields general guidelines rather than rigid prescriptions for imitation.[2]

The power of recordings to demonstrate forgotten or neglected alternative approaches to works and styles should be valuable in the teaching of performance—not as models for imitation, but as stimuli for imaginative rethinking of generic modern approaches to standard works. In a musical world where too many performers seem to view their role as a passive one, analogous to a stylus tracking a record groove, the study of historical performance might serve to stimulate individuality—as, for not unrelated reasons, has the use of historical instruments. In either case, the challenge is to avoid plodding, lifeless performances based on rote or rules.

Historically, the performance of new music has provided stimuli to performance practice. People who play new music have to "invent" its sound—they cannot just

[2] Will Crutchfield, "Vocal Ornamentation in Verdi: The Phonographic Evidence," *19th-Century Music*, 7 (1983), 3–54.

run through what they remember from recordings; there are no such crutches. And when these people turn to older music, the best of them continue to exercise the skills honed in learning and performing new music. That is why performances of standard repertory by such artists as Bethany Beardslee, Ursula Oppens, the late Jan DeGaetani, Paul Jacobs, and Robert Miller—not to mention my colleagues on this panel, Raphael Hillyer and Gunther Schuller—have so often been vital, imaginative, and healthy.

Thus, to its potentially destructive effects on our musical life, the phonograph also offers a counterbalance, through its ability to preserve and revive a wondrous variety of stylistic and interpretive possibilities. If I have a single message for music librarians, it is to encourage them to build collections of recordings that will make possible many encounters of this stimulating kind among performers and listeners of several generations.

A Composer's View

Milton Babbitt

Since we are gathered in this hall in a spirit of scholarly inquiry, celebrating the central instrument of such inquiry, I think I can best begin—at least, I dare to begin—by posing a question: "What am I doing here?" I do not come here as a scholar, I come here as a composer. If I seem to be somewhat aporetic, I assure you it is not because I feel in the presence of so many librarians the way Wystan Auden once said he felt in the presence of scientists. He said that he felt like a ragged mendicant in the presence of merchant princes. Well, I don't feel that way: I simply feel like a ragged mendicant. The aporia actually results from pondering the complex problem that must have beset the planning committee in choosing speakers. Surely they had to imagine what manner of composer would be so quixotic, so foolhardy, so abandoned as to presume to tell other composers that they should submit their fragile afflatuses to the conflict, to the battle, and to the insult of the thoughtful word, particularly about music, to expose them to such an unsettling influence. Who am I to dare direct any composer, particularly one of our prelapsarian composers (that is, a composer who aspires to compose in a prelapsarian mode), to enter the library and perhaps, in fact undoubtedly, to encounter if not the music, at least the name of, let us say, Eduard Grell, that supreme prelapsarian who insisted that music had its fall from grace when musical instruments dared to intrude upon the virginity, the purity, of the human voice. Eduard Grell I mention in this case because our prelapsarian pikers would do very well to go back and examine what has happened to his music. Apparently, even having been a friend of Brahms's hasn't helped his music survive, and very few of us can boast that we are friends of Brahms's. The problem here is to determine what composers should wander into what libraries. Would you like to lead the already overburdened, apatetic composers into libraries, where they would have to adjust to yet another atmosphere, to yet another environment, in order to be all things to all people?

Milton Babbitt is professor of composition at the Juilliard School and William Shuabel Conant Professor Emeritus at Princeton University. He is currently holder of a John D. and Catherine T. MacArthur Foundation fellowship. Among his recent compositions are *Transfigured Notes*, for string orchestra (1986; premiered 8 February 1991 by the Boston Composers Orchestra, conducted by Gunther Schuller) and *Consortini*, for 5 instruments (1990; recording to be released by Gunmar Music).

I was very puzzled by a statement made by John Braine, the novelist, apropos of libraries. He said, "Being a writer in a library is rather like being a eunuch in a harem."[1] I pondered that: What does it mean? Does it mean that—I wonder to what extent I dare say what I was going to say—does it mean the writer is disinterested, or uninterested, or merely rather wistful? Now if you consider the composer under those conditions, it's really much worse. Therefore, I was trying to find an analogy, but it's beyond my medical knowledge. After all, the writer in the library, even if surrounded by these forgotten books, can pick them up and read them. But

1 Quoted by Robert Gutwillig, "A Talk in London with John Braine," *The New York Times Book Review*, 7 Oct. 1962, p. 5.

consider the composer who wanders through the library and sees these mounds of scores which, after all, are unheard, unperformed, and therefore, scarcely music anymore. What can the composer hope for, in all statistical sobriety? That some Ph.D. student of the future—someone who is desperately seeking a subject—might indeed write a thesis that will have a lifespan as fugacious as the music itself.

In spite of all of that, in spite of the hazards, I must confess that I have stumbled into a library or two, or at least stumbled around a library or two. I am very grateful to libraries for, among many other things, having supplied me with a modest, not specifically musical discovery with regard to the novelist Somerset Maugham. When Maugham had reached a rather advanced age, someone decided to place another honor upon his head. He arrived at the point where he was supposed to make a little speech, rose very slowly, and said, "You know, old age is not without its advantages—" There he stopped, as I just did before, and everyone thought, "The poor old man has finally had it." And then he continued, "—but on second thought, I can't think of any."[2] As a matter of fact, I can think of one. It is the moral prerogative for a writer or a composer of a certain age to engage in nostalgia (although even nostalgia isn't what it used to be). So I shall indulge in my nostalgia. Unfortunately, I can't go back as far as Raphael Hillyer did, because I didn't have such an exotic childhood. I've still never been to Budapest, and I was seventy when I first entered the Moscow Conservatory Library.

I shall go back only to old East Fifty-eighth Street in New York, when I first came to the City in 1934. On East Fifty-eighth Street was a branch of the Public Library. On the second floor of that public library was a circulating library of scores (figure 1), and many of us took everything we ever learned out of that library. But tucked away in a corner was a little fiefdom of scores that were not allowed to circulate, that were not obtainable or available anywhere else, that were really classified "for eyes only," because there was absolutely no way you could hear them except to sit and look at them. Sitting in a corner of that corner of the library was a woman, a magnificently benevolent despot, named Dorothy Lawton. I realize in retrospect that I really should not have thought of her as "Madame LaFarge," because what she had in her hand was not a knitting needle but a pencil. But she sat there watching us intently, and if anyone so much as put a thumbprint on a page of a score, or was led to shed a tear on a score, heads would roll. She had every right to be so protective of these scores, because they were the means by which most of us heard a great deal of music that we couldn't hear in any other way. In Brahms's opinion, it was the best way to hear music. We had to concoct these ideal performances in our own heads—heaven knows how accurate they were, particulary at that stage of our lives—but it had to be that way. So we sat there peering over these scores, which of course had never been recorded (virtually nothing had been recorded except the Bach Brandenburg Concertos), and they were the most exotic, recondite things we could imagine. And by the way, that is the only way I have heard most of those scores, even to this day.

We have not developed a repertory in this country, although I hoped for many years that one of our conservatories would become a repertory conservatory. When Gunther Schuller headed the New England Conservatory, he began to develop one. At the Juilliard School, the "focus weeks" require repertory companies, but only

2 This story was told to me by Mel Powell.

Figure 1. The East Fifty-eighth Street Music Library, New York City, in an undated photograph.

for that one week a year. We have no repertory performance whatsoever of music from the 1930s, that most varied, incredible, pluralistic period (with the possible exception of our own), because most of that music disappeared—not for musical reasons but for other, rather more horrible reasons.

I also recall another New York library, the central facility on Forty-second Street. During my earliest days in the City, one of my first discoveries was of another tiny room that housed a music library. It was tucked away in the northwestmost corner of the building—a little, dimly-lit room with a few dimly-lit tables at which few people ever sat. Surrounded by walls of periodicals, you handed in your call slips to have books retrieved for you. I sat one day in that tiny room when I was seventeen years old, just out of the Deep South, having had very little experience or exposure to such things. I handed in my slips for books—who knew for what: Marcia Davenport, Ernest Newman, I don't know, Robert Haven Schauffler—and while I was waiting for them to be retrieved from this incredible dungeon where they were kept (you never, ever saw the stacks!), a very strange thing happened. Now I am not romanticizing—it had a tremendous effect on my life, and it happened very suddenly. Someone had forgotten to return the *Bach-Jahrbuch* for 1909 to the desk, and I picked it up. I read German only academically (I still read German only academically), but I could read this; it was in Gothic script, and I felt very proud of myself because I had been taught German in Gothic. I immediately became so excited about an article by Robert Handke on the linear principle in Bach[3] that I put in slips for lots of other *Bach-Jahrbücher*. Among them was a 1921 article by Reinhold Oppel on Bach's fugal technique (figure 2).[4] These two articles really did change the course of my life. They made it possible for me to realize that thinking *about* music can transmute into thinking *in* music. The only thinking about music that I had done before then was learning to read music when I was four, playing the violin, all of those things, so what did I know of thinking about music? I learned from Thomas Tapper's *First Year Melody Writing* and from Arthur Foote and Walter Spalding's *Modern Harmony*.[5] The two *Bach-Jahrbuch* articles never became distinguished; they are not listed in the bibliography of the *New Grove Dictionary* article on fugue, but then neither is Heinrich Schenker's famous article on the "organic" in Bach's fugues.[6] (Ebenezer Prout's writings, which *are* listed there, must then be the most important works on fugue[7]—so, you see, there will always be a *Grove's Dictionary*.) The authors were neither celebrated at the time nor remembered since, except perhaps in a class or two of mine at Princeton. The two have not become household names even now, after forty years or so, when we have other household names, such as Joseph Riepel and Simon Sechter and Moritz Hauptman and other music theorists whose tribe has increased so since I began reading articles. But as I taught these two articles in my history of theory course, I realized not only that they were special articles for me personally, but that the authors had looked at music in a new way. In fact, none of the articles I read at the Forty-second Street library had anything explicitly to do with my central concern at the moment, which was contemporary music—above all, my own—but they did have to do with things that I could extrapolate to my own concerns.

I stand here as a surviving composer of the mid-thirties. There were very few of us in New York at that time. It's hard to realize that with thirty-five thousand people now classified, or at least documented, as composers at the American Music Center, there were only about a dozen of us in New York when the American Composers' Alliance was formed. Some of us were university people, some of us were not, and of course, we got to know each other. We had already begun to consider the problems involved with music that we would now call context-dependent, self-referential, automorphic, and syncategorematic—any of the terms that are perfectly reasonable descriptions of a music that in some relative sense has lost a kind of technical communality. In very simple terms, people were talking about restoring common practice, but we were concerned with the kinds of assumptions one brings to a piece and the premises with which one begins a piece. We became convinced that the coherence of such music was very sensitive to, and dependent on, its initial conditions. And what in traditional terms is a more explicit statement of initial conditions than a fugue subject? This view is exactly what Handke and Oppel were adumbrating in very restricting and restrictive terms. We thought about

3 Robert Handke, "Das Linearprinzip J. S. Bachs," *Bach-Jahrbuch*, 6 (1909), 1–11.

4 Reinhold Oppel, "Zur Fugentechnik Bachs," *Bach-Jahrbuch*, 18 (1921), 9–48.

5 Thomas Tappper, *First Year Melody Writing* (Boston: A. P. Schmidt, 1911); Arthur Foote and Walter R. Spalding, *Modern Harmony in Its Theory and Practice* (Boston: A. P. Schmidt, 1905).

6 Heinrich Schenker, "Das Organische der Fuge," in his *Das Meisterwerk in der Musik* (Munich: Drei Masken Verlag, 1925–30), 2: 55–95.

7 Ebenezer Prout, *Fugue* (London: Augener, 1891) and *Fugal Analysis* (London: Augener, 1892).

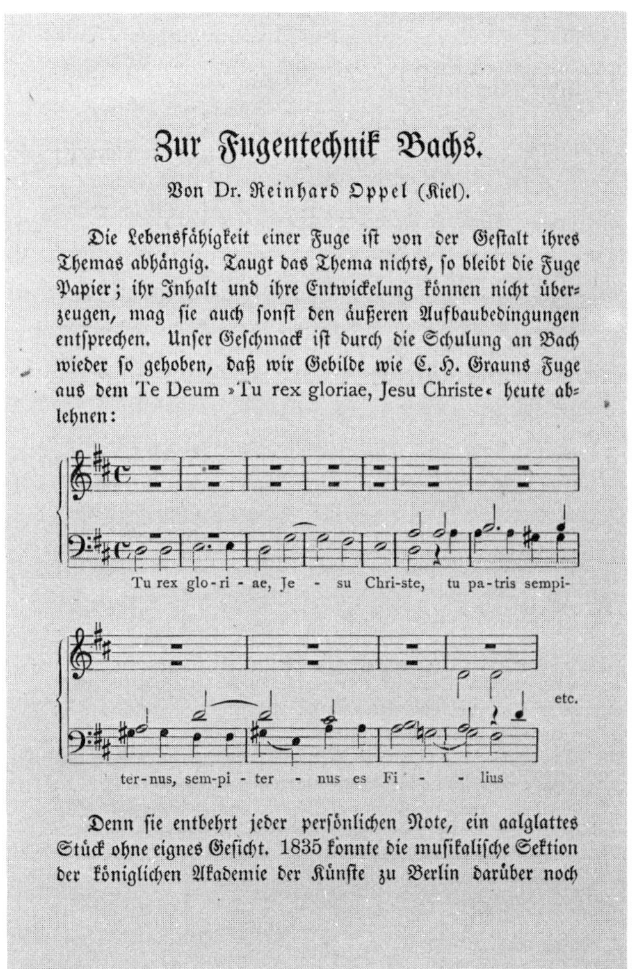

Zur Fugentechnik Bachs.

Von Dr. Reinhard Oppel (Kiel).

Die Lebensfähigkeit einer Fuge ist von der Gestalt ihres Themas abhängig. Taugt das Thema nichts, so bleibt die Fuge Papier; ihr Inhalt und ihre Entwickelung können nicht überzeugen, mag sie auch sonst den äußeren Aufbaubedingungen entsprechen. Unser Geschmack ist durch die Schulung an Bach wieder so gehoben, daß wir Gebilde wie C. H. Grauns Fuge aus dem Te Deum »Tu rex gloriae, Jesu Christe« heute ablehnen:

Denn sie entbehrt jeder persönlichen Note, ein aalglattes Stück ohne eignes Gesicht. 1835 konnte die musikalische Sektion der königlichen Akademie der Künste zu Berlin darüber noch

Figure 2. Opening page of Reinhard Oppel's "Zur Fugentechnik Bachs" in the 1921 Bach-Jahrbuch.

a piece being crescive—growing and taking shape. To us, analysis was not a matter of placing chord symbols above all, nor was it a matter of simply identifying a theme's appearance in very well-known transformations—not the sort of thing you would have found in Prout (in spite of *The New Grove*). Such notions were terribly suggestive to those of us who conceived of ongoing pieces rather than fugal form, or of units that were simply transformed as fixed entities. Indeed, we had something in mind that could begin to indicate where the piece was going harmonically—the fugue subject as prolepsis, to use what I think is probably the best word to describe it. It was proleptic in the sense that it predicted where the piece would go in many different dimensions. The term that we now use, of course, is dimensional imaging, a perfectly reasonable term that describes how one dimension begins to affect another that begins to shape another.

There were other important *Bach-Jahrbuch* articles, such as one in 1917 on motive structure in Bach by Ernst Kurth, who is now very celebrated.[8] There you had, purely with regard to Bach, something that was of fundamental concern to composers five years later. A devastatingly saturated series of conversations about motivic saturation began to appear in journals, so much so that the string quartet of Ludwig Weber—has anyone today even heard of the work?—was hailed in 1927 as a masterpiece (if a rather evanescent one) because it was analyzed. An entire issue of *Melos*

[8] Ernst Kurth, "Zur Motivbildung Bachs," *Bach-Jahrbuch*, 14 (1917), 80–136.

was devoted to it, and every little thing about the piece was taken apart. The quartet derived from a three-note motive (I've never forgotten that three-note motive). The work became the model of what was called motivic saturation. One found in the Kurth article exactly the same concerns, even the same identities, and the same identification of transformations. Another significant article by August Halm, who had been associated with Kurth, was concerned with Bach's concerto form.[9] Halm never became well known in this country, but he wrote some analytical books that were influential mainly in Germany and Austria. In that Halm was very much on his own and very anti-modern, he had something in common with Heinrich Schenker. Also, like Schenker, he used the term *Zug* to describe a certain overall—what we would now call a middleground—motion. Gunther Schuller might say that every German sentence contains the word *Zug,* but this was a rather special application of the word that indicated a concern with line—that linear question again—when people were talking about linear counterpoint. I once asked Ernst Krenek about the harmonic control of linear counterpoint. He said there *was* no concern with harmonic control, and he was right. But the article also introduced the notion of a relationship between the *Gattung*—the species or the type—and the individual work, and the idea of hearing a piece in terms of its communality. These were crucial issues to us, but they were not being dealt with in any contemporary literature because there was none: there was no place where one could publish an article on contemporary music or contemporary issues. So here I found them in these particular articles by these particular theorists in these most unlikely places. If I introduce the names of Oppel, Halm, and Handke (and I seem to be name dropping), it is because they probably survive only in history of theory courses—and there, not very well—but they deserve to be read.

But that is not my point here today. This is, after all, a celebrative occasion, so I can indulge in all kinds of nostalgia (in spite of Somerset Maugham), specifically with regard to Heinrich Schenker, another name that was making its mark. I think of him in response to remarks made earlier in this symposium about the immigrant influence. The immigrant influence on the literature about music was at least as considerable as its influence on the music itself. I have lived long enough to be amazed by—of all things—the Schenker phenomenon, because it was brought here essentially by a few refugees, among them two dear friends of mine, Hans Weisse and Oswald Jonas. I will tell an indiscreet story to show you what the world was like at that time. Walter Piston was also a dear friend of mine and therefore I believe I have a right to tell this story. When Oswald Jonas came to this country, he was absolutely penniless. He was a remarkable musician; he had been a student of Schenker's, and because of that became very much the guru. I apply that term in the friendliest possible fashion and to any number of famous performers who went to work with Schenker, as later they did with Ernst Oster. A friend of Jonas's who was a graduate student at Harvard met Jonas and was very impressed. "Look, why don't you come to Harvard," he said to Jonas, "and I'll take you to Piston's seminar; perhaps he can do something for you." So they sat in on the seminar, where Piston was analyzing a Chopin mazurka, writing down chord numbers according to his system.[10] Afterwards, the student asked Jonas, who could hardly speak English

[9] August Halm, "Über J. S. Bachs Konzertform," *Bach-Jahrbuch*, 16 (1919), 1–44.

[10] Walter Piston, *Harmony* (New York: Norton, 1941).

at the time, "Now may I introduce you to Piston?" to which Jonas replied (probably in German), "I won't talk to someone who analyzes like that." This will give you some idea not only of the climate but also of Schenker's position—it was very underground and very subversive. Anyone who has anything to do with a music library knows how much Schenkerian analysis influenced music theory in this country and that it changed from the heretic to the hieratic. It now finds its lip service in every elementary harmony book and it has just worked its way back to England through the journal *Music Analysis*.

No influence has caused a greater transformation of our thinking about music than Schenker's, be it in reaction to or in reaction with. Schenker influenced some of us who, though we might have agreed with him that Brahms was the last great master of German music, did not agree that Brahms was therefore the last great master of music. Our approach to Schenker was very much like my approach to the articles in the *Bach-Jahrbuch*—that is, we found ways of extrapolating and inferring from Schenker ideas of which he would never approve, ideas that concerned us not at all except for their tremendously suggestive power to affect our thinking about our own music, which was so, so far removed. Such ideas include the whole notion of diminution technique and the notion of how one perceives a musical work. For me, Schenker has always offered the most powerful hypotheses about how our musical memory functions and how we can take in a piece as a whole, particularly at a time when, as composers, an idea *for* a piece was very much an idea *of* a piece. Schenker allowed us to view how a piece of music takes shape on various temporal and structural levels in a cumulative way—cumulative containment, or successive subsumption, if you will—thus making it possible for musical memory to function and musical works to be perceived in their entirety. This is not, however, what the Schenker students and those who were devoted to every aspect of his ideology would regard as the crucial Schenker. It was, nonetheless, for us the most influential of all the indirect and inexplicit influences.

Harold Bloom talks about the anxiety of influence, which he thinks is stimulating for creative artists.[11] As we try to bury our ancestors and attempt to exorcise their influence, we purposely misinterpret them by eccentrically reinterpreting them in our own terms, making them something very different from what they thought they were or from what others thought they were. Both Schenker and Arnold Schoenberg themselves were capable of this process. Schenker and Schoenberg are two vertices of my own Viennese triangle (if not my Trinity), and they both carried out that tradition of "misinterpretation," as Bloom calls it. What they were very much concerned with in their particular sense of history was minimum mutilation. They belonged to the past and, indeed, identified themselves with the past by identifying the past with themselves: in the case of Schenker, with Carl Philipp Emanuel Bach and the anti-Rameau theorists; in the case of Schoenberg, with Johann Sebastian Bach, his predecessor as a contrapuntalist, and with Brahms, his fellow progressive. This was the atmosphere in which most of us lived and worked in the thirties, the forties, and the fifties. Now that Schenker theory has become orthodoxy—at least, a certain kind of orthodoxy—the arguments are no longer about Schenker, but about whose Schenker analysis is right (whether you

[11] Harold Bloom, *The Anxiety of Influence: A Theory of Poetry* (Oxford: Oxford University Press, 1973).

can have an ascending *Urlinie*, for instance). The world has changed and changed and changed.

I am reminded of Hugo Leichtentritt of Harvard University asking Schoenberg in the late thirties for the titles of books that he thought composers should read. Schoenberg sent back an interesting list of twelve authors, adding that he was not much of a reader but that he found many good ideas in those books.[12] One book on the list has a special relation to my life: Hermann Erpf's studies in harmony, *Studien zur Harmonie- und Klangtechnik der neueren Musik.*[13] There is a curious historical aspect to this book. When it came out in 1927 (it dealt of course, with new music), it included near the beginning a chart of the harmonic regions that was derived from Hugo Riemann, or rather, it extended Riemann's work. (Coincidentally, Schoenberg's 1954 *Structural Functions of Harmony*[14] contains essentially the same chart. Although Schoenberg probably based it on Riemann's work as well, he does not include Riemann among the authors on his list.) In his extremely serious book, which is one of the most curious ever written, Erpf begins by analyzing in the most straightforward, Riemann-like chordal fashion (very much as Schoenberg did later in *The Structural Functions*) works by Mozart and Beethoven, and then moves chronologically forward to newer music until he reaches Schoenberg's Opus 19 and other such pieces of that era. At that point Erpf states, though not unequivocally, that this analytical method no longer works and one must find some other way of dealing with these pieces. If they make any sense at all, they must make sense in different terms, and thus Erpf begins applying what we would call contextual analysis. We witness in this book a theorist going through his own evolution. Not surprisingly, the book was totally disregarded for thirty or forty years, but then it suddenly reappeared in a second edition.[15] I found that somewhat remarkable because I hadn't seen any references to it in the meantime, but someone must have thought it was a book to be read. Schoenberg was obviously impressed by it; he may have seen in Erpf's evolution from Mozart to Schoenberg his own evolution from *Verklärte Nacht* to the String Trio. The point of Schoenberg's list of books lies in his claim that he had gotten many good ideas from them, and we'd like to know what the ideas were. He mentions "above all . . . all Heinrich Schenker's writings," commenting "although I disagree with almost everything."[16] Schoenberg himself, however, knew the books on the list only "very superficially," according to the same letter to Leichtentritt. He probably derived his opinion of Schenker not from the graphs or the analysis, not even probably from much of the text, but from the *Vermischtes* in the back of the books—the miscellaneous notes on life, love, and the German Empire. I can understand, then, why Schoenberg was impressed, although I don't know how much of Schenker he actually knew.

There is an apocryphal story that I'd like to put to rest. It is alleged that a student showed Schoenberg a Schenker analysis of Beethoven's *Eroica*. Schenker, of course, devotes an entire volume to the *Eroica* in his *Meisterwerke*,[17] and because

[12] Arnold Schoenberg, *Letters*, ed. Erwin Stein, trans. Eithne Wilkins and Ernst Kaiser (Berkeley and Los Angeles: University of California Press, 1964), pp. 206–207.

[13] Leipig: Breitkopf & Härtel, 1927.

[14] Arnold Schoenberg, *Structural Functions of Harmony* (New York: Norton, 1954).

[15] Wiesbaden: Breitkopf & Härtel, 1969.

[16] Schoenberg, *Letters*, p. 207.

[17] See note 6.

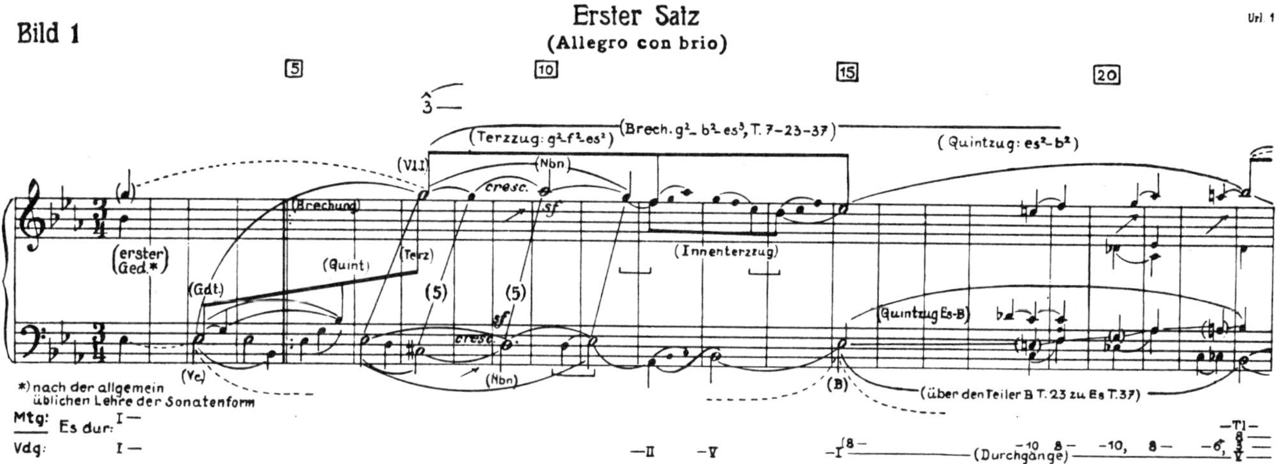

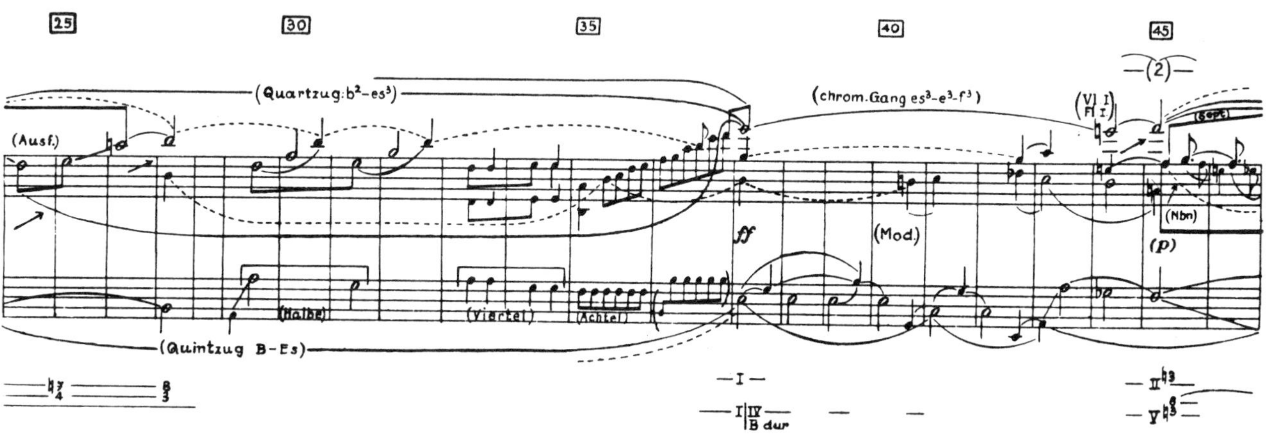

Figure 3. Heinrich Schenker's analysis (1930) of Beethoven's Eroica *Symphony, opening measures.*

there are many, many, many pages, it is next to impossible to "show" a Schenker analysis to someone. But let's assume that Schoenberg at least saw the first page (figure 3). He is alleged to have pointed to something and said, "But where are my favorite places?" Now this story is supposed to illustrate the free-spirited creative artist confronting the dry theorist, but apparently it never happened. I wish it had, though, and I wish I could have been there to confront Schoenberg and say, "Ah! But would these be your favorite places in Rimski-Korsakov's *Sheherazade* or Tchaikovsky's Second Symphony? They may be your very favorite places in the *Eroica* and in its context, but who provides that context better, who describes it more cogently, if not completely, than Schenker?"

In closing, I will indulge in another bit of nostalgia. This remembrance takes me back to the 42nd Street library, which in those days held musical performances. It was there that I heard the first performance of Schoenberg's Fourth String Quartet played by the Kolisch Quartet in a little room, pervaded by the noise of the Fifth Avenue buses outside. There were about fifty of us present at this historic event, which I have never forgotten. (Anyone who has ever read a word I have written about music will know that I've never forgotten the event.) This was a time, in the early and mid-thirties, when most of the contemporary music we could hear came through the radio, broadcast from the Library of Congress—the Coolidge Quartet had already been formed at LC. Just a year after that performance of the Schoenberg Fourth Quartet, I went to teach at Princeton. The senior historian there—in fact the only historian—was Oliver Strunk, who had just left his position as the chief of LC's Music Division. Strunk's interest in contemporary music stopped with his having beer with Paul Hindemith, but he nevertheless told me proudly how, in his role as chief, he had written to Alban Berg offering him a commission of a string quartet. Berg had written back that he was terribly sorry, but he could not, unfortunately, undertake writing a quartet under such stringent time constraints. So Strunk sent a telegram offering the same commission to Sergei Prokofiev, who probably sent his quartet back by return mail. The Library of Congress became our repertory theatre, providing composers with commissions, performances, and talented performing groups, such as the Juilliard String Quartet, to play their music.

So we have the library and all of its functions, not only as a repository of erudite knowledge, but as an active force that has done so much in our lives. Raphael Hillyer documents this so well in his presentation, and I share his feelings of gratitude. I do want to say that some of my best friends are music librarians, from Gottfried Leibniz, to Oliver Strunk, to so many of the attendees at this symposium. Therefore, in the name of that friendship, I ask that should any young composers wander into your library precincts—perhaps in search of nothing more than the solace of discovering that Mozart didn't get a Guggenheim the first time he applied—after informing them of their rights, you also remind them that anything they read will be held against them. That is all I have to say, except one final word of thanks to a very dear friend and colleague over many of these years, Richard French, who, in the words of the great American philosopher Yogi Berra, has "made this occasion necessary."

Questions and Discussion, Part 4

Gunther Schuller, Chair

MARK DEVOTO (Tufts University): Milton Babbitt didn't finish the story about Schoenberg and his favorite passages in the *Eroica*: Schoenberg is said to have looked over the chart and then remarked, "Ah, there they are, in the little notes."

BABBITT: I have looked into that whole story very carefully. We know the name of the person who originally told it and who alleged that he had shown the Schenker analysis to Schoenberg. He was the only one who really knew Schenker theory at the time, and he even had a copy of *Meisterwerke*. (Let's face it, it wasn't easy to get in those days.) Mark Devoto's form of the story is one that I've heard, of course. But if the whole point of the story lies in Schoenberg's spotting his favorite places in the little notes, then he must have looked way ahead in the book.

BRIAN NEWHOUSE (Princeton University): David Hamilton gave us an idea of what music librarians can do that we may not be doing enough of. Are there any further suggestions from the panel?

Gunther Schuller, composer and conductor, is president of Margun Music, Inc. and former president of the New England Conservatory of Music. He is author of *The Swing Era*, volume 2 of his *History of Jazz*. His most recent recording is John Knowles Paine's oratorio, *Saint Peter*.

BABBITT: I take that question very seriously. I live closely with libraries, particularly the record collections at Princeton and the Library of Congress. I can't think of anything a librarian might be expected to do that the librarians I know have not already done. And Dorothy Lawton, whom I mentioned earlier, occupies a special place in my heart because she accommodated us in a special way. Many of us lived through times when we had to fight our way to get a score, to look at a score, to study a score. To hear a score was impossible, and if it hadn't been for the librarians, we couldn't have done so at all. College students at the time were not supposed to use the central collections of the New York Public Library, but the librarians broke the rules and allowed me in, despite my looking young, perhaps because I was such a southern gentleman. In truth, everything I have ever needed from a librarian has been done, and that has been very important to me.

HILLYER: If music librarians could see to it that the individual volumes of composers' complete works and other such collections bore the contents on the spine, they would be taking care of the only annoyance in using libraries that I can think of.

SCHULLER: As I travel around the country speaking and lecturing and visiting, particularly at universities, I get the impression that young people today take much less advantage of library resources than those of our generation did. Some of us have been reminiscing about our early years, about how much time we spent in libraries and how much we learned there. I am dismayed that the enormous recording, book, and score collections at major libraries and universities just sit there underused. The libraries are not actually devoid of students, because many use them to complete assignments for particular classes.

Now, in answer to the question: I often wonder whether there isn't something that librarians, professors, and university administrators could do nowadays to stimulate the curiosity and interest of students to explore these wonderful resources. I have no prescription for doing this, and it is certainly not the burden of librarians alone. The irony is that in the older days, when so much less material was available, we used libraries voraciously. As a young composer, I had to resort to transcribing the last half of Alban Berg's Violin Concerto from the recording because no score was available.

BABBITT: I remember when Stravinsky's *Sacre du Printemps* was available only in a piano-four-hand version and his Piano Concerto only in a version for piano solo with piano reduction. We had no full scores for any of Stravinsky's works or any of Berg's. A great deal of the music was not available in any notated form. We couldn't hear it either, because it also wasn't recorded. Libraries certainly afford us a great deal more now than they did in our day.

PATRICK MAXFIELD (New England Conservatory of Music): When I was a student at the New England Conservatory, shortly after Gunther Schuller left, I knew nothing about the library and never used it. It scared me to death: it was huge, there was so much in there, and I didn't know how to find anything. Now the library has an intensive bibliographic instruction program. The librarians work with the faculty, class by class. We start in the freshman history classes, showing students the basic tools and encouraging them to come see us. We tell them, "We don't want to hear you say that the library doesn't have something. We don't want to hear a card catalog drawer slam in frustration. We don't want to see you hit 'return' on the computer and walk out empty-handed. Bother us, please bother us." We take an active role with students and faculty members. When we hear someone saying, "It's not here; maybe some other library has it," we ask what they cannot find. We ask new faculty members what repertoire the library needs that it does not have. Like library professionals elsewhere, we allow ourselves to be interrupted constantly and work to go that extra mile.

WILLIAM COSCARELLI (University of Georgia): The last twenty years have surely seen a decline in browsing of the collections—not to look for anything specific, just to see what there is, pull it off the shelf, and take it to a practice room. I have been associated with three universities and noticed the same trend at all of them. Perhaps core curricula are taking up more of the undergraduate's time, but the curiosity to see what's new, what's out there, seems to be lacking. At the University of Georgia, librarians attend the student convocation at the beginning of the year to give students positive feelings about the library, tell them what we have to offer, let them know that we're there to help them, and invite them to come bother us so that we can point them in the right direction. We now make a strong effort to reach freshmen, after hearing junior and senior music history students in our bibliographic instruction program tell us that they had no idea such useful material existed. Part of the problem lies in the students' not leaving the music school to come to the main library, where the music library is located. Faculty could help by trying to motivate their students to "get over to the library and find something!"

BABBITT: Just a quick comment on the critical issue of where music libraries should be located. The question caused a great stir at Princeton when Oliver Strunk insisted absolutely that all the scores and books (though not the records, which were kept in the music building) should be housed in the main library, because that was where the thinking was done.

JOEL COHEN (Boston Camerata): The intensity of library use is cyclical. I remember going to the Bibliothèque nationale twenty years ago and finding the music reading room empty; I was literally the only person there. Nowadays we find a whole generation of young French musicians copying music out by hand, because photocopying is not allowed. There is no equivalent self-initiated activity on this side of the ocean. Without question this country is, at least in the short term, in a downswing, which is unsettling for the future of American cultural life in general. Let us hope it's not a deep downswing, but it is definitely present and we have to face it. American music librarians could help change the situation by finding ways to get the curiosity level up and running.

DAWN THISTLE (College of the Holy Cross): I work in a very small library that supports the music department in a small liberal arts college. The situation is very different from that at the New England Conservatory, where Patrick Maxfield is preaching to the initiated—those who are there to study music. At our institution, students have very little background in music and we have to rely heavily on the music department faculty to encourage students to come in and use our materials. It is frustrating for librarians to see the students spoon-fed, told exactly what to study, with every item they need put on reserve. We want the faculty to encourage students to browse the shelves and to do additional listening, even if the students think they are too stretched to afford the time required for such activities.

BABBITT: Does Richard French consider the students at Juilliard to be the initiated, to whom one can preach in a bibliography course? I suspect that many of the performers are more resistant to using the library resources than liberal arts students are.

FRENCH: Juilliard students are just as resistant as any bibliography student is during the first six weeks—no more, no less—because the whole thing appears impossible to students: they can't read those languages, and they are convinced that there's nothing in those books that matters anyway. But given a patient teacher, about the seventh week they eventually come around.

JANE GOTTLIEB (The Juilliard School): Performers are resistant to bibliography in the way that performers are resistant to anything other than practicing their instruments. But being musicians, they don't have to be broken in to the music library. Like the New England Conservatory librarians, we make sure that the students let us know of their needs. Juilliard students come to the library because they need to use the materials it houses.

French: Students who don't use the libraries display an interesting problem: they may listen to a recording of a Brandenburg Concerto (for example) and assume that what they hear through their ears is the same as what is written on the page—that the score is a kind of printout of the sound. But the score isn't that at all, and the great lesson that Milton Babbitt and I remember from our generation is that we had no choice but to sit in the corner and look at the scores. Why can we read open clefs and open scores? Because that is how we had to study Palestrina; there were no editions of Palestrina in G clefs and F clefs. We had to put the music on the piano and hope we could get through it somehow. Many people today encounter what I consider a fundamental difficulty—that it's now too easy to ingest music. If what we hear is what's on the page, then we don't need to look at the page, we just need to listen to it. And that, of course, is the opposite of how music comes into existence.

Coda: Keeping the Faith

Richard F. French

We have spent the last two days examining the identity of the American music librarian, not an identity bounded, as it often is, by cards, computers, catalogs, and all the other clutter euphemistically called "professional concerns." This is neither the identity we have sought, nor is it the one we have found. Indeed, this conference was designed to avoid the protection of the familiar, to let us break through that prophylactic shield—despite the danger, and just for the fun of it. What would happen, we thought, if we threw away caution and put on a rollicking good time right out in the open for all to see and hear? Surely the campus police could never imagine disorder conceived here, by this profession, and in this hall. They could never have dreamed of the lengthy procession we have witnessed, the disorderly parade of ideas, challenges, opportunities, and performances that has come marching out of our past, through our present, and off into our future. It was a great party, and we thank the planners for asking us to come.

But to what end? Was the whole party just another western on a wide screen, just another hifalutin' professional binge? What happens when the last sound recedes into silence, and the last fiddler falls dead in the dust? When we wake up, what will remain? Just the stale memory of a night before? Or can we imagine a different kind of morning after? We, at least, have to try to imagine one, because the party deserves that we do so. Perhaps we may all ask ourselves next Monday morning how what we have heard here relates to our daily working lives. To put it another way, must the memory of this conference remain only a part of our past, or can it find in us a present and a future? And if so, how?

Following is an exchange of correspondence I recently had with a young pianist. The context will be clear from the contents:

> Dear Bob,
>
> Thank you again for coming to play for Donald last Saturday. This was the first time I had heard you since you left Yale as a student. You were always a good player, but you were a student nevertheless, and played like one. No more.
>
> One of the hardest things to explain to young performers is that they must cross a very fine line from being imitators to becoming artists, from following instructions to daring to frame their own, with due regard, of course, to all the other things they have to consider. It's a balancing act without any balance except that of their own making. It's the most frightening kind of indecent exposure imaginable. To cross the line they must first know that they have to do it, then they must dare to do it, and finally, they must do it. They also have to become "older" than they were before and suffer a lot in the process of growing up. All these things you have done.
>
> If I had a young son who wanted to be a pianist, I'd entrust him all to you.

Richard F. French is director of doctoral studies in music at The Juilliard School and professor of music *emeritus* at the School of Music and the Institute of Sacred Music, Yale University. He edited *Music and Criticism: A Symposium* (Harvard University Press, 1948) and recently translated *A Book about Stravinsky* by Boris Asaf'ev. This talk has also been published in *Notes*, 46 (1990), 846–848.

The reply:

> Dear Richard,
>
> Many thanks for your kind note, which touched me deeply. It's going into my "Keep Forever" file, to be re-read at moments of doubt or uncertainty, of which there are plenty. That's another thing that's hard to explain to young performers, probably impossible—that no matter how hard you try, you will never be sure—of your career, of an interpretation, of how best to deal with a student. It's always in flux, which is probably the reason live performance is so interesting, since it represents the *present, never-before-known moment* [emphasis added].
>
> Know that I value your friendship and support greatly. Hell, that note might even go into a frame on my wall!

Now I will reproduce a statement made by Charles Wuorinen in an interview with Joan Peyser in June 1988. Often one has to crack through the hard shell of Wuorinen's hyperbole to find the nut of plain wisdom:

> It is not only that serious music is now pop; even Beethoven gets marketed for the masses. A great work like a Beethoven symphony becomes like a blob of toothpaste. There is the bored orchestra. There are the indifferent audiences. They wait it through. They applaud. They leave. *The symphony is wrapped in such a way that nobody can find how demanding it is* [emphasis added]. The Beethoven Fifth is a fierce, not terribly pleasant work, but it is packaged in such a way that it doesn't bother anyone.[1]

These items represent the alpha and omega of most musical performance in our time: born in anguish, buried in respectability. First, we have a young man reflecting on the perilous rite of live performance: frightened by it, fascinated by it, frustrated by its devilish unpredictability—even tempted, like Caspar in act 2 of *Freischütz*, to call in a loud whisper: "Samiel, Samiel"—but sensing that he can survive only by enduring. And, once he has done so, aghast that he has to start over each time. Second, we reflect on live musical performance that has only the surface charm of its cosmetic packaging, but is lifeless at the core, like a corpse at a wake.

What is this musical art, anyway? What exactly is it that you have in your libraries—on your shelves, in your cassettes, in your acid-free archival boxes? I am reminded of a good friend, a librarian at a New York seminary in the 1960s, who would be happiest if all his materials were on the shelves, the lights out, and the doors locked. A real imprisonment. Unfortunately he never heard all the noise going on between those covers. "What noise?" you ask, "We don't hear it." Yes, you do. Think, and listen. The scores on your shelves are not respectable, lifeless corpses, got up for posterity. They are messy, often only moderately successful and maybe even unreadable attempts to invent new musical languages. In them composers and performers may find new ways to ask new questions about music, forever. What the seminary librarian mistook for the answers—all the materials that he felt deserved to be protected—were really the eternally active questions, screaming to be let loose, attended to, and heard. What our young pianist discovered, therefore, is that the world rewards not the answerer but the questioner, not the imprisoner but the liberator; that great art, like great scholarship, great teaching, and great performance, does not provide answers but shows us only how to begin to interrogate the world in a new way.

[1] *The New York Times*, 5 June 1988.

That is what we have tried to do in this symposium: to suggest new ways in which to interrogate the world. Doing so is always very difficult, but the difficulty is always worth the effort.

Bertrand Russell, writing on the value of philosophy, puts it in his own gentle, wise way:

> The man who has no tincture of philosophy goes through life imprisoned in the prejudices derived from common sense, from the habitual beliefs of his age or his nation, and from convictions which have grown up in his mind without the co-operation or consent of his deliberate reason. To such a man the world tends to become definite, finite, obvious; common objects rouse no questions, and unfamiliar possibilities are contemptuously rejected. As soon as we begin to philosophize, on the contrary, we find . . . that even the most everyday things lead to problems to which only very incomplete answers can be given. Philosophy, though unable to tell us with certainty what is the true answer to the doubts which it raises, is able to suggest many possibilities which enlarge our thoughts and free them from the tyranny of custom. Thus, while diminishing our feeling of certainty as to what things are, it greatly increases our knowledge of what they may be . . . *and it keeps alive our sense of wonder by showing familiar things in an unfamiliar aspect* [emphasis added].[2]

We salute you, music librarians, custodians of our past, provokers of our present, sustainers of our sense of wonder, keepers of all those unanswered questions, that endless parade of imperfect and noisy interrogations that constitutes the substance, the story, and the glory of our culture. Few professionals can hope to champion so noble an enterprise. We wish you well.

[2] Bertrand Russell, *The Problems of Philosophy* (London: Oxford University Press, 1912), pp. 156–157.

Epilogue: *Respice, Adspice, Prospice*

Michael Ochs

Respice, adspice, prospice is the motto of my alma mater, the City College of New York. The three words exhort us to "look back, look at, and look ahead." Looking back, American music librarianship dates to the appointment in 1897 of Walter Rose Whittlesey as first Chief of the Music Division at the Library of Congress. That was nearly a century ago—longer than even the most senior and venerated among us can remember—yet the first substantive look at the history of our profession, in the form of a doctoral dissertation by Carol June Bradley, took place only in 1978[1] (recently enough that some of us may indeed find her volume still lodged in our cataloging backlogs). Since then, Bradley and others have contributed a few additional historical writings,[2] but looking back seems to remain quite low on our list of priorities.

Michael Ochs, the editor of this volume, is Richard F. French Librarian of the Eda Kuhn Loeb Music Library at Harvard University and Senior Lecturer on Music. He has been editor since 1987 of *Notes,* the journal of the Music Library Association.

We have some good reasons for stopping so rarely to examine the past. For one thing, music librarians are kept busy tending to the urgent problems of the day. We juggle inadequate budgets to provide the collections and services that our patrons require. We select materials in a marketplace that threatens to stretch our pocketbooks—if not our imaginations—to the breaking point. We process a barrage of incoming books, scores, serials, recordings, and micromaterials using the most advanced bibliographic techniques and the most up-to-date computer hardware and software on earth (while perhaps harboring nostalgic memories of sitting for an hour at a dilapidated Underwood typewriter and cataloging a dozen scores that we had unpacked minutes earlier). We expend great effort and not a little money to replace typewritten card catalog records with their machine-readable counterparts. We write reports describing the space crises in our stacks (reports that are often duly added to different kinds of stacks—that is, stacks of similar reports describing space crises in other library units). We provide more and more public service in an age when more and more of our patrons are less and less equipped to use our resources. And finally, in what we euphemistically call our "spare time," we compile bio-bibliographies and other reference tools that by their sheer number and diversity serve to enlarge the very same bibliographical quagmire through which they guide our patrons.

1 Carol June Bradley, "The Genesis of American Music Librarianship, 1902–1942" (Ph.D. dissertation, Florida State University, 1978).

2 See especially Carol June Bradley, *American Music Librarianship: A Biographical and Historical Survey* (New York: Greenwood Press, 1990), and *Modern Music Librarianship: Essays in Honor of Ruth Watanabe,* ed. Alfred Mann (Stuyvesant, N.Y.: Pendragon Press, 1989).

Besides being busy, there are other reasons we do not look back (or, in the locution of students at City College, "re-spice"[3]). One is that we tacitly buy into the stereotype of librarianship as a "secondary" profession, dependent for its very existence on "real" professions such as college teaching, medicine, law, or even school teaching. (And with classical music already regarded by most of our society as a frill, music librarianship must really be the handmaiden's handmaiden!) Like nursing, child care, secretarial work, and other service occupations, librarianship is thought of by most people—when they think of it at all—as "women's work," in the most old-fashioned, menial sense of the term. Just picture the librarian of fiction and humor: a dowdy spinster of indeterminate age with unfashionable glasses and sensible shoes, mouse-brown (or mouse-gray) hair tied back in a bun, alternately charging out books and shushing people in the reading room. Moreover, I would wager that there's hardly a person in the profession who said as a child, "I want to be a librarian when I grow up": librarianship does not top many children's lists of dreams. It is safe to assume, then, that at least some of us felt we had to settle for second best. Never mind that we *chose* to enter library school—but perhaps that was only after we had given up the dream of becoming a singer or pianist or conductor or musicologist or whatever. If that is indeed the view of our profession we harbor, then it is plain why we spend little time delving into its history.

Figure 1. Seal of the City College of New York.

Finally, some of us might question if there is a market for studies about music librarianship and even if there is, whether anything can be learned from what our predecessors thought and did. After all, hasn't the profession undergone so many changes in this generation alone that the work of our forerunners can have no more than curiosity value? To address this latter issue, let us examine this excerpt from a recently published obituary for a music librarian:

> His confidence in administering the functions of librarianship, his broad knowledge of books and their contents, and his "sense of direction" about books, which enabled him to assign every single one to its proper place and to find it again in a moment wherever it was, were *remarkable* attributes of his. A *lovable* attribute, however, was that he placed his skills at the disposal of others, at all times and with inexhaustible willingness. No day—no hour—passed during which some musician or young author did not make demands on him; he imparted advice and gave them information far beyond the dictates of his position. To some beginners he provided the entire stock of literary resources needed for some project of theirs, and also took over a substantial portion of the work—on which they then prided themselves as though it had been their own.

That obituary was published in December 1988 in the translated version above[4] and, if the gender may be changed, could describe almost any recently-deceased member of our profession. It originally appeared, however, in 1858, the year its subject, Siegfried Wilhelm Dehn, passed away. So we can see that in certain essentials music librarianship has changed very little in a century and a half. As for there not being a market, editors of *Notes* have long pleaded for interesting, informative, and well-written papers about music librarianship—past, present, and future.

3 The seal of the college (figure 1) depicts a woman with three aspects: one facing left, one facing the viewer, and one facing right. The motto is placed around the top and sides of the seal so that it appears to name the three aspects, which students—hardly any of whom had studied Latin—always referred to as Re-spice, Ad-spice, and Pro-spice. Freshmen were solemnly informed that there was a fourth, hidden aspect, facing away from us, known as Allspice.

4 *Notes,* 45 (1988), 417–418.

The image problem referred to above can also be solved. If we ask ourselves whether we can ever be happy in a secondary profession, we pose a question that itself raises a barrier to any solution. As long as we keep focusing on the status of librarianship, we will find *prima facie* dissatisfaction in our work. So our objective must be to do what we do best—serve our patrons as interested, knowledgeable, competent, and helpful members of a socially valuable profession and take pride in our abilities and our considerable accomplishments. Among these achievements are: conserving and disseminating a portion of the world's cultural heritage; helping interpret that heritage to others; and participating in the musical and musicological discourse of the day. When we have collectively gained a greater respect for our work and for ourselves, we will naturally take a greater interest in the history and workings of our own field.

The exhortation *adspice* is to look at where we find ourselves now. Scrutinizing our profession in the mirror of the present, we can gain deep satisfaction that we are sharing our work and ideas with one another: through the meetings and committee work of the Music Library Association and its international and local counterparts (the International Association of Music Libraries, the regional chapters of MLA, the Music OCLC Users' Group, the Associated Music Libraries Group, the Boston Area Music Librarians, and others); through publication in *Notes, Fontes,* and elsewhere; through joint projects and cataloging networks; through symposia and special conferences; and through our informal contacts by phone, fax, electronic mail, and other less hectic forms of communication. We can be pleased about the services we are able to offer to musicologists, music theorists, performers, composers, critics, members of the general public, and perhaps above all, to students.

Adspice was the *raison d'être* for this symposium. Previously the only major investigation of "the state of the profession" was undertaken in 1960 in *Music Libraries and Librarianship,* a special issue of *Library Trends* edited by the redoubtable Vincent Duckles.[5] The volume contains fourteen articles by various specialists, including Duckles's own "The Music Librarian in 1960."[6] That sixty years passed before our first full-length look in the mirror and another thirty before our second suggests that we don't like to do this too often. It is not clear just how—or how much—that issue of *Library Trends* influenced our thinking about music librarianship, but almost everyone who plied the trade in the 1960s and 1970s kept a desk copy at hand and its contents were assigned and excitedly devoured by a whole generation of incipient music librarians in our schools of learning. We can hope that these symposium proceedings are disseminated just as widely and that the many ideas expressed in these pages will serve as points of departure for future research and discussion.

We have, of course, just segued into *prospice,* looking toward the future. One of our chief tasks is to insure that music librarianship really *has* a future. At the most basic level, the establishment of the Richard F. French Librarianship, which this symposium celebrates, guarantees that there will always be at least one music librarian in the United States. More important, the mere presence of this endowment at a university with the prestige of Harvard raises the stock and visibility of music librarianship everywhere. The chair can serve as an inspiration for other

[5] *Library Trends,* 8 (1960), 495–616.

[6] Ibid., 495–501.

institutions to follow suit. A network of such chairs could help bring the concerns of the profession to the attention of academic and public library administrators in ways that our national and local associations may not be able to achieve. Such chairs can promote activities central to the profession—colloquia, lectures, conferences—that can help keep it vital. We can even hope that the good publicity generated by this endowment will draw new talent into the field.

We face real challenges: in the seemingly endless stream of publications beckoning to be purchased; in the worthwhile materials that are deteriorating on our shelves before our very eyes; in the computers and automated systems that sometimes exacerbate rather than alleviate our paper jams; and in the perennial budget problems that seem designed to frustrate all our efforts to address the other challenges. Yet I am confident that we will be equal to them, and that we will not only continue to meet the demands of our most demanding users but that we will enjoy doing so.

The following, in which the words *respice, adspice, prospice* are applied in a highly personal way, represents the editor's personal coda.

Fifty years ago, on 5 September 1939, Professor A. Tillman Merritt of the Harvard University Music Department arrived at the Port of New York on the S.S. *President Roosevelt,* returning from a summer in Europe. In one of those stranger-than-fiction coincidences, my family and I were traveling on the same ship, fleeing—along with many other Jewish refugees—from Nazi Germany. We were privileged to be granted haven in the United States, and my profound gratitude to the people of this country for that act of mercy can never be adequately expressed. Since that time I have had many other occasions for being grateful: for the excellent free education I received both in the public schools of New York City and at C.C.N.Y.; for the chance, at the latter institution, to work in a music library for the first time, under the mentorship of Melva Peterson; and for this opportunity to acknowledge publicly the great debt I owe her for guiding me into this wonderful profession. (And thank you, Melva, for "not noticing" the inordinate amount of time it took me to shelve a cartful of books whenever Carol Blumenthal—or Carol Ochs, as she has been known since 1959—was also working in the stacks.) I am also grateful to Christoph Wolff, whose confidence a dozen years ago in my ability to help the Harvard Music Library led to my initial appointment here. My introduction to Harvard and to what was then the almost new Eda Kuhn Loeb Music Library took place in 1959, when I followed my musicology mentor, Gustave Reese, to Cambridge. I spent many happy hours that July and August under the benevolently watchful eye of Larry G. Mowers, poring over microfilms in "his" Isham Memorial Library (which was then located in Memorial Church in Harvard Yard; figure 2). Not in my wildest dreams did I imagine then that one day I would be named to an endowed chair at this University, charged with overseeing both of these great libraries.

Which brings me to the personal present. The endowed chair we have celebrated through this symposium did not fall from the sky, it had to be created. I have come to know well its self-effacing creator, Richard F. French, and it is a particular honor and source of pride to carry his name as part of my title. His support of the Music Library at Harvard and, by extension, of music librarianship everywhere has been longstanding, generous, and altogether exemplary. He has never shirked from

Figure 2. Professor A. Tillman Merritt (left), curator of the Isham Memorial Library, with Larry G. Mowers, librarian, conversing in the Library's original quarters above the portico of Memorial Church in Harvard Yard, in a photograph from the 1960s.

becoming actively involved in library problems when his advice was needed. At the same time, he has consistently followed the practice of providing philanthropic help with no strings attached, leaving all decisions to the judgment of the librarian.

Prospice—looking ahead—at the personal level is easy, because I feel my own future to be intimately connected with that of our profession, in which I have already expressed my confidence. So I look ahead with genuine optimism. As we might say in Latin, *successimus, succedimus, succedebimus:* We have succeeded, we are doing well, and our future shall be filled with beautiful music.